MOCKING JUSTICE

MOCKING JUSTICE
America's Biggest Drug Scandal

Hamilton E. Davis

CROWN PUBLISHERS, INC. NEW YORK

Printed in the United States of America
Published simultaneously in Canada by
General Publishing Company Limited

Book Design: Huguette Franco

Library of Congress Cataloging In Publication Data

Davis, Hamilton E
Mocking justice.

1. Narcotics, Control of—Vermont—St. Albans.
2. Lawrence, Paul 1944. 3. Criminal justice,
Administration of—Vermont—St. Albans. I. Title.

HV5833.S23D38   353.4'5'0974313   77-27370
ISBN 0-517-52895-9

For my mother and father
and for Candy

Acknowledgments

MANY ATTORNEYS, PUBLIC OFFICIALS, AND PRIVATE individuals in Vermont and Rhode Island gave hours of their time to answer my questions on the Lawrence case. I wish to thank particularly James Levy, whose outrage in the face of injustice was for a time virtually the last vestige of justice present in St. Albans; Francis X. Murray, the prosecutor primarily responsible for bringing Paul Lawrence to ground; and Robert Gensberg, the special prosecutor who unraveled the twisted skein of Lawrence's depredations. Without their help, the book could not have been written.

I wish also to acknowledge the willingness of Kimberly Cheney, a former attorney general of Vermont, and Ronald Kilburn, a local prosecutor in St. Albans, to discuss their roles candidly with me even though they realized that this book would highlight shortcomings in their performances as public officials.

I am also grateful for the assistance of several individuals who suffered at Lawrence's hands or who grew up with him and were thus familiar with Lawrence's background and character.

Finally, I wish to thank my editor, Sig Moglen, for his skill, sensitivity, and encouragement in completing this work.

Contents

MOCKING JUSTICE

Christine's Day

TUESDAY, MARCH 5, 1974. CHRISTINE CURREY WAS COLD. A chill wind, the remnant of a harsh Vermont winter, gusted down the road, still edged with dirty snow, and blew against her cardboard sign that pleaded "Burlington." To her left, Lindholm's Diner offered a haven, but she had to get back to school. A research paper had to be written that afternoon, and her standing as a graduate student in psychology at the University of Vermont was none too secure.

An occasional car came up the hill on Rutland's Main Street and passed her, headed north. She hunched deeper into her coat. It was eleven o'clock before a blue Ford Mustang, driven by a young man with long hair and a moustache, veered to the side of the road and stopped. She ran to the car and opened the door.

"Where are you going?"

"St. Albans."

"Oh, good. I'm going to Burlington," she said.

"Great."

Christine put her suitcase into the back of the car, then sank into the seat with a sense of relief. It was a two-hour drive to Burlington, but this guy would have to go through there to get to St. Albans. That would leave only a few hours for the paper, which she was reluctant to write anyhow. She couldn't have afforded to spend much more time in Rutland.

"I'm Paul," the man said, as he swung back onto the highway. "Is it okay if I stop at the cleaner's?"

"Sure."

Paul pulled into the parking lot of the cleaning establishment on the outskirts of the city. "I'll be back in a minute," he said.

He seems like a nice guy, she thought while he was gone. Quiet, not pushy or tough. And not unattractive. Which would make the trip a lot easier. Hitchhiking carried some risk when you were as attractive as Christine Currey: long dark blonde hair, even features, a figure that turned heads. A quiet elegance.

"Sorry I took so long," he said when he got back to the car.

"I'm Christy," she introduced herself, as they drove north.

"Have you been skiing?" he asked. He had seen the back of the cardboard sign with "Wilmington," a southern Vermont ski resort, lettered on it.

"I've skied some," she said, "but I've never been to Wilmington." She had intended to go there for the weekend, but had not made it.

"I really like it there," Paul said, and he described the atmosphere of the resort. "Lots of action there," he said.

"In fact, I ran into this girl there who turned me onto coke. I really dug it," he said. "Have you ever tried it?"

"A couple of times, a few years ago," she replied.

He dropped the subject then, and her attention wandered to the countryside mosaic of dull browns and dark greens, with patches of snow on the hillsides.

The road wound through a long valley, flanked by the foothills of the Green Mountains to the east, and a narrow range of hills blocking the view of Lake Champlain to the west. The old and the new stood side by side: now an old farm with the classic farm house and big barn, then a tiny, pastel ranch. Commercial life along Route 7 ran to truck stops and diners, fronted by gravel parking lots.

The Mustang passed through town after town—Pittsford, then Brandon—tiny villages that spoke of a warm community life in sharp contrast to the cold and loneliness of the valley farms. They were approaching Middlebury, the road rising as it left the valley for the foothills, when Paul mentioned drugs again.

"Do you want to do some coke?" he asked. "I didn't mention it before because I thought you might be a narc," he said.

"I'm not a narc," she said.

He produced a tinfoil package containing a plastic bag filled with a white powder.

"How do you do it?" she asked. "Right from the bag?"

"Yes," he said, as he took a one dollar bill from his pocket and rolled it into a narrow tube. He stuck the tube into the bag, inhaled deeply, and handed the bill and the package to her.

She placed the rolled up bill in the package and inhaled. A wave of good feeling, at once mellowing and exhilarating, swept over her. She passed the apparatus back, and they traded snorts until the bag was gone.

Paul chatted quietly as they drove, talking about the weather and the countryside. But she was able to relax only partially. The research paper was a cloud over her day.

It was nearly noon when they bumped across the railroad track at New Haven Junction and began to climb the long hill that leads into Ferrisburg. Both were dry from snorting cocaine, and they agreed to stop at Dakin Farms, a long, low store catering to the stream of tourists that flows along Route 7.

Paul bought a bottle of rose wine, a corkscrew, and paper cups, and they returned to the car. It was clear by this time that Paul wanted to make a day of it, but he was neither pushy nor particularly assertive.

For her part, Christine was intrigued by the man. He was clearly into the drug traffic in a serious way. He was knowledgeable about it and charismatic too: a representative from another world. They talked about four Burlington area people who had just been arrested on charges of selling fifteen thousand dollars' worth of cocaine to a federal undercover agent. The story had been in the Burlington *Free Press*. Christine knew of one of those who had been arrested; he was Nat Gold, the owner of a record shop in Burlington. She had seen him in the shop.

Christine herself had come into only marginal contact with the drug world. There was always someone who had soft drugs, such as marijuana, or knew how to get them. It was also not hard to get pills of various sorts, amphetamines and barbiturates, "uppers" and "downers," they were called. Most were on sale at pharmacies if one had a prescription, and there was a sizeable illegal traffic in them. Cocaine was also trickling in, particularly for the wealthy. Christine had tried cocaine at parties on a couple of occasions a few years previously.

Beyond all this, however, was a shadow world of connections to drug sources in South America, Asia, and Europe. Christine had heard stories about this world, and she recounted some of them as they rode. There was someone who had bought dope in Peru, another who had made two hundred thousand dollars on drugs purchased in Nepal . . . they were just tales to her, but they had their fascination. She had never before actually met anyone tied to the international drug world. This soft-spoken, dark-eyed man apparently was.

"I'm going to St. Albans," Paul said presently. "Why don't you come with me? It's a nice drive. I'll bring you back and drop you off in Burlington after we go to St. Albans."

"Okay," she said.

She knew that she ought to write her paper, that she was procrastinating. But he was attractive and fascinating and she wanted to hear more about drug intrigue.

It was nearly one when they got off the Interstate and drove into St. Albans, an old railroad town. The main street was lined on one side with small stores, on the other by a tree-lined park.

Paul told her he had to leave her for a time. He had to talk to some people about drugs, he told her, and he could not afford to bring her along.

"My friends might get paranoid, uptight," he said. "I'll let you out at Pud's Restaurant, and I'll be back to pick you up."

She got out of the car and went into the restaurant, feeling slightly uneasy, and also guilty about the research paper. She ordered a cup of coffee, then another, occasionally staring at the clock. She finished the second cup, and decided to leave and return to Burlington alone.

She was walking down the street when she saw the blue Mustang approaching.

"Sorry I took so long," he said, as they headed back toward the Interstate and headed south. When he got onto the highway, he took from his pocket another package of cocaine. He must have bought it in St. Albans, she thought.

He then took out two one-hundred-dollar bills, gave her one, and rolled up his. They sniffed the cocaine until it was gone, and the euphoria returned.

"Look," he said, "I'd like to go to Stowe for dinner. What do you say?"

"I have this paper to do," she said.

But he urged her. They could have dinner, then he would drive her home to Burlington. It would be an ideal way to end the day— Stowe was great.

She agreed; the paper was dead for today anyway. They settled down for the ride, passed the Burlington exits, and, swinging south and east, headed for the central part of the state. Forty minutes later, they pulled off the Interstate and drove north on Route 100.

Shortly after they left the Interstate, Paul pulled into a combination gas station– grocery store to buy gas. But after the attendant had filled the tank, they found he could not change a hundred-dollar bill. That was all Paul had. He must have made a big sale in St. Albans, Christine thought.

Paul talked the man into letting them go to a place up the road to change the bill, and they drove on to the Mouse Trap, a gaudy tourist trap crammed to the eaves with souvenirs. Paul bought a bottle of wine and a few souvenirs, but the clerk there could not change the hundred dollars either. The clerk called the owner, who came down and made change.

As they left, Christine told Paul she thought he had got less change than he had coming to him, but he shrugged it off. He seemed to care nothing about the money.

When they got to Stowe, they drove up the road toward the horseshoe-shaped mountain that towers over the town. The road to the mountain is lined with lodges and resorts. Nearer the mountain, these give way to deep forest, cut by streams.

Paul and Christine parked the Mustang at the side of the road near one of these, and, slipping on the still deep snow, they followed a trail to Bingham Falls, a cascading stream a few hundred yards away. Then they returned to the car and headed for a more popular stopping-off point for travelers on the Mountain Road—Sister Kate's, a bar redolent of the rustic, European atmosphere of the resort. Sister Kate's was filled with leathered nooks with soft chairs, and tables with hammered copper tops. A fire blazed in the huge stone hearth. They took a table and ordered drinks: she had white wine, he had Scotch. They had another round. She had a "Sombrero" mixed for her.

She sank back into the luxury of it all. He had all the money they could use and the research paper could be done later.

"Let's get something to eat," he said.

They left the bar and drove back up the Mountain Road to the Hob Nob, an expensive restaurant on a high knoll off the road. She skimmed the menu—price would be no object. She ordered roast duck; he ordered filet mignon. He ordered a bottle of wine, and when they were through eating, they had after-dinner drinks. He gave the waiter a dollar tip for each of the drinks.

Christine was somewhat uneasy, however, She had been fascinated by Paul's talk about the drug traffic; she had liked the cocaine; although she came from an affluent background, as a student she was not used to the good life and she had reveled in the luxury of having unlimited money to spend in a place like Stowe. But Paul was likely to be interested in more than that, and though she liked him, she wasn't ready for anything more.

"The night is young," he said when they got up to leave. "We could get a motel . . ."

"No, I don't think I'd better," she said.

He didn't press her, but he asked her where she lived.

"16 Colchester Avenue," she said quietly.

"14 Colchester?" he asked.

She didn't correct him. She also gave him an incorrect phone number, and he wrote that and the address in a matchbook cover.

They said little on the drive back to Burlington. He dropped her off near the University of Vermont campus, not far from her apartment.

She went in alone to face the research paper.

It was midafternoon on April 3 when Christine Currey's life fell apart. She was picked up by the Burlington Police and taken to the station. They said they wanted to talk to her. They took her to a room on the second floor. She was in the room when a policeman and a policewoman from St. Albans entered and told her she was under arrest.

"For what?" she demanded.

"Sale of a regulated drug," the officer said.

He handed her a copy of the warrant for her arrest.

She was too stunned to argue. They allowed her to stop at her room and pick up a change of clothing and a few books. On the way to

St. Albans, the two cops explained to her that she was under arrest for the sale of heroin to an undercover agent named Paul Lawrence.

She could not believe it—*heroin*. She had never known anyone who had anything to do with heroin. She had never seen heroin, for that matter. As for Paul, who could Paul be? Could it be the Paul in the blue Mustang?

She had snorted coke with the man, but that had been his idea and his coke. And even if she was guilty of that, what did it have to do with heroin? She still could not make sense of it when they locked her up in the Franklin County jail.

She was twenty-three years old and in very serious trouble.

Paul Lawrence, an undercover narcotics agent for the St. Albans Police Department, told a strikingly different story of his day with Christine Currey. His report, written in the laconic, convoluted prose of the policeman, began this way:

> On March 5, 1974 at approximately 1100 hours this officer was traveling north on North Main Street in the City of Rutland, Vermont, and upon approaching the intersection of West Street and North Main Street this officer observed the accused hitchhiking in a northerly direction on North Main Street in front of Lindholm's Diner. The accused was carrying a sign and displaying the sign to oncoming traffic which stated "Burlington" on the sign. This officer then proceeded to stop and pick up the accused at which time the accused stated that she travelling [*sic*] to Burlington . . .
>
> Upon travelling a short distance the accused while engaging in conversation with this officer advised me that a group of her friends had just been busted for selling a large quantity of cocaine to an undercover agent in Burlington. This officer recalled the incident from reading the morning edition of the Burlington Free Press which indicated that John Henderson, Esther C. Nadeau, Martin Gold, and Victor R. Bellucci had all been arrested by agents from the drug enforcement administration for the sale of one pound of cocaine. At this time the accused advised this officer that upon hearing of the arrest of her friends, she had left the Burlington area and attempted to go to Wilmington, Vermont and while hitchhiking had

been picked up by a group of hippies from Rutland, Vermont who had taken her to their residence where she spent the night. She further advised this officer that while spending the night with the group of hippies that she became involved in an argument with one of the girls who was allegedly going out with the person she was sleeping with that night. This officer proceeded to continue north on Route 7 and upon entering the area of Middlebury, Vermont, the accused asked if it was alright if she did some drugs. I then advised her that it was, at which time the accused produced from a blue colored piece of luggage which she was carrying a tin foil wrapper and produced from within the tin foil wrapper a small clear colored plastic wrapper containing a quantity of white powder which she stated was pure cocaine. At this time the accused inquired from this officer if I had a dollar bill at which time I proceeded to give her a dollar bill and she proceeded to roll the dollar bill up in a tight fashion so as to resemble a straw. At this time the accused proceeded to .stick one end of the rolled-up dollar bill in her nose and the other in the bag of alleged cocaine and began to snort a quantity of cocaine into her nostrils. Upon reaching Burlington, Vermont area the accused inquired from this officer where I was going at which time I advised her that I was going to the St. Albans, Vermont area in an effort to acquire some dope. The accused stated that if I didn't mind she would go along with me and that she had some friends in the St. Albans, Vermont area who had a quantity of really good dope. Upon reaching the city of St. Albans, Vermont the accused directed this officer to a location located at 11½ Lake Street at which time she advised me to wait while she went inside and that if she brought me in with her, her friends may become uptight. After a brief period of time the accused appeared back at the vehicle operated by this officer and advised that she had some really good smack if I were interested. Upon advising the accused that I would be interested in purchasing the alleged heroin, she returned back into the apartment and later returned back to this officer's vehicle at which time she stated she would need $360 for the heroin in that she had just laid out the money out [sic] herself. I then advised the accused that I did not have the cash at this time but

that I had a quantity of dope which I was going to drop off
and that I would have the money after that transaction. At
this time I advised the accused that I could not take her
with me and left her off at Pud's Restaurant which is
located on the north side of police headquarters. Upon
leaving the accused off at this area, this officer observed
Sgt. James Thibault, who was directing traffic at this time.
This officer then proceeded to the residence of Chief George
Hebert and advised the chief of the situation and requested
a quantity of drug purchase money. Upon leaving the
residence of the chief, this officer also requested that a
surveillance be established in the area of Pud's Restaurant
so that upon picking up the accused, it could be observed by
the surveillance team. At approximately 1415 hours, this
officer proceeded to the downtown area of St. Albans, Vermont and observed the accused standing on the corner of
Kingman Street and North Main Street at which time this
officer proceeded to pick her up and begin to travel south on
South Main Street. At this time the accused proceeded to
produce from her pocket a large tin foil wrapper containing
a quantity of glassine envelopes which were each sealed
with tape and containing a white powder. This officer then
proceeded to pay the accused $360 in cash consisting of
three one hundred dollar bills, one fifty dollar bill and one
ten dollar bill. The accused then advised that if I were
interested she knew where I could get a quantity of really
good cocaine. This officer then assumed the accused was
talking about possibly an ounce or less of cocaine and
advised her I was interested in purchasing the cocaine at
which time the accused stated we would have to go to
Stowe, Vermont. During the course of the trip from St.
Albans, Vermont to the Stowe, Vermont area, the accused
advised this officer that for approximately five or six years
she had been really heavily involved in narcotics trafficing
in the State of Vermont, New York and various mid-
western states. She further advised this officer that she
was a courier with a group which had just been busted in
the Burlington, Vermont area and for various groups in
the Buffalo, New York area. She further stated that she
had a short time ago gone to Lima, Peru and purchased a
large quantity of cocaine at which time she delivered the
cocaine to a subject in Corsica and from there the cocaine

was later smuggled into the U.S. where it was distributed to various locations. The accused stated that the people she was working for had made approximately $465,000 cash from this cocaine deal and that they had recently deposited it in Swiss bank accounts in Switzerland. Upon arriving in the Stowe, Vermont area we proceeded to Sister Kate's Restaurant and Bar, which is located just off the mountain access road in Stowe, Vermont. After a short time the accused proceeded to go to the telephone and make a call and then came back and advised that the cocaine would be there shortly. At approximately 1745 hours, this officer observed two male subjects enter Sister Kate's, one male subject being approximately six feet tall with blonde curly hair and approximately 35 to 40 years of age. The other male subject being approximately five foot ten to six feet tall having long brown hair and approximately 30 years old in age. At this time both male subjects were greeted by the accused who was sitting with this officer at which time this officer was introduced to both the male subjects. Both of the male subjects and the accused then advised this officer to come out of Sister Kate's restaurant as we proceeded toward a Brown colored Mercedes-Benz vehicle, which was parked in the parking lot. At this time this officer observed that the vehicle had no front license plate or other markings. At this time the blonde haired subject advised me to look in the front seat of the vehicle at which time I looked in the front driver's compartment of the vehicle from the passenger side and observed on the front floor two large clear colored plastic bags containing a large quantity of white powder. I was then advised by both of the unidentified male subjects that each of the bags contained a pound of cocaine. They then stated that the price of the pound was $16,000 per pound or a total of $32,000 for the two pounds. I then advised both of the male subjects and the accused that I did not have that kind of cash on hand with me but that I possibly could see some people and raise the cash at a later time. At this point both of the male subjects entered their vehicle and proceeded to leave the area of Sister Kate's at which time I proceeded back into Sister Kate's with the accused. After conversing with the accused for approximately three more hours, I proceeded to leave the area of Stowe, Vermont and returned the accused

to a location which she directed me to drive to in Burlington, Vermont at which time she was dropped off in the
vicinity of the University of Vermont on Colchester Avenue. Upon leaving the accused off, she proceeded to write
on a piece of matchbook cover, her name and address and
telephone number and advised me to call her at a later date
if I were interested in purchasing any of the larger quantities of cocaine.

At the time Christine was arrested, she knew only that she had
been charged with the sale of heroin to Paul Lawrence; she knew
nothing of the story that the man told of their day together. That
would come out later, when her lawyer began looking into the
charges. She called her family in Buffalo when she got to St. Albans.
Her father, an executive with a large company, was in Europe, but
her family immediately arranged for a local attorney to represent
her. He was John Kissane, perhaps the best lawyer in the city. Her
bail was set at five thousand dollars, very high for someone who
almost certainly would not have fled.

Christine got the first indication of the community's attitude
toward drug sellers when she went before Judge Carl S. Gregg for a
bail hearing. Kissane had known Gregg for years, but that didn't help
at all. Gregg told Kissane that Christine had to be turned over to the
custody of someone responsible in order to win release. So Kissane
suggested his married daughter, a substantial member of the community.

"Oh, no, we're not going to have anything like that," Gregg said
harshly. To Kissane, it sounded as if Gregg had already decided she
was guilty. Gregg finally consented to release her, but on unusually
strict conditions. She was to reside only in Franklin or Chittenden
County, the latter being the location of the university. She was not to
leave her room except during daylight hours and then only to go to
classes or to the library. She was also ordered not to use drugs unless
they were prescribed by a doctor.

"You wouldn't do that for somebody charged with murder," Kissane said later. "She couldn't have been treated any more shabbily if
they had caught her inside a liquor store with a gun holding them
up." At one point later in the spring, Kissane spent several hours
tracking down a probation officer to get permission for Christine to
attend a concert on the university campus in the evening.

On July 1, 1974, some three months after Christine Currey was arrested, the St. Albans police picked up Tony Badamo, a young hippie who was living at a drug rehabilitation center called "Threshold" in Sheldon Springs, north of St. Albans. Badamo was on parole for a drug conviction at the time.

He was one of the more unusual characters to inhabit the St. Albans street scene at the time. He looked like what the kids called a speed freak—thin, wiry, nervous: the impression was that he was taking amphetamines. Badamo wore lots of rings, spent hours working out, and was a karate expert. He also told the other hippies in town that he knew people connected with the Mafia.

When Badamo was arrested, he said that he was innocent. But the report filed by undercover agent Paul Lawrence seemed to fit Badamo to the letter. Lawrence said he had picked up Badamo hitchhiking on the morning of May 21, and that Badamo had told him that he was deeply involved in the illegal drug trade. Lawrence's report said Badamo told him that a shipment of more than twenty pounds of heroin was coming into St. Albans, and that he, Badamo, had a major role in the shipment. Badamo had a friend in Cambridge, Massachusetts, who was helping out in the deal, the story went. Moreover, Lawrence said, Badamo told him that he knew how to get a large quantity of marijuana or hashish; a shipment was due in the Portland, Maine, harbor aboard the Italian fishing boat *San Tio*. Lawrence said in his report that Badamo told him he knew these things because he was a courier for the Cosa Nostra. He had smuggled heroin into the United States in the past, Lawrence said Badamo told him.

In the light of the conversation in the car, Lawrence said he would like to buy some heroin from Badamo and he arranged to meet him later at a parking lot on Lake Street. About 9:45, the Lawrence report said, he met Badamo in the parking lot and bought a quarter ounce of heroin from him for four hundred fifty dollars.

One of the people surprised when the story about this supposed transaction ran in the St. Albans *Messenger* was Andrew Brown, Badamo's probation officer. He had thought Badamo was getting out of the drug traffic; in fact, Brown had helped him get into "Threshold." Bothered about the report of the heroin sale, Brown checked his log for the late May period.

The log showed that Badamo had been in his office, together with Brown's supervisor, Avery J. Smith, for much of the day of the supposed sale, including the time that Lawrence said he had made the buy. Brown remembered picking Badamo up early that morning—Badamo had been in his pajamas when he arrived—and driving him to the court building. How could Lawrence have made a buy from Badamo at 9:45? Brown could not remember Badamo leaving the office at all that morning. And even if he had, how could Badamo have been hitchhiking at the time Lawrence said he was?

It was shortly after ten o'clock in the morning on Oct. 24, 1973, when Edward "Sonny" Cross was awakened by a wild banging on his door. He was groggy and hung over from a night of drinking. His first thought was that whoever wanted to get into his store, the Sand Castles Arts and Crafts Shop, was certainly anxious about it. They were hammering on the door so hard that splinters were flying from it, but Sonny had a bar against the door, and the bar was holding.

He got up and went to the window and pulled aside the curtain. He was staring down the barrel of a gun held by a police officer. Other police officers were hammering on the door. He let them in, and they handcuffed him and quickly searched his store. They took him to the police station and told him what he was accused of—selling heroin, Demerol, cocaine, and MDA to Paul Lawrence, a St. Albans undercover agent.

Cross thought at first that the whole thing was a joke. He didn't know what Demerol was, and he had never seen cocaine or heroin. He had dealt in some drugs on a small scale, but it had been pot or speed, nothing hard. He had recently pleaded guilty to selling ten dollars' worth of speed to a state police undercover agent, and he was under a suspended sentence of up to three years. Sonny had admitted the speed sale; those charges had been accurate and so had the circumstances set forth by the agent. But Sonny claimed this charge was a total mystery. He didn't know any Paul Lawrence, and he had not sold any drugs since his conviction several weeks earlier. And while he could see how the police could make a mistake about a sale of marijuana or speed, the idea that he had sold heroin and cocaine was farfetched. As far as the Demerol went, he had no idea what Demerol was.

Sonny Cross, Christine Currey, Tony Badamo. Three people, all young, linked, over a period of several months, by serious drug charges—sales of heroin and cocaine. Dozens of others were arrested in the same period, some on major charges, some on charges as minor as the sale of a few dollars' worth of LSD. Were they part of some ring, some huge scheme to market hard drugs in northwest Vermont?

Had the ubiquitous soft drugs of the counterculture, marijuana and the like, led to reliance on the drugs of addiction? If there was such a plague threatening the region, when did it begin? And who could be behind it?

Cross, Currey, and Badamo seemed to have no relationship to one another, yet the reports by Paul Lawrence fit their backgrounds quite well. Christine Currey had used cocaine in the past; she was a well-educated, affluent young woman and cocaine was just coming into vogue as the drug of the wealthy and the intellectual. The sale she was charged with involved heroin, but much of Lawrence's story centered on the cocaine connection he said she had set up in Stowe.

Cross was a young hippie, a well-known member of the street culture in St. Albans. The local police had long suspected his tiny shop as being a front for the sale of drugs. In fact, just before he was arrested on the Lawrence charges, Cross had been convicted of the sale of a small amount of speed, or methamphetamine. Badamo was also a notorious member of the street scene in St. Albans; and he, like Cross, had a prior drug conviction at the time he was arrested by Lawrence. Lawrence's report that Badamo was a courier for the Mafia had the ring of plausibility. Badamo had often boasted to his companions that he knew people in the crime organization.

The reports submitted by Paul Lawrence, the young narcotics agent for the St. Albans Police Department, were detailed, specific, persuasive. He recounted conversations with suspects, their mannerisms, their looks, the coloring of their clothing and possessions, the makes and colors of cars, the times that things happened.

These reports both pleased and frightened the people of the community for which Lawrence worked. They were pleased that he had been able to penetrate the counterculture of the area. The circumstances of his locating the drug sellers was random—Christine Currey was a chance encounter on a busy street in central Vermont, Badamo was hitchhiking near St. Albans, Cross was tending his store. Yet, Lawrence was getting so many of these cases that he must be onto some sort of web, some sort of drug structure that spanned a significant area.

The drugs he was buying were horrifying. Cocaine and

heroin—particularly heroin—were the drugs of the big cities. Judge Gregg's harsh bail conditions for Christine Currey were just one indication of the community's attitude. Heroin was a spectre looming over the city and the countryside. It evoked visions of young people with needle-tracked arms losing their lives to an endless addiction.

The presence of these hard drugs lent an air of desperate urgency to the simmering community resentment at the other manifestations of the counterculture—the long hair, the sloppy clothes, the nasty language, the rebellious refusal to honor the ideals of work and other traditional values.

Lawrence seemed to move easily among these people. The rebellious young seemed maddeningly impervious to the normal community pressures—they laughed at the values the straight people held most dear. They were unknowable and unreachable, and thus threatening. The politicians and the public expected the police to deal with this threat, but the police for the most part had great difficulty doing so.

The police understood traditional criminals, but they were as baffled by the relatively sudden appearance of this human scourge as was anyone else. The police were offended by dirty clothes and obscene language and easy sex, but what were they supposed to do about it? If hippies swarmed through the streets and lazed around public places, was that a police problem? The hippies were breaking all the rules, but for the most part they were social rules and not laws: the kids did not work, but they did not indulge in armed robbery either. They enjoyed sex, but they did not go in for assault.

The one set of *laws* they seemed to break most often were the drug laws, but in dealing with this, the police had but little experience. To penetrate the drug trade, the police would have to work undercover, to know the street society from within. For most cops, that was impossible.

That was not the case, however, with Lawrence. He could reach the kids. His reports indicated clearly that he had talked to them, and that he was able to win their confidence; yet, he was as relentless as the straight people themselves would like to be in sweeping this scum off the streets. A few of the politicians and other officials Lawrence dealt with were faintly uneasy about him; they were not convinced that the drug problem was as serious as his charges indicated. But Lawrence inspired great confidence in most officials. He was obviously intelligent, and he was certain of his facts. He was young, like the people he was arresting, and he looked a little like a hippie—he had longish hair and a moustache, but those were necessary for his work. In his conversation with his superiors and in his work itself, he made it clear that he had a deep commitment to solving the drug problem. He was what the city officials needed to save their community.

To the young, like Badamo, Currey, and Cross, the presence of Paul Lawrence fell over their lives, suddenly, like a shadow. A few, like Christine Currey, knew him briefly and accidentally—a quiet-spoken young man who seemed to know a great deal about drugs. To many others, he was not known at all—he was a name on a police warrant, a hand on the shoulder. The charges he made bewildered them. They had often been where he said they had been, or at least it was possible they had been, but they protested frantically that the charges were false. Those with prior drug convictions were as vehement as those who had no such convictions.

But to the street people, the Lawrence charges did not have the ring of plausibility—they had, in fact, just the opposite. The drugs were all wrong. All the street people knew there was no heroin and very little if any cocaine in northwestern Vermont. It was not that the counterculture youth were afraid of them. They simply could not afford such expensive drugs. Finally the word spread among the street people that there was something strange about the charges; they knew that there was a sizeable traffic in soft drugs and many of their number had been convicted for sale or possession of these drugs. In most cases, they admitted these transgressions with little reluctance. Now, each person arrested was saying he was innocent.

"Did you do it?"

"Hell, no."

"What were you charged with?"

"Heroin. *Heroin!*"

"Who is this guy Lawrence, what is he trying to do?"

A sense of fear, of terror even, settled over the counterculture in the face of the Lawrence campaign. Even after people began to recognize his face, because of newspaper photographs or court appearances, the arrests based on his charges went on. *You are under arrest. For selling drugs, heroin, cocaine, methamphetamine. . . . On such and such a day, this officer, while working undercover on illicit drug*

*activity in the city of St. Albans, Vermont, Swanton, Vermont, Bur-
lington, Vermont, saw the accused. . . . He offered me . . . I advised
him . . . I gave him the money. . . .* On and on, the arrests mounting,
week after week, month after month . . .

For years, northwestern Vermont had been a haven for the
counterculture. Life was hard there: the winters were cold and there
was little easy money, but life could also be very cheap, and the
rolling hills and hardwood forests were beautiful. It was a refuge from
the corporation, from the pressures of schools and careers, from the
dangers of the big city slums, from a country at war with a smaller
country, at war with itself.

Now, in early 1974, a heavy sense of menace hung over the
shacks in the hills, the old farmhouses, the rundown apartments of
Lake and Center streets in St. Albans, the seedy bars that dotted St.
Albans and marked the crossroads of the small towns between there
and the Canadian border. No one could tell when there would be a
knock on the door.

Green Mountain State

INTERSTATE ROUTE 89 BEGINS AT AN INTERCHANGE WITH I-93 south of Concord, New Hampshire, and carries traffic from Boston and southern New England to the northwest, through rolling country, to the Connecticut River and into Vermont. The road rises after it leaves the Connecticut, swings across the valley of the White River, and knifes into the Green Mountains. Range after range of hills spill away to the east and west: snow-covered in winter, with patches of dark green spruce and pine alternating with the gray bristle of hardwoods; all green, dark and light, in the summer.

Through the center of the state, the road runs along a high ridge, and to the west lies a long, narrow valley with an occasional white-spired village and meadows patching the hillsides. Still farther north and west, the road follows the Winooski River, which has cut a long, steep-walled valley through the spine of the mountains. This canyon yields to the wide expanse of the north- and south-running Champlain Valley, giving the traveler a breathtaking view of Lake Champlain and the jagged summits of the Adirondacks in New York State. The road turns north at Burlington, the state's only sizeable city, and runs to the Canadian border, and finally to Montreal.

The traveler along this road is likely to be struck by the sheer physical beauty of the region. Indeed, I-89 has often been described as the most scenic interstate highway in the country. Physical beauty is one of the reasons why Vermont has become a mecca for people seeking the new virtues of the last decade—a simpler life, an escape from the urban scramble, a chance to live close to the woods, mountains, lakes, and streams. For the young, this impulse was often expressed in the back-to-the-land movement; in the 1960s, communes began to spring up back in the hills. Many of these are gone now, but their founders can be seen working in the proliferating craft shops and small businesses and living in rejuvenated small farms. They are not as alienated as they once were, but they have retained a simpler set of values.

Gurus to this generation were Helen and Scott Nearing, two New Yorkers who came to the mountains of southern Vermont in the early 1930s and built their own home and outbuildings and fashioned a life-style independent of the overall economy. The Nearings are gone now—they moved to Maine in the 1950s—but their writings inspired a generation to seek a self-sufficient way of life; and many of those people are in Vermont.

It was not just the dropouts who were attracted to Vermont, however. Businessmen and industrialists have moved there too, attracted by the beautiful countryside, plentiful land on which to build, a willing pool of low-priced labor, and easy commuting and transportation. Much of this development has taken place in northwest Vermont, around Burlington. The outstanding example is the big International Business Machines plant in Essex Junction, just east of Burlington.

Explosive growth has become a fact of life in that part of Vermont, too. The state's population in 1970 was about half a million, and of that number, a hundred thousand lived in Chittenden County. That number is expected to rise to 185,000 by 1990. Less than ten years ago, the cows in Vermont outnumbered the people. Dairy farming is still a major industry, but it is not as dominant as it once was.

However, Vermont is much more than Chittenden County. In fact, it is several distinct regions, each with sharply etched characteristics.

Some two hours' drive from Burlington, for example, is a three-county area called the Northeast Kingdom, a seemingly endless expanse of forest and bog: a land of dirt-poor farms and logging camps dotted with small towns and villages whose inhabitants work in the occasional sawmill or factory for minimum wages. In the early 1970s, the median family income was $7,200, at a time when the federal poverty level was $7,300. Twenty percent of the region's nearly fifty thousand people were poor, and many of those were desperately poor. In 1968, an organization, the Citizens Board on Hunger and Malnutrition in the United States, found that there was real hunger in Orleans County. The only other such counties in New England were in northern Maine. Two towns in this region obtained electricity for the first time in 1960. There are whole townships without a single paved road.

This is magnificent country for three of the four seasons. The great sprawling spruce forests, mountains, lakes, and streams provide an unexplored and uncrowded playground for hikers and fishermen and campers, city people who want an inexpensive retreat in the country. It also attracted many of the communards of the 1960s. One of their sites was Earth People's Park, a haven for young people that was purchased in the wake of the Woodstock concert of the late 1960s. Many of the young seekers are gone now, and one of the major reasons is the fourth season of the year.

Winter, which can begin as early as October and runs to at least April, is savage here as well as in much of northern Vermont. Temperatures can drop to thirty-five degrees below zero. The air becomes clear and cold and sharp as glass. The snow sifts in early and deep and lasts: it creaks under foot in the cold. Water and sewer pipes freeze and break. Vehicles won't start, and when they do, they often bog down. Simply keeping warm becomes a problem, and, if you are poor, often an insurmountable problem. The antipoverty agency in the Northeast Kingdom distributes food and firewood to the poor. Happiness in this country can be a reliable four-wheel-drive pickup and a supply of dry wood. Luxury is a snowmobile. Life contracts.

The climate is similar in other parts of the state, but life is not so harsh. Much of central Vermont is still the land of the *Vermont Life* magazine calendar photograph: picturesque hill farms, tiny quaint villages, cows wandering into the barnyard, smoke curling from the chimneys of the maple-sugar houses, lichened stone walls trailing across the hillsides.

Southern Vermont, which in the Nearings' time was similar to the Northeast Kingdom, has been effectively colonized by affluent expatriates from New York and New Jersey and southern New England—many of them live there only part time. But they have poured money into the refurbishing of the old, colonial farmhouses and the sprawling old mansions of the small towns. Many of them are skiers, and the area around Mount Snow and Stratton Mountain is now dotted by chalets, some tacky, some not, and by condominiums. These people coexist more or less harmoniously with the young people who began moving in around the 1960s. The city of Brattleboro, particularly, has a faintly funky, back-to-the-land air.

Because of its rugged grandeur and its cheap land, Vermont has become a site for the confluence of two generations: the deeply conservative older generation, the liberal-to-radical young. In some regions, these generations have meshed; in others they have clashed, with differences in life-style and outlook generating savage tensions.

Chittenden County, whose center is the city of Burlington, is one extreme. It is suburban America. The city has a population of some forty thousand persons and is the home of the University of Vermont and two smaller colleges. The surrounding suburbs are heavily populated by well-educated, well-paid people—engineers from General Electric and IBM, stockbrokers, lawyers, real estate people, businessmen, and academics. The living is easy—one can live in a village that is rural, by northeastern standards, and commute to one's office in Burlington in fifteen minutes.

The city itself has good restaurants and excellent bars. It has the warm ambience of a small town and the many amenities of a larger city. The area supports one of the country's better Shakespeare festivals; there are museums, concerts, plays. The university hockey team is a major winter attraction. Boston is four hours by interstate highway; Montreal, less than two.

For some young people, there has been another signal advantage to living in Burlington—a relatively relaxed attitude toward the drug traffic. There has for years been a sizeable traffic in drugs there, most of them soft—marijuana, hashish, barbiturates; very little heroin.

The Burlington Police Department established a drug unit about 1970, but there never was the fierce public pressure to stamp out drugs that was felt in other parts of the state. Although there never was a written policy, Chittenden County State's Attorney Patrick Leahy, the local prosecutor, was thought to be the first state's attorney in Vermont to decline to prosecute young people for possession of small amounts of marijuana. That is not to say there was no anti-drug effort in the Burlington area; there was. But if you were a small-time user and not a dealer, the level of your anxiety was not likely to be as high in Burlington as elsewhere.

Leahy, who did much to modernize the local prosecutor's office and to professionalize as well as liberalize law enforcement, was a symbol of the local attitude. He gained national attention in the early 1970s by writing a hilarious directive to local police departments containing guidelines on circumstances under which nude swimmers ought to be arrested. If the officer had to walk miles through the woods, climbing over fallen trees and fighting his way through the brush to capture someone swimming nude in a remote mountain stream, perhaps he ought to be doing something else with his time. In other Vermont jurisdictions, such swimmers continued to be arrested.

Politically, Burlington and much of Chittenden County is Democratic, due partly to the blue-collar workers who have lived there for generations and who formerly were a Democratic island in a Republican sea, and due to the influx of liberals and radicals that came both from industrial growth and the region's role as a home for alienated young people. In 1962, Philip Hoff, a Burlington lawyer and a native of Massachusetts, became the first Democratic governor in Vermont since Reconstruction days. In 1974, Patrick Leahy, likewise a Burlington Democrat, won the United States Senate seat vacated by the retiring Republican patriarch, George Aiken.

Burlington has thus been the focal point for Vermont's slow swing from the Republican heritage that made it one of the most conservative states in the union. Chittenden County casts about 25 percent of the state's vote, but by 1974, Democrats had penetrated enough constituencies in other parts of the state to swing the Vermont House of Representatives to their control for the first time in this century.

Even Republican officeholders have begun to shift ground. James Jeffords, the state's lone congressman, has become a thorn in the side of the major oil companies since his election in 1974. And Senator Robert Stafford, a conservative as a young man, has in recent years fashioned so liberal a record, particularly on labor issues, that the AFL-CIO declined in 1976 to endorse his Democratic opponent, which is usually a formality.

The state's increasing liberality is also reflected in the relative success of the Liberty Union party, a feisty splinter group that grew out of the antiwar movement and has shifted its focus now to economic power and organization. They have pressed such issues as the public ownership of the utility companies; and while they have not succeeded in winning an election, their candidates have received 5 percent of the vote often enough to give them the right under state law to a primary election.

The liberal impulse in the state has given Vermont some of the nation's most progressive legislation. In the field of land use and development, for example, Vermont's Act 250 is the most advanced legislation in the country aimed at controlling development. Vermont has banned billboards and throwaway bottles and cans. In the field of social legislation, Vermont has for some years operated a "Tooth Fairy" program under which poor youngsters get free dental care; some of them never before had any dental care.

Nonetheless, this liberalizing trend has not supplanted the deep-rooted conservatism in much of the state. The Vermont town meeting is still the form of local government for most of the communities in the state, and in these forums few advanced ideas are likely to find easy going. There is also a dark side to the Vermont experience. Bigotry and intolerance flourish as they can in any insular community.

A striking example of these attitudes took place in 1968 in the tiny hamlet of Irasburg in the Northeast Kingdom. David L. Johnson, a black minister, moved to town with his wife and four children. Accompanying them was a white woman with her two young children. Mr. Johnson, a strongly opinionated man, rented a house in the town and moved in.

Shortly thereafter, a carload of men fired a barrage of shotgun blasts at the house one night, shattering several windows. Larry Conley of nearby Glover, a young army sergeant home on leave, later was arrested in connection with the attack. He had been incensed by the presence of the black Johnsons and had suggested to some of his friends that they "go up and scare the niggers."

Young Conley, the son of a prominent man in Glover, was given a suspended sentence of from six to eighteen months on the charge, but the local prosecutor and the local contingent of the Vermont State Police were so reluctant to bring the charges that Governor Philip Hoff ultimately established a special commission to study the case.

The actual prosecution was carried out by the office of Vermont Attorney General James Oakes, who stepped in to take it over from the local prosecutor.

Meanwhile, the black man and the white woman were arrested on a charge of adultery. The Vermont state trooper who had been stationed in the Johnson home, supposedly to protect the occupants from any more nightriding attacks, said he had observed the two together early one morning. The woman subsequently pleaded no contest to the charge and the charge against the minister was dropped. It was clear to the commission that studied the case that, while the adultery charge might have been technically justified, the primary aim of the state was to drive the Johnsons from the area. No adultery charges had been brought by the state police in years.

The hostility to what was seen as alien was experienced by Stephen Terry, then a political writer for the Rutland *Herald,* who was traveling with James Oakes one day when he went into Irasburg. Terry sat for a while on the front porch of the Johnson home and while he was there, several cars passed the house slowly, their occupants yelling, "Nigger lovers!" at the people in the yard. When Terry drove out of town, he was followed closely by a car bearing Vermont plates and with a Confederate flag displayed on the window.

The same sort of reaction, though muted, took place when Governor Philip Hoff brought more than two hundred black youngsters from Harlem to Vermont for a vacation in a program worked out with then New York Mayor John Lindsay. The program grew out of Hoff's sympathetic reaction to the Kerner Commission report, which had warned that riots in American cities in the late 1960s presaged a divided society, black and white.

The Hoff action represented the state's liberal and progressive instincts; the anger and hatred it spawned, similar to that generated in Irasburg by the presence of the Johnson family, spoke for the other side.

Neither Hoff nor James Oakes, now a federal judge, won office again in Vermont after 1968, although other liberal politicians later did.

The strains of the racial issues of the 1960s touched Vermont only marginally. The state was more directly affected by the back-to-the-land and protest movements of the sixties and early seventies. In Chittenden County, these pressures were absorbed in the processes of urban and suburban growth; in southern Vermont, they blended, finally, into the area's faintly bohemian atmosphere. But in the northern, rural areas of the state, the influx of newcomers often brought a harsh reaction.

The townspeople of Norton, for example, hated and feared the people who drifted into Earth People's Park, the big, loosely structured commune on the Canadian border. Some of the young people who came there tried to get along with the townsfolk, but others tramped across the farmers' fields and shouted and caroused in town. At times, this conflict came near to open violence. On one occasion, a farmer fired a couple of warning shots at people crossing his field; later they threatened him in his farmyard; an open flare-up was prevented by the police. The prospect of a rock festival in the Northeast Kingdom, common in the early seventies, inevitably drew angry protests and calls for additional police protection. Some prospective festivals had to be canceled. These confrontations were political to a degree. Some radical theorists argued in the 1960s that communes and settlements of people committed to alternative life-styles would provide a political base for some kind of revolution in the United States. Tom Hayden called for the creation of "free territories in the Mother Country," and "rural Vermont" was one of the sites he suggested. He said these territories "should be centers from which a challenge to the whole Establishment is mounted." The magazine *Playboy* contributed to this speculation by running an article about the prospect of hippies taking over Vermont because of their sheer numbers there. But such a takeover never was a serious prospect.

The critical source of tension was the challenge to prevailing values and life-styles posed by the newcomers to the state. The communes were foreign to native Vermonters; so were the drugs some of the hippies brought with them. The older native Vermonters could see their own children's hair lengthening and beards sprouting, and they could see them adopting the drug habits, particularly the use of marijuana, and other characteristics of a nationwide counterculture.

The dress of the young grew sloppier; they were sloughing off traditional ideas about sex and marriage; they felt differently about going to church; their language took on an aggressively vulgar and obscene aspect. Equally important was the attitude of many hippies, native or immigrant, toward work. Poverty has been pervasive in Vermont for generations—making a living on its rocky, hillside farms and in its endless forests has never been easy and has often been close to impossible. Many towns had a poor farm where indigents could go, and welfare for urban residents has been common, too. But it has always been a matter of shame, something to be hidden. For people, especially young and vigorous people, to refuse to work, indeed to appear to refuse *on principle* to work, raised for some Vermonters the threat of collapse of their way of life.

A Cop's Credentials

TWO YEARS BEFORE THE FIRST ST. ALBANS ARRESTS, IN the early morning hours of September 8, 1971, three young men climbed into a pickup truck and drove down Route 4 in Rutland, Vermont, headed for the Farrell Distributing Company, a big soft-drink wholesaler. The three men had carried out a series of burglaries in the Rutland area in the previous year. This night they would hit the Farrell warehouse.

The warehouse, they knew, was protected by a silent burglar alarm, but there was a night deposit box on the warehouse wall, and they thought they could breach that. It was nearly 3:00 A.M. when the truck rolled into the warehouse parking lot. The driver swung the truck around, then backed up to the deposit hatch. The trio got out and hooked up a heavy chain from the back of the truck to the hatch cover. The driver pulled slowly ahead; the chain stretched taut—and snapped.

The driver cursed. His companions threw the chain into the truck and hurried back into the cab. The driver then pulled the vehicle back onto the roadway, but the three men were reluctant to abandon the enterprise. They would wait for twenty minutes or so; if no one appeared by then, it would be clear the alarm had not been tripped, and they could try again.

Moments later, they saw a Vermont State Police cruiser racing down Route 4. The cruiser turned into the Farrell Distributing Company parking lot. The three men drove away quickly, the night's work aborted.

The driver of the state police car was Trooper Paul Lawrence. He had been at the Rutland hospital when the alarm had sounded from Farrell and was ordered to the warehouse.

Lawrence said that when he got to Farrell's, he saw a man with a red shirt and dark trousers standing at the point where the Farrell driveway joined the highway. When he got to the warehouse, Lawrence later reported, he saw lights in the warehouse office and he thought he saw three men in the southwest corner of the building.

Lawrence pulled his cruiser up to the warehouse, halted, and radioed the barracks for help. He opened the door and got out; as he did so, the office lights went out. Then, he said, he saw a figure appear at an upstairs window and aim a rifle or shotgun at him. Lawrence said he took cover behind the cruiser door.

"Within the next few seconds, a volley of blasts were heard by this officer and the driver's side window of the patrol car was shattered by some type of projectile, and also this officer heard some type of projectile strike the roof of the patrol car," Lawrence wrote in his report.

Lawrence then fired at the upstairs window with a shotgun of his own. He retreated to a trash barrel, took cover, and fired another round at the window. He then raced to the warehouse door to keep anyone from escaping, then back to the patrol car to radio for help again.

By this time, the gunfire and the frantic radio calls for help drew policemen from all over the area—state police, Rutland city police, and sheriff's department officers. They flooded the warehouse area with light and surrounded the building, calling on the people inside to surrender. When no one came out, they filled the building with tear gas. This got no response either, so they searched the building. They found no one.

The Farrell Distributing case was never officially solved, but a year later a young man was arrested by police and questioned by the Rutland County state's attorney about several robberies in the area. He cooperated in order to secure a lighter sentence, and he told about the activities of himself and his friends. One of the incidents was the attempt on Farrell Distributing. The man took a lie detector test, and the examiner concluded that his story about the night at Farrell's was true.

The story appeared to confirm the serious doubts that had arisen about the gunshot-filled night at Farrell's. The window on the driver's side of Lawrence's cruiser had been almost entirely blown out. Normally, a shot fired from a distance will leave a hole in the window with a web of cracks radiating from it. The muzzle blast from a shot fired at close range, on the other hand, would shatter the window. Moreover, there was a crease in the roof of the cruiser and a 38-caliber bullet, the caliber used by policemen, fit in it perfectly.

The state police took no official action concerning the Farrell incident, but stories about it quickly showed up on the law enforcement grapevine in Vermont. John Gladding, a part-time television reporter for WCAX in Burlington heard about it, and he told his friends at the TV station. Many cops and prosecutors in the state heard about it also.

Some of them were not surprised. Lawrence had been a policeman since 1966, and wherever he went his performance would be impressive then, somehow, questionable. Early in his state police career, he had worked as an undercover agent in Brattleboro. Half a dozen suspected drug dealers were convicted on the basis of his testimony, but then discrepancies showed up in his court testimony and the Windham County state's attorney, M. Jerome Diamond, refused to prosecute any more Lawrence cases. The state police took Lawrence out of Windham County then, but wherever he went in the next couple of years, the people he arrested protested their innocence vigorously, or said that drug sales they had made occurred differently from the way he described them.

There were other bits and pieces of odd behavior in Lawrence's career: he beat a handcuffed prisoner with a flashlight; he was embroiled in constant controversy during the five months he served as police chief of Vergennes.

Lawrence always seemed to stand out: apparently more successful than other cops, but one who raised more questions, too. Who was this man?

Paul David Lawrence was born in Fall River, Massachusetts, on

December 11, 1944, and grew up in Barrington, Rhode Island, a suburb of Providence. He attended La Salle Academy, a Catholic High School for boys in Providence, for one year, and spent the rest of his high school years at Barrington High School, graduating at the age of nineteen.

As a schoolboy, Lawrence was a heavy drinker and it got him into trouble with the authorities. It was against the law for youths under twenty-one to drink then, and Lawrence was arrested once, on a charge of possession of malt beverages (beer), and given a nine-month suspended sentence. This charge was the only untoward thing that showed up on his record in his early years in Vermont.

Lawrence drifted after high school. He worked in 1964 and 1965 as a carpenter's helper in Barrington and on Cape Cod. On October 29, 1965, he enlisted in the United States Army, and underwent basic training at Fort Dix, New Jersey. He got excellent ratings on his performance. Then he went into advanced infantry training.

In January of 1966, Lawrence collapsed in his barracks and was taken to Walson Army Hospital where he was operated on for the removal of his appendix. Doctors concluded on examination that his appendix was normal, but they took it out anyway, which is standard medical procedure. Lawrence recovered uneventfully, and went back to his barracks. His assignment was "light duty." At that point his military career began to unravel.

Two weeks after his operation, he left the post without permission, returning after eleven days. He was charged with being absent without leave (AWOL) and punished under Article 15, which permits commanders to administer penalties for minor infractions without going through a court-martial. If a soldier desires, however, he can demand a court-martial, in effect a trial, if he wants to contest the charges.

Lawrence's military records show that he went AWOL on February 18, 1966, and returned on February 28 voluntarily. He was ordered to forfeit twenty dollars per month of his pay for one month, and he was restricted to his company area for fourteen days and ordered to carry out extra duty for fourteen days. He was also recycled to a new unit.

On March 7, Lawrence went AWOL again, returning, again voluntarily, on March 16. This time he was ordered to forfeit twenty dollars a month for two months, and to remain in his company area for thirty days. On March 26, Lawrence went AWOL again, for four days, returning March 30. This time he was fined thirty-five dollars a month for two months, and ordered to remain in his company area for the remainder of his assignment, but not to exceed sixty days.

It was clear by this time that Lawrence intended to get out of the army as soon as possible. He had returned to the hospital in early 1966, complaining of a pain in his side, near the location of his recent operation. No medical problem could be found; he also kept going to the hospital with a variety of other medical complaints not related to the appendectomy. Lawrence had also told his superior officer that he hated the army and wanted to get out.

After his third AWOL, the army initiated discharge proceedings. Lawrence was interviewed by a psychiatrist, John W. Rosenberger, a captain at the Mental Hygiene Consultation Service at the Walson Army Hospital.

On May 16, 1966, Rosenberger and Captain Paul A. D'Oronzio, a social worker, issued the following report:

1. This is the report of neuropsychiatric examination in the case of:
   LAWRENCE, Paul D. RA11 463 585 Pvt. Co. K, 1st AIT Bde.

2. PERTINENT HISTORY: This 21 year old single Caucasian enlistee with five months service was referred by his commanding officer prior to administrative action. He is described as chronically AWOL, and refusing to train. The EM (enlisted man Lawrence) states that he "hates it here," and wants to be home. . . . In the past the EM has been able to avoid facing the unpleasant consequences of his decisions by familial intervention. His decision to enlist was impulsive and a poorly considered effort to avoid being drafted.

3. MENTAL STATUS: Subject presents as a quiet, though somewhat guarded, young man who is candid about his desire to get out of the service. No thinking disorder is present. Affect is constricted but in general appropriate with mild depression. Intelligence is average, memory intact, and impulse control poor.

4. DIAGNOSIS: Passive-dependent personality.

5. <u>FINDINGS:</u>
   a. In my opinion, the above-named person was and is mentally responsible, able to distinguish right from wrong and to adhere to the right, and has the mental capacity to understand and participate in board proceedings.
   b. The above-named person has no mental disease or defect sufficient to warrant disposition through medical channels.
   c. This condition is not amenable to treatment, counseling, disciplinary action, transfer or change of duty.

6. <u>RECOMMENDATION:</u> Whether this man is separation [*sic*] from service or not is a command decision. However, it is our recommendation that this individual should be separated under the appropriate administrative regulation. Retention on active duty can be expected to result in continued ineffectiveness and disciplinary infractions.

Both Rosenberger and D'Oronzio signed the report.

In addition to the psychiatric report, army authorities obtained statements from four of Lawrence's superiors to the effect that they would not trust him, and that they did not want him in their commands.

"I would not want Pvt. Lawrence in my unit at any time," wrote Captain Anthony J. Curcio, Jr., the commander of Co. K. "I feel it would be of benefit to the U.S. Army to release Pvt. Lawrence from the military as soon as possible."

Lawrence's first sergeant in Co. K said essentially the same thing: "What I observed of this EM while he was assigned to this unit was that I would not want to be associated with him at any time. Private Lawrence cannot be trusted with any of the duties required of a soldier."

He was discharged under the provisions of Army Regulation 635-209, which allows for the release of enlisted men for character and behavior disorders and apathy. None of this involved medical disabilities; and, moreover, it precludes the soldier's right to veterans' benefits and is normally a bar to reenlistment in the armed forces. His discharge was a general one, under honorable conditions, which in itself was a serious matter—anything less than an honorable discharge can follow a man for life.

There was no doubt that Lawrence understood the nature of the actions being taken against him. On June 8, 1966, Lieutenant Rolf Erickson met with Lawrence to advise him of his rights and of the nature of the army's case against him. Lawrence signed a receipt acknowledging that he had been given the statements of his four superiors. Erickson told him he was being discharged because of character and behavior disorders and apathy; that likewise was acknowledged. Lawrence also said he was in good health.

Lawrence did not have to accept this outcome, but he did so willingly. He waived his right to a lawyer and to a formal hearing. In June, Paul Lawrence left the army. He had been a soldier just over seven months, and he had a badly flawed record. Twenty-six days after his discharge, he applied for a job with the Burlington Police Department.

He was successful and went to work there on August 14, 1966. The department did not check his military record, and they accepted his version of his arrest in Barrington as a schoolboy prank. Lawrence's career in Burlington was uneventful for the most part. He impressed Chief Arthur J. Caron with his ability, although some of his fellow officers felt he was unnecessarily enthusiastic when he arrested the drunks and vagrants around City Hall, the center of his beat. Some also resented the fact that he spent all his service on the day shift, even though most rookies had to work nights.

Still, he had no serious problems. Lawrence was very likable, and was considered to be an effective cop. He was not a college graduate, but neither are most local cops, and in fact, Lawrence was seen as highly intelligent. He also gave the impression that he was a rugged guy with nerve, although he did not seem mean; he lacked the swaggering, aggressive posture of some cops. He weighed about 190 pounds, and stood five feet eleven inches tall. He made lots of arrests, although Chief Caron observed that he got into trouble more than most officers.

On May 27, 1967, Lawrence left the Burlington department to join the Vermont State Police. The state police also did not check Lawrence's military records. They did check his credit rating in Burlington, and it was acceptable. They also got a letter from the guidance director at Barrington High School, stating that Lawrence had graduated on June 4, 1964. The officer making the check said in his remarks that "the writer was unable to find anything derogatory about the applicant around Burlington."

Lawrence's superior was Lieutenant John Poljacik, the troop commander in Rutland, who liked Lawrence. Lawrence always was neat and clean, his shoes and the leatherwork on his uniform gleamed. The man never refused an assignment, which likewise impressed Poljacik. In fact, he often volunteered to go out on calls or cases; nothing was too rough or dirty, the tougher the better. Lawrence was very respectful to Poljacik, an older man.

At the time, the Vermont State Police, like police in many jurisdictions, were just getting into drug work in a serious way. Few cops had any experience with it, yet drugs were becoming so pervasive that almost anyone could be an undercover agent; in that sense it was different from gambling or organized crime—no expertise was required, only nerve. Lawrence in effect, therefore, was working without supervision. And his methods were not out of the ordinary.

The cops called them "one-on-one buys." Lawrence would say that he discovered or bought drugs from a person, and that statement, plus the drugs themselves, would consist of the case against the suspect. There would be no corroboration in most instances, either by another officer or through the use of electronic devices. There was no serious effort in the early days to preclude the possibility that a bad cop, or even an overzealous one, could step outside the law and manufacture a phony case.

From the beginning of his career, however, Lawrence drew more complaints from victims than any of the other narcotics cops, although other people arrested by the state police claimed they were innocent. Two cases in St. Johnsbury will serve to make the point.

In the winter of 1969–70, Lawrence and another state trooper went into a local bar to try to buy some marijuana from a waitress they had heard was a dealer. The two men asked the waitress if they could buy some marijuana, but she said she had none. After some conversation, it became obvious to Lawrence's partner that they could not make the buy, so he suggested they leave.

But Lawrence insisted on staying and his partner left. Five minutes later, Lawrence walked out of the bar with a napkin containing marijuana. He said he made the buy for five dollars. The woman insisted she was innocent, but she was tried before a jury and convicted.

In a second case, Lawrence said he had gone alone to the apartment of a college student who was suspected of dealing in drugs. He said that the suspect and his girlfriend were in the apartment and that he had bought some LSD from the two of them. Lawrence said he had told the primary suspect that he wanted to buy some acid, and the man had instructed the girl to get the sugar cubes, impregnated with the drug. Lawrence said she did so, returning with a tin of cubes and giving some to him while he paid the main suspect.

Robert Gensberg, the local state's attorney, charged both the man and his girlfriend with the sale. The main suspect pleaded guilty and after he was sentenced, the man and his attorney told Gensberg that while Lawrence's basic story about the sale was true, the girl had not even been in the apartment when the sale took place. The woman offered to take a lie detector test, and the state police examiner concluded she was telling the truth. Gensberg's successor, Dale Gray, thereupon dropped the charges against the girl.

In the early summer of 1970, Lawrence arrived in Brattleboro to continue his undercover work for the state police. Jerry Diamond was the state's attorney there, new to the job and under heavy pressure from the community to do something about the drug menace in the area. Brattleboro was a haven for the counterculture, and there was lots of marijuana in town. The use of and sale of marijuana was considered a serious offense at the time, and Diamond wanted to do something about it.

Diamond was very shrewd, a politically ambitious Democrat, and a hard-liner on crime. But until Lawrence showed up, working for the state police, Diamond had no resources to deal with drug abuse. Lawrence began making a series of arrests shortly after he arrived in town. Diamond was immediately impressed with the man. He was the most knowledgeable drug agent Diamond had ever met. He seemed to know about the technical side of drugs, the prices, the street customs surrounding their use, the way the drug traffic worked. The defense attorneys in these early cases contended their clients were innocent, but they could not prove it, and the juries were convicting the suspects. Many of them had been thought for months to be drug dealers, but the local police had never been able to make a case against them.

By the end of the summer, Diamond and his assistants began to have problems with Lawrence. There was no question in their minds that the people he was arresting were pushers; still, Lawrence seemed to have problems remembering the events surrounding various arrests. One of the characteristics of his reports was detailed descriptions of conversations with people. But as time went on, his stories seemed to change. Lawrence's excuse was that he was so busy he did not have time to read his reports when testifying on a given case. But Diamond was still uneasy.

The process of an arrest was naturally a drawn-out one. Lawrence would file an affidavit of probable cause when the person was arraigned; he would file a police report at a different time; there would be a probable cause hearing, possibly several weeks later; defense attorneys, at still another time, could question Lawrence in detail, under oath, in what is called a deposition; and there would be the trial itself, still further removed from the alleged crime. Lawrence could tell his story each step of the way. As the summer wore on, the defense attorneys built an increasing store of Lawrence stories and statements, and any change or contradictions in them could be fatal to the prosecution.

At first, the peculiarities involved not the fact that buys had taken place, but rather the circumstances of them—in the way, for instance, that prosecutors had noticed in two St. Johnsbury cases. In one instance, Lawrence said he bought some marijuana from two girls on the campus of Windham College. He said they came up to him and offered him a marijuana cigarette. He said he pretended to smoke it, then bought some for himself. The girls in question told a different story. They admitted selling him the marijuana, but they said he had offered them a cigarette one day, then made the buy from them a week later. Diamond traced down a witness to the sale and she said that Lawrence's story, except for the transaction itself, was false.

On August 11, 1970, Lawrence reported that he had bought some hashish from a man named Allen V. Daley of Brattleboro. There was no corroboration. Daley was arrested September 4, in accordance with Lawrence's normal practice. Lawrence would make several buys without arresting anyone, then arrest them later. The idea was to gain people's confidence, to find as many links in the drug traffic as possible, and to avoid having his "cover" destroyed. In this instance, Daley swore he was somewhere else at the time of the alleged sale, but he went to trial on September 12, and the jury convicted him. Jerry Diamond prosecuted the case.

The trial was watched with keen interest by many of the hippies in the area, and during a recess in the trial, someone called Lawrence a pig outside of the courtroom. Lawrence grabbed one of the youths, Howard Lieberman, slammed him up against a door, and broke his glasses. Then he arrested the man for disorderly conduct.

Lawrence wanted Diamond to prosecute the disorderly conduct case, but Diamond wanted a witness. Another state trooper had seen the youth assault him, Lawrence said, but when Diamond talked to the other officer, he said he had not in fact seen it. What the kids in the hallway told Diamond was that Lawrence had roughed up Lieberman after someone in the crowd had called Lawrence a name. Lieberman subsequently sued Lawrence for brutality and won a $2,500 judgment, which the insurance carrier for the state police paid.

Meanwhile, another Lawrence case was coming to trial, that of Aaron Struthers. When Lawrence took the stand, he told the jury he had made the Struthers buy at precisely the time he had said he made the Daley buy—at a different location. Edward John, Struthers' attorney, caught the discrepancy, brought it out in court, and his client was acquitted.

All this was too much for Diamond. He told Lawrence that unless he would take a lie detector test, he, Diamond, would not prosecute any more of Lawrence's cases. Lawrence refused, and he left Windham County. Diamond's deputy, Garvan Murtha, wrote a letter to State Police Lieutenant Robert Iverson outlining the problems their office had had with Lawrence. He got no answer.

The action by Diamond and Murtha was the first serious impeachment of Paul Lawrence as a policeman. It was possible of course that the discrepancy in his court testimony in the Daley and Struthers cases was simply an honest mistake, but it came on top of numerous other mistakes—mistakes that were becoming so common that Diamond no longer believed the man.

But no one followed the issue any further, neither Diamond, who was happy to see Lawrence gone, nor the state police, who now had a formal, on-the-record complaint by a county prosecutor that one of their best undercover men might be untrustworthy. Lawrence could not work as a narc in Windham County, but that left the remainder of the state . . .

By early 1971, however, the state police took Lawrence out of undercover work, for reasons that have never been quite clear. Major

Glenn Davis, the number-two man in the state police hierarchy, said later that taking a man out of undercover work after a year or two is simply an administrative move. There was nothing about Lawrence's work that caused the state police to lose confidence in him, Davis said.

Davis was evasive, however, about the complaint made by Diamond's office. He had heard of it, he said, but he could not remember what had been done about it. He added, though, that "We don't ignore that kind of thing." The state police's handling of the Lawrence case over the nine months following his transfer back to uniformed service indicated that the department had become disillusioned with the man, but his fall from favor was cloaked from public view, a fact that made much of his later career possible.

For despite the reports and incidents that seriously clouded his background, Lawrence's public record was clear. His resumé, which he would present to future potential employers, contained state police efficiency reports that sang his praises and bulged with commendations about his work as a state trooper.

His immmediate commander, Poljacik, rated Lawrence outstanding in most categories, fully satisfactory in the handful of others, for the period from November 1, 1969, to November 1, 1970. Under "Quality of Work," Poljacik rated Lawrence outstanding, the highest rating, and noted that he was "Very neat and thorough[ly] accurate—little need for review." In his overall comments, Poljacik noted that Lawrence had been assigned to drug work in Troop C, but that he had been so good at it he had helped in drug investigations in other parts of the state.

"He has made many cases in buying of drugs and users as well," Poljacik wrote. "His productivity and conviction record is high. He has demonstrated the ability in Court Trials on the cases too. He is an outstanding officer in this field and has the potentials for more responsible duties."

The prosecutors that Lawrence worked for felt the same way. Neil S. Moss, then a county prosecutor in Bennington County, wrote to Poljacik on December 14, 1970, to comment on Lawrence's transfer back to uniformed duty. "In my dealings with Paul I have found him to be utterly dedicated, dependable, professional, and honest without exception," Moss wrote. "Paul worked such long hours and was involved in so many different cases that I am frankly awed by the competence he displayed under such circumstances."

Stephen L. Klein, an assistant state's attorney in Rutland County, was equally effusive. He said in a letter that Lawrence would later use as a reference that Lawrence was "one of the most outstanding, if not the most outstanding, of the officers with whom I have dealt. . . .

"There were many times when Paul arrested someone on a serious felony at 3 a.m. and I would find on my desk at 8 a.m. the same morning, a five or six page type-written report, including statements of witnesses, pictures, and a full and complete police record of the defendant, the latter needed to support any recommendation for bail at the arraignment.

"I have found in my experience as a prosecutor that once an arrest is made, many police officers consider the case closed, even though there may be a great deal of investigation to be completed in order to secure a conviction," Klein's letter continued. "Paul never stopped at the arrest. On his own volition, in addition to his other current duties, he continued to secure statements of witnesses, collect evidence and secure those detailed bits of evidence which I felt were invaluable in achieving the ultimate result."

Klein went on to write that Lawrence was particularly experienced as a drug agent and that he would be "an immeasurable asset to any police department."

These comments could be expected to carry weight with future employers of Lawrence. There was no way to tell from his official record that Lawrence was in trouble with the state police administration. Nonetheless on August 13, 1971, Lawrence was ordered to move from Rutland to a subtroop in Bethel, Vermont, a considerable distance to the northeast. The transfer was to be effective September 15.

Later, knowledgeable observers like Jerry Diamond would contend that this sort of transfer was the way the state police dealt with its problem children. Lawrence's reaction to the order was one of anger and resentment. He argued that his wife, Carole, had a good job in Rutland that she wanted to keep and that it would be difficult for him to find acceptable housing in the Bethel area.

The commander at Bethel had established a rule that troopers assigned to his office live in either Bethel or nearby Randolph. One reason was that the station was short of patrol cars and the commander wanted his men nearby and available for emergency calls. But the letters that Lawrence wrote to the police administration disclose an unusual inflexibility on the part of the police administration toward his requests for time to work out his housing problems. Finally, he decided he would resign.

The letter of resignation is instructive. Lawrence complained bitterly about the housing question, noting that others were given a chance to work out some arrangement on commuting. The administration's refusal to let him do the same "indicates clearly to me that I no longer have your support and continuing efforts by me would result only in further frustration," he wrote.

He concluded: "I have decided, as I intimated to you earlier, to return to college and complete my education. Although you told me a leave of absence may not be available under such circumstances, if it is, I ask that you regard this letter as a request for a leave of absence rather than a tender of resignation."

One may read between the lines here and infer that the administration was, in its own way, forcing Lawrence to resign. But there was no such indication on the record. Later, Captain Harold Dean of the state police would comment that Lawrence should have been given the lowest possible rating, but that judgment did not prevail at the time. Commissioner Edward Corcoran and Glenn Davis, the number-two man, apparently made the judgment that Lawrence should be allowed to go quietly.

No one knows why they chose that route. Perhaps they did not wish to shut Lawrence out from other law enforcement positions. Perhaps it would have introduced a strain into their own organization: men like Poljacik and some of the troopers Lawrence worked with thought highly of him. Perhaps the hierarchy feared that the image of the state police would suffer damage. The only thing that is certain is that Lawrence emerged from the Vermont State Police with his record and his reputation intact.

Before he left, however, he had one more problem. In the early morning hours of September 25, Lawrence and two other troopers responded to a complaint by a Bethel woman that a drunken man had wandered into her trailer and had gone to sleep in her bed. The three troopers went to the trailer and tried to wake the man up. When they succeeded, he arose from the bed, swinging wildly. They subdued him, handcuffed him, and led him from the trailer. The woman later told police that when two of the troopers were leading the man toward the door, while he was handcuffed, Lawrence had struck the man on the head with a flashlight and had kneed him in the stomach.

Sergeant George Nickerson later investigated the case and concluded that "Tpr. Lawrence was unnecessarily rough," and that he (Nickerson) felt "that there was no need for the use of the flashlight to make this apprehension." The woman agreed to take a lie detector test, and the examiner concluded that her story about the assault on the drunk was true. Nothing was done about this flashlight assault, but Paul Lawrence was gone shortly thereafter—he was no longer the state police's problem.

A Town Divided

DIANE VOUDRIEN DIED ON JUNE 16, 1973, TWO WEEKS before her eighteenth birthday. A beautiful, highly intelligent girl, she had lived in foster homes for most of her life. She had recently returned to St. Albans to attend Bellows Free Academy (BFA), the local high school, and to be near her mother, Rosemary, who lived at 29A Catherine Avenue, at the rear of the St. Albans House, now known as Benson's, an ancient and decrepit former hotel.

Diane had attended BFA in the spring semester, but she had not graduated. She told her friends she was going to attend an Upward Bound program at Johnson State College and get her high school diploma that way. Meanwhile, she had fallen easily into the St. Albans counterculture, working now and then, drifting around the park, often with her dog Safflower. Much of her time was spent with the members of the Graefe band, a group of hard rock musicians who had become notorious in the town. Some were from Sheldon, a tiny Franklin County community, and they all lived in an apartment at 11 Rublee Street in St. Albans.

Her friends disagree on the extent to which Diane was a drug user, but there are indications that she used methamphetamine, or speed, and she, like virtually all of the other street people, used marijuana. Her friends doubt that she bought many drugs; she was friendly and popular and she probably got whatever drugs she used for nothing. At the time, Diane apparently was a deeply unhappy girl, despite whatever happy exterior she presented to the world.

In her room, she kept a small, flower-covered spiral notebook, with a long poem that limned the pressures and sorrow of an unhappy life:

> I don't want to see anyone any more. Wish I could just
> lock myself in this closet for ever.
> Wonder what Deb and Emmett are doing? I'd like to see
> them, but if I did, what would I say or do.
> Do I really miss them, or is it that I think I do?
> Sometimes I think I know everything, but don't.
> I should keep my mouth shut.
> What should I do?
> What is real and what isn't?
> Lots of times I find myself in a dream world, even when
> small
> I hurt, not in feeling but in feelings
> Wish I could crawl in a corner someplace where no one
> will find me.
> But who would want to?
> Wonder if someone really likes me or is it all part of a
> joke on DIANE DIANE, yes lets see her
> Looks in a looking glass and sees herself. But still
> doesn't know what she looks like.
> DIANE doesn't belong here.
> But what is she doing here.
> Not supposed to be here,
> Lots of us aren't supposed to be here
> I don't like DIANE
> She is as bad as the rest
> It's funny but there are 2 or 3 of something
> One is DIANE
> another is me
> I know what DIANE is and does, but she doesn't know me
> DIANE loves people and does what they do
> But I don't

I mess with her a lot.
I show her things that she doesn't see
I make her feel things in feelings that she doesn't know
I wish I could get out of her and just wander
Can't stand it
I'm always fighting with her
She knows I'm here
You know when I want to smash something someone
DIANE stops me
When I say yes, she says no
Wish we could get together or just leave each other
The only way to do that is for DIANE to kill herself.
I tell her to do so but she said no
I want to leave her, want to see things
DIANE is very tired
But I won't let her go to sleep
I know what I want
DIANE wants to learn by books, but I want to learn by
    listening, seeing and touching
But we won't let it happen and don't get anywhere
Sometimes I let her book learn and DIANE lets me see,
    touch, listen, feel.
But if we don't give each other a chance to come out then
    nothing gets done.

On Sunday, the sixteenth, Diane was seen in the park about four in the afternoon; later that evening, about 7:30, a friend who saw her said she was "on something." Still later, she appeared at the Graefe apartment and began to undergo a violent physical reaction to something. Someone at the apartment finally called an ambulance, but she was dead when it arrived. Her death was ascribed to an overdose of the drug MDA.

To her friends, Diane's death was a shock and a tragedy. It sobered many of the street people, who had been dabbling happily in whatever drugs they could find. Otto Kremer, the proprietor of Tuner's Place, a local bar, was particularly shaken. He had been Diane's mother's social worker when he worked in the welfare department. He could see in the girl the stirrings of literary ambition, which pleased him. When she died, he wrote a bitter, angry poem about her death and gave it to John Howland, the reporter for the St.

Albans *Messenger;* Howland got it printed on page one of the paper.

> *A young friend of mine died today*
> *In a small county in the U.S.A.*
> *Her name was called I heard some say*
> *But I don't give a damn*
>
> *It was MDA that knocked her down*
> *Chained her beauty to a silent cloud*
> *Inside I'm screaming who made that pill*
> *My young friend's gone she's gone*
>
> *Children of love*
> *Children of God*
> *Beware of the demon wherever you are*
> *Who comes disguised in powder and pills*
> *Promising salvation cold and still*

If Diane's death was a tragedy to the small circle of friends she had in St. Albans, it was much more than that to the community at large. She became a symbol, a goad. For St. Albans was a city under siege. For months, the city's highly conservative establishment had been viewing with distaste, then alarm, then with a virulent hatred the encroachment of the drug culture on their community. This cultural and generational conflict had been experienced all over the United States, beginning with the civil rights movement in the 1950s and 1960s and developing into the Vietnam War upheavals of the sixties and early seventies. The sharp changes in life-style of the protest generation—the use of drugs and a more relaxed attitude toward sex and employment—generated deep conflicts between young and old, liberal and conservative.

St. Albans was particularly fertile ground for such a clash. The city lies along the northeast shore of Lake Champlain, just fifteen miles or so south of the Canadian border. Interstate 89 now passes close by the city on its way to the border and thence to Montreal, but even before the Interstate was built, St. Albans was affected by its location. Since the turn of the century, it was a railroad center. The Central Vermont Railroad had its headquarters and its yards here. The CV facilities sprawl over the lowlands to the west of Main Street:

low-slung warehouses, bunkhouses for train crews, dirty brick sheds that housed the trains and maintenance operations, workshops, the cavernous high ceilinged administration buildings with their old, polished woodwork.

The lake, too, has been a line of communication between north and south. One can go by water from Montreal, on the St. Lawrence River, to the Richelieu River and down it to Lake Champlain, then south to Whitehall, New York, and on into the Hudson by canal. During Prohibition the normal bustle generated by the railroad was joined by a heavy traffic of bootleggers, moving over the highways and down the lake with contraband whiskey. Even today, there are legends about treasures of sunken booze, thrown overboard by boot-leggers being pressed by revenue agents.

St. Albans thrived through all of this. There was prosperity, but an air of violence hung over the town, spawned by the bootleggers in their days, and by the hard-handed railroaders. The railroaders, many of them French Canadians and Irish, lived in the blocks of wooden tenements that lined the area west of Main Street and surrounded the Charlie Vermont yards. They roistered and filled the bars, but they had jobs. And the gentry built their magnificent homes on the hill to the east of town, with the Green Mountains to their backs, St. Albans and the lake to the west.

In the early 1960s, however, St. Albans suffered a heavy blow. The Central Vermont Railroad, long owned by the Canadian National rail system, moved most of its operations to Montreal. Hundreds of people were thrown out of work. The "blocks," once the home of the blue-collar workers, turned to prisons for bitter, underemployed or unemployed people. The Central Vermont pullout did more than that: it eliminated at a stroke much of the city's community leadership. If a man was big at the railroad, he was big in the community. Suddenly, many were gone. The gentry that was left was also affected. There were still the elegant old homes on the hill, but the economic vitality was leaching out of the city, hurting everyone. Even the professionals seemed to be affected. More than in most places, the doctors and the lawyers appear to spend an inordinate amount of time trying to go into business, buying bars and slum housing.

"The whole town seems to consist of people trying to get rich selling real estate to one another," says Phil Chapman, a local reporter who grew up in Richford, a small border town, and who moved to St. Albans. "Mean Streets, U.S.A." is what Chris O'Shea, the young editor of the Franklin County Newspapers, calls St. Albans. In fact, the town often evokes that feeling: crabbed, mean, bitter. "Drinking and getting laid are the main pastimes," says a girl who went away to college and returned to live.

There is no culture to speak of—a single movie theatre, a narrow-minded, reactionary newspaper owned by William Loeb, the right-wing owner of the Manchester, New Hampshire, *Union Leader*. Some people feel that the newspaper is a major factor in the grim atmosphere of the town. Russ Greene, the head of the Franklin Grand Isle Regional Planning Commission, believes that the St. Albans *Messenger*'s treatment of public affairs kept many capable people from participating in the life of the community. When the paper's editor disagreed with a city official, he hammered him unmercifully. "Our leaders were subject to that type of abuse whenever the paper hit the street," Green says.

The loss of the railroad not only cost hundreds of jobs, but it eliminated the apprenticeship programs for machinists, pipefitters and the like—the high-quality blue-collar occupations that provided a way out of the blocks. What remained was a handful of firms, most of which paid low wages. The Union Carbide plant north of town paid the best wages and employed about five hundred persons; Fonda Container Company, a maker of paper plates, hired about the same number; other major employers were the H. P. Hood Creamery, which made cheese and shipped bulk milk to the Boston market; an Agway chemical division plant and grain elevator; the St. Albans Cooperative Creamery and the Leader Evaporator, a small firm that manufactured maple-sugar-making equipment. There were not enough jobs available in these firms and the wages, for the most part, were below the levels paid in Chittenden County to the south. St. Albans unemployment figures were always the worst, or nearly the worst, in the state.

The surrounding area, Franklin County, is rural America. The floor of the Champlain Valley is a patchwork of dairy farms, and there are farms too in the hills that rise to the east. These hills are heavily forested with sugar maples, and the groves provide a cottage industry for residents; St. Albans is the site of a maple festival, held each spring when the sap is running. There is considerable poverty in the rural areas, and although the atmosphere is somehow less grim than in St. Albans, there is little to keep the young here. Mostly they leave, drifting to St. Albans, to Burlington, or beyond.

In the early 1970s, the waves of social change that had affected the rest of the country for years began washing over St. Albans. Young people, many of them long-haired and scraggly, began to hang around town, congregating first near Pud's Restaurant on Main Street, then in Taylor Park, a lovely patch of green that slopes upward from the Main Street to the old red brick courthouse on the hill.

Of course, people had for generations been lounging in the park; on summer nights particularly it provided a refuge for the "blockers" who, it goes without saying, had no air conditioning in their steaming tenements. Drinking in the park was nothing new, either, but in the early seventies the use of drugs escalated. For the most part it was soft drugs: marijuana, hashish, and pills — or speed, and the various sedatives and diet pills that could be had by prescription under normal circumstances. There was no cocaine, the high-priced drug of the affluent, or heroin, the hard drug of the big city ghettos. Still, the soft drugs were easily sufficient to frighten and enrage the St. Albans establishment.

In early March of 1973, the clash of social forces in St. Albans found a focal point. It was Tuner's Place, a bar operated by Otto Kremer and two other men, Richard Carr and Carlos Compeau. The key man was Kremer, a heavyset, bearded man who had drifted into St. Albans after a career as a social activist and political gadfly. A New Jersey native, Kremer had attended Rutgers University and the University of Cincinnati and had then worked as a neighborhood organizer in Cincinnati and Newport, Kentucky. He obtained status as a conscientious objector and had worked in menial jobs in Vermont and on the West Coast. In August of 1968, he came to St. Albans to work in the area, as a welfare worker, VISTA volunteer, and antipoverty organizer, until he opened the bar.

Otto was twenty-nine when he opened the bar, older than most of the hippies in the park, and at bottom, he was more serious: interested in politics, in art and music, in writing poetry. In fact, he said later, one of the things that led him to the bar venture was that it would make him a businessman, a member of the community rather than just a social irritant; he wanted to be part of the social fabric. But in St. Albans, Otto's political radicalism was as much of an irritant as his association with long-hairs and the drug culture.

Early the previous year, for example, Otto had circulated a questionnaire at the local high school, asking the students views on such issues as communal living, the extent to which they trusted their teachers, and whether they liked drugs. Otto enlisted five students to help him distribute the questionnaire to students; the school administration knew nothing of it.

Otto got about a hundred replies from the 1,250 or so students. He gave the results of the first seventy to a reporter for the Burlington *Free Press,* whose lead on the story said that BFA students were "overwhelmingly in favor of commune living, are heavy drug users, and believe the rich control America." Some of the questions were innocuous — are there enough water fountains in school, for example. But many were pointed, indeed. On the question of whether the *Mercury,* the school newspaper, printed the whole truth about issues, eight replied yes, and sixty-seven said no. Most of those polled estimated that at least 30 percent of BFA students used drugs. On the question of how many of their teachers the students trusted, five said all and seventeen said none. Half the remaining said they trusted more than half the teachers, 49 percent trusted less than half. Fifty-eight said communes were a "sensible way to live and learn together." Eleven said they were not. Seventy-two said there should be a free birth-control clinic for persons under eighteen; nine said there should not. Seventy-eight said industry was more interested in money than in ecology; two said the reverse.

This survey did not sit well with the town'e establishment. Kremer said that its purpose was to stimulate some thought about social issues, and while it may have done that, the suggestions that the students were deeply interested in drugs and sex, thought communes the best living arrangement, and had a low view of American industry generated more outrage than reflection. Many of the residents who called the town's radio talk show called the survey a Communist plot.

When Tuner's opened, it quickly became a hangout for the counterculture in St. Albans. The bar was located on Main Street, in the middle of the town, and directly across the street from Taylor Park. It was on the first floor of the Thompson Hotel building, a five-story, red-brick haven for derelicts and drifters. Next door, on the corner of

Lake Street, was the first-floor real estate office of Keith Campbell, a member of the St. Albans City Council. Around the corner, on Lake Street, was the hippie establishment, Sand Castles, an arts and crafts shop run by Edward "Sonny" Cross.

The owners of Tuner's first closed off its connection with the Thompson Hotel, much to the distress of the hotel's owner, Irene Irish. "You're making a big mistake," she told Otto. "These old drunks (her boarders) might get a whiff of fresh air when they go out the door and get enough strength to go down to Benson's. You'll lose 'em for the whole day."

Once nominally free of the Thompson Hotel, the owners went ahead and decorated the former hotel bar in their own eclectic style. The decor was red and black—red walls with black panels and the trim was black. On the wall across from the bar they hung a series of Eskimo lithographs and mounted a Polynesian totem pole on the other side of the room. There was a stage and a piano in the front of the bar, and in the curtained front window Otto hung dozens of plants. In the rear was the coin-operated pool table, a kitchen, and restrooms. Otto lived in a small room off the bar.

In an unpublished manuscript, Otto described his clientele: a cross section of St. Albans, lacking only what he called "the ruling class."

> The late morning hours were for the older people, mainly men retired of [sic] living on a public assistance pension. The afternoons were taken over by rednecks and blockers. The evening brought on the hippy invasion. Generally speaking, all three groups got along well, and as time passed, a certain harmony developed between heretofore conflicting factions. Over the months that I presided over the bar, I watched a slow process of assimilation take place between the rednecks and the hippies. The older people seemed to like anybody who showed them the least little respect like saying, "Hello. How are you?"
>
> I trust the reader has some idea what I mean when I say rednecks and hippies. No slur is intended. Both groups have one thing in common. They are not the ruling class. They are not the merchants or the farm owners or the school teachers or the social workers or the local executives at the Fonda Container factory or the Union Carbide plant or the computer programmers and engineers down at IBM.

Instead they are the part-time workers, the roofers, rough carpenters, outlaws, greasers, ice fishermen, tenant farmers, general assistance recipients, unemployed, unemployables, pool shooters, garage mechanics, waitresses, cleaning ladies, nickle-dime pot dealers, musicians, warehousemen and $2.25 an hour custodians barely getting by . . . not expecting much more out of life than a good time, food, a roof over their heads and maybe a second hand car or van to ride around in. That is, if they haven't lost their license for drunk driving. Of course there were a few merchants, lawyers, food co-op people, transvestites, tourists, school teachers and the like who frequented the place . . . but like I said . . . they were the financial cream.

And then there were the transients, most of them mad rejects, bent coins, foreign currency . . . madder than the rest. They came to Tuner's because of the hotel upstairs, a flea bag operation with broken baths and sheetless beds. It was an ideal place for the folks who lived there as they need only stumble up or down stairs to reach one of their two basic needs . . . that being sleep or drink.

The straight residents of St. Albans, the "ruling class," quickly concluded that Tuner's was a haven for drug dealers and users, a conclusion that distressed Otto, although he was aware that drugs were consumed there. For himself, he would smoke pot, but he was done with the rest—acid, speed, downers. He described in his book the experience that led him to quit hard drugs, in terms that evoked his literary idol, Hunter Thompson. . . .

"Then one day coming back from Cincinnati in my old green scout high on sunshine it happened . . . the old short circuit . . . death itself come to pay a quick visit . . . catatonic in a Howard Johnson not knowing if I was hot or cold, alive or dead . . . what a feeling.

"I should have known to stop putting all that crap into my body right there and then, but I had to see if that bummer was just a fluke. It wasn't. The old nervous system had had it. I was over-amped. Two more times on a dash out to the West Coast with crazy John I lost it again whirling through high winding vortexes of horror . . . the white light fading as the tarantulas of illusion appeared. The third time this happened, five days after the second time, convinced me the game was up. Time now to try and patch up the damage and take these many experiences and transform them into something useful. This all happened years before I ever thought of opening Tuner's."

Drugs were not what Otto was looking for . . . music was more like it, and endless conversation, poetry if you could get it, but most of all, music. The Tea Company on Lake Street, a bar and dance hall, also featured live entertainment, but it was mostly rock music. Otto was more interested in indigenous music, some of it akin to the bluegrass music of the southern mountains. Franklin County was alive with this sort of music—musicians doing their own thing, mostly without the heavy amplification of standard rock. In fact, the tiny village of East Fairfield was virtually a musicians' colony. There was "Home Brew," a rock band; the John Cassell Band, a group of studio quality musicians that played jazz; Automatic Slim and the Fat Boys, and Otto's friend, Mike Hurley, a song writer and musician who often played at Tuner's. There was always music at the bar, live or on tape. At times, several groups from around the state would be lined up to play on the tiny stage.

It was not surprising that the bar with its hippie owners, cheap drinks, and endless music became a center for the town's longhaired youth. They jammed the place in the spring and early summer evenings, drinking, wandering back and forth to the park, hanging out on the corner of Lake and Main: yelling, some drunk, some stoned, some simply obnoxious. "It was so noisy," Otto says sorrowfully. "You wouldn't believe the noise. It was outrageous."

The noise, the long hair, the drinking, the powerful suspicion that drugs could be had in the bar—all built the confrontation between the generations in the town. Still, the reactions of the established townspeople varied considerably. Some were worried about the effects that drugs were having on the young; and of these effects there was considerable evidence. The youth of St. Albans, coming into contact with drugs for the first time, were like kids in a candy store. They tried whatever they could find, in every bizarre combination.

Chris O'Shea, a young newspaper editor from Enosberg Falls who had used soft drugs himself, was appalled by the kids' reckless use of drugs. He ran into one youngster who told him that he had just taken seventeen hits of MDA and drunk a case of beer. They are lucky that only one kid had died, O'Shea thought. Otto himself was concerned. Someone drinking liquor and taking "downs," illegal sedatives, could fall right off the bar stool. One day, one of Otto's friends, stoned on something, borrowed a car, wrecked it in another part of town, and wandered back to the bar, streaming blood. These were the exceptions, of course. For the most part, the kids could get hold of marijuana easily, and barbiturates only infrequently. The thing that kept the lid on it as much as anything was the sheer lack of money: most of the street people in St. Albans subsisted on public assistance, fifteen or twenty dollars a week, or did odd jobs.

To Richard Allard, a young member of the St. Albans city council, these kids needed protection and help. He was not particularly repelled by the street people; he had grown up in the "blocks" himself, and he still liked to hang out in the local bars occasionally. His urge was to stop the flow of drugs into the city.

Other members of the establishment, however, saw the drug scene as an enormous threat that loomed over *their* town and *their* lives. Mayor Melvin ("Ken") Kaye, the owner of a Main Street shoe store, deeply disliked the fact that young people were going on welfare, and he, and others also, felt that the laws favored criminals, that the police had their hands tied behind their backs. These "criminals," youths who were rowdy, noisy, frightening to people on the street, were bad for business.

Finally, there was an implied political threat by the counterculture, although it was hard sometimes to take it seriously. There was Otto's survey at BFA; and during the previous year Larry Ellsworth, a local musician, along with Otto and others, had run a slide show in the window of the Sand Castles Arts and Crafts Shop on the subject of substandard housing. The pictures went on and on, sometimes for twenty-four hours at a stretch, one dreary scene after another. People need to see what the problems are, Ellsworth said. One of the pictures in the show was an aerial view of the airport in Atlanta, Georgia, but that didn't bother Otto or the other sponsors. Ellsworth, they could explain, operates on a different wavelength from other people.

The activists got involved in other, more serious issues in 1972 and 1973. In December of 1972, the Vermont Health Systems, Inc., held a hearing on the problem of health care in the region. Federal funds were available, but no one was sure how to spend them. Otto, then a VISTA worker, proposed allocating ten thousand dollars to hire twenty people to make a house-to-house survey of the area and to delineate the problem that way. Earlier, Ellsworth had organized the St. Albans Tenants Union to demonstrate in favor of jobs for people in the area. "Vermonters have been the storekeepers and the custodians for out-of-state businesses for long enough," Ellsworth said when a reporter asked him why he was running the demonstration.

This sort of activity tended to unsettle the establishment. It struck at the heart of many of the commercial arrangements in the town, in such areas as real estate and housing; it tended to support the proposition that those who were on welfare or had poor jobs were the victims of those who were better off. If people did not get the medical care they needed, perhaps doctors were at fault. And people like Otto and Ellsworth never seemed to let up, even though an individual campaign might not be taken seriously.

Ellsworth even decided to run for mayor. He got an old washtub, painted it red, white, and blue, and campaigned in places like Tuner's. A tall cadaverous man with burning black eyes, Ellsworth was an alien presence for St. Albans. Otto thought the cops were afraid of Larry so they always left him alone. His campaign for mayor consisted primarily of forays into places such as Tuner's, carrying his tub and setting up a chant:

"When Ellsworth is mayor, I'm going to grab Chief Hebert [the police chief], strip him naked in the middle of the street, paint a yellow swastika on his belly and one on his back and make him dance to the music of my .45, cuz we're going to get things done and have fun when Ellsworth is mayor."

Ellsworth got into trouble in town just once. That was when Otto and his partners forced him to quit playing his harmonica in the bar. A harmonica, when played over the bar's sound system, gave out an unholy screech, and the police came around to tell them to quiet down. One thing led to another, and the owners finally threw Ellsworth out.

"I ain't livin' in America, I'm livin' in Russia," Ellsworth bellowed as he left the bar. Still in a rage as he strode down Main Street, he kicked in the window of the National Bell Store. The cops arrested Ellsworth for it, the only time they ever went after him.

When Tuner's Place opened in March, Otto, ever the politician despite his radical leanings, went to see Keith Campbell, a conservative member of the city council. He appealed to Campbell by saying that he was not sure he was cut out for the bar business—that he had often thought of buying some land and building a greenhouse. Campbell applauded that idea. He was in the business of selling land, for one thing, and for another he was glad to see Otto was not committed to a long-term partnership with Richard Carr, with whom Campbell had had some disagreements.

But there was nothing that Otto could do about the basic conflict with Campbell. He had all he could do to control what went on in his bar; there was nothing he could do about hippies on the street corner. Furthermore, the hippies delighted in mocking and baiting Campbell. They hooted at him and threw paint on his windows. They knew he hated them, and they hated him in return, and Otto could do little about any of it, though he continued to try.

During warm weather, Otto instituted cleanups on Friday afternoons as a means of placating Campbell and the other politicians and merchants who were angry about the street people. Otto would send a couple of dozen longhairs out with garbage bags to pick up the trash in Taylor Park, giving them fifteen-cent beers when they returned. This did not help much. The city council members grumbled that the hippies had put the trash there in the first place.

Campbell leaned hard on Otto to do something about the hippies on the corner. "I don't want them there," he insisted. But Otto, who had heard that Campbell was plotting to have Tuner's closed, finally gave up.

"I've done favors for you, Otto," Campbell said at one of their meetings.

"You never did anything for me," Otto replied. They did not talk much after that.

Otto was also having trouble with Irene Irish, the owner of the Thompson Hotel. She came in one day to say the rent was going up. Otto exploded, accusing her and the other landlords in town of milking their properties, sucking out the rents and never putting any money into the buildings. The two argued bitterly, even scuffled briefly, the Irene stalked out of the bar. "I'm going to the police," she said.

Nothing came of this incident, but Otto feared that the police were getting the impression that dangerous, irrational people were running Tuner's Place.

Whatever the local police thought, the St. Albans City Council was clearly worried. The council was a six-member body consisting of Stan Cummings, Campbell, Richard Allard, Mrs. Cecilia Gamache,

Robert Hill, and Bill Bessette. Campbell, Bessette, and Hill were thought to be the most conservative; Gamache and Cummings the most liberal, and Allard a swing man.

All were concerned about drugs, but the level of their concern varied widely. Campbell was the most outspoken. He is a tall, beefy man with short-clipped white hair, given to sport jackets and pipe. A devout Roman Catholic, he married late in life, and now can be seen at mass at Saint Mary's Church, near the park, with a flock of young children. Campbell's colleagues liked him well enough, but they thought him obsessed by the hippies and the drug problem. He saw the issue in apocalyptic terms: the hippies were not only noisy and obscene, they were promiscuous, almost depraved.

Mrs. Gamache and Stan Cummings didn't feel that way. There were drugs about, that was true, they felt, but the kids were simply not that bad. Cummings thought they often passed a brown paper bag amongst a group in the park, drinking from it as though it were liquor when actually it was soda. Not that they would not drink beer, but they knew Campbell was watching them, and they loved to annoy him.

Nonetheless, Campbell was the strongest personality on the council and he insisted that the members do something about the drug menace.

"What are we going to do about the drug problem?" Campbell would demand of the members.

"Well, Campbell, just what drug problem are you talking about?" Cummings would inquire.

"It's all around us," Campbell would reply.

Campbell also insisted that Tuner's had to be forced to stop playing music so loudly, and that Otto Kremer be required to clear the hippies off the street corner. They were frightening old people, and making obscene, suggestive remarks to women passing by.

The police would not get them off the street, Campbell said, so it was up to Otto.

"If the police can't do it, how can you expect Otto to?" Mrs. Gamache wanted to know.

Campbell would not be deterred, however, and he was carrying a majority of the council with him. In the spring, he circulated a letter of intent to the members of the council to the effect that the city ought to hire an undercover narcotics agent. The statement was handled secretly; there was no mention of it in the city council minutes, or in the press coverage of the council action.

The statement did not specify how such an agent was to be hired, but some of the members understood the agent or agents would be college students, hired for the summer. Neither Cummings nor Mrs. Gamache would sign the statement, but the other members did. There was no provision for such a procedure in the council rules—and, in fact, the hiring of the agent would have to be formally authorized later—but Chief George Hebert got the message. He would have to hire a narc. . . .

The chief had been quoted previously as saying the city had no drug problem, a statement that had become a source of considerable embarrassment. It had subsequently become clear there was a drug problem, but his department could do little about it. He knew nothing about drugs and neither did his men. The letter of intent by the council was the go-ahead he needed; he would start working on a narc right away, but the use of a few college boys wasn't the way to do it. What they needed was a professional.

By June, spring had finally arrived. That development never seems quite certain in Vermont. The bone-deep cold gives up its hold on the country reluctantly, a warm day in early spring, so bright with promise, is often followed by cold, slashing rains, or, even into May, by snow. But by June, the leaves were on the trees, the grass in Taylor Park was a bright green, the days were long and easy. And the street people swarmed along the main streets of the town, lolling in large numbers on the street corners and lazing in the park.

The increasing number of hippies on the streets and in the middle of town exacerbated the tensions that had been growing through the early part of the year. The strolling hippies passed by Keith Campbell's office, and hung around his corner of Main Street. Next door, Tuner's was jammed from midmorning till late at night; kids wandered in and out, drinking and listening to the music that never seemed to cease.

It was in late June that Diane Voudrien died. Her death gave Campbell and the people who felt as he did the evidence they needed that the town faced a drug menace of enormous proportions. *This was what they had been warning people about.*

For Stan Cummings and Mrs. Gamache, the Voudrien death

sounded a knell for common sense and moderation. No longer was it possible to say publicly that the drug problem was not as serious as Campbell and the others contended. Increasingly, the only credible line for a politician was a hard line. . . . Cummings signed the statement on the undercover agent. Only Mrs. Gamache continued to hold out.

The council members were not sure what Chief Hebert was doing about the undercover agent; secrecy was obviously the essence of such an operation. But Campbell was not content to leave the issue alone. On July 25, he asked the council to pass an ordinance prohibiting drinking or loitering in Taylor Park. He asked that bicycles be forbidden there, and that there be a curfew in the park from midnight until six in the morning.

"It's an outdoor whorehouse," Campbell said of the park. The kids were buying beer in a saloon—he did not name Tuner's but that was clearly what he meant—and taking it into the park to drink,

A few weeks later, the council's legislative committee agreed to draft such an ordinance, but Campbell rowled them for moving too slowly. "The park is being overrun by a bunch of bums who don't pay taxes," he said as he walked angrily out of the meeting. They needed "strong action to keep those filthy characters out of the way."

Hiring an undercover agent was one thing, but placing sharp restrictions on the right of everyone to use the park generated opposition from the fading liberal wing of the council. Cummings thought that the ordinance Campbell wanted might be unconstitutional. A curfew would be an effort to discriminate against people with long hair and old clothes. "Where do my rights begin and where do their rights end?" Cummings wondered as Campbell left the session.

Meanwhile, Campbell urged city work crews to cut away some of the branches and greenery around the monument in Taylor Park. The kids are hiding there to fornicate, he said.

All of this appeared in the newspapers, and the kids mocked Campbell unmercifully. They threw paint on his building, and they loved to speculate that Campbell was a repressed old man who sat in his office watching young people enjoying themselves, resentful that he could not enjoy himself too.

This theme was captured by John Howland, the reporter for the St. Albans *Messenger,* who wrote a song about Campbell. The song was entitled "The Taylor Park Whorehouse" and was supposed to be sung to the tune of the old Kingston Trio number, "Charley on the MTA." It went like this:

> Oh, let me tell you of a story
> Bout a man name of Campbell
> On a tragic and fateful day
> He put ten bucks in his pocket
> Went to the Taylor Park Whorehouse
> To have himself a lay
>
> Did he ever return, no, he never returned,
> And his fate is still unlearned,
> He may search forever
> For that Taylor Park Whorehouse
> He's the man who never returned.

The song went on like this for several more stanzas, all with the theme of a frustrated man looking for a little "sweet release." Someone slipped a copy of the song under Campbell's door. No one could say what his reaction to this was, but the speculation among the street people was that he was outraged.

The street people may have been right about that, but they probably did not understand Campbell or people like him very well. There was a deep gulf between the establishment and the hippies: not only did they disagree about many things, but they were unable to communicate with or even to understand one another. The street people saw Campbell as one of a small group of powerful people who wielded the power of society. They controlled the money, the police, the courts, the way the law was enforced.

Ragging them, as they did Campbell, was just a harmless diversion, a stone hurled against the side of a tank. Campbell clearly saw it differently, and in terms that made sense to him. The people who were rebelling against law and order and decency, the touchstones of society, were *dangerous* and not only dangerous in some nebulously ideological way, but physically dangerous. They were a threat to order, an enormous challenge to law enforcement. Keith Campbell would keep a gun on hand.

This clash was due not only to misconceptions on each side. Even if the street people and the Keith Campbells had understood one another, the fact was that they intruded on one another's turf. The hippies were not something that the establishment could ignore: they were on the street corners, on the welfare rolls, in the stores, rowdying in the bars, there was all that noise. . . . The hippies, on the other hand, believed that they had as much right to be on the streets as did Keith Campbell and the police. Why should they be harassed by the police and driven from Taylor Park?

To people like Chris O'Shea, it was time to leave town. He had enjoyed hanging out at Tuner's, but some kind of trouble was coming, he thought. Otto Kremer and some of the other counterculture people simply don't understand St. Albans, O'Shea thought. But O'Shea, who had been brought up in the region, did. He knew that all this baiting and noise and open use of drugs was driving the town pillars into a rage.

Actually, Otto Kremer was deeply worried. A source of his in the police department had warned him that "something could happen." During the dog days of August, he spent much of his time hanging over the bar, warning some of the people he knew were dealing a little to stay cool. He even contemplated getting out of the bar business altogether.

The growing tensions in the town, and the portents of trouble, did little to quiet the noise and the roistering that went on in the bars, on Main Street, and in Taylor Park. The use of soft drugs was as open and blatant as ever. One day, Otto came upon one of the street people sitting at a table in a hallway of the Thompson Hotel, weighing and bagging marijuana without a thought of concealment.

On Labor Day, Mayor Kaye gave a speech in which he said fervently that the drug problem would be solved—people could count on that. And the city council continued to move on suppression of drugs and the counterculture generally. On September 10, the council formally authorized the hiring of an undercover narcotics agent by the St. Albans Police Department. And on September 19, the members took up the antiloitering ordinance for Taylor Park.

The September 19 session was an uproarious one. Campbell insisted the kids had to be excluded from the park at night. "I want to prevent them from buying dope," he said. "I want to prevent them from making love."

"You ought to be castrated," Cummings shouted at him, and the two very nearly came to blows. The council passed the measure, with just Cummings and Gamache voting no. The council would not hesitate any longer: they would mount a full-scale war against drugs in the city.

At the time of the council debates in September, Paul Lawrence, the ex-state trooper and former police chief of Vergennes, Vermont, had been working undercover in St. Albans for more than a month. Only a handful of people knew about it: Chief Hebert, who had hired him, a few key subordinates in the police department, perhaps Keith Campbell, and Raeldon Barker, the city manager.

Lawrence had long hair and a moustache and wore old clothes. Most of the time he drove a 1974 blue Ford Mustang; occasionally he drove a Volkswagen. He moved quietly through the street scene in the weeks of August and September. No one knew for sure what he was doing.

The St. Albans Raid

BY MID-OCTOBER, SUMMER HAD LEFT VERMONT. EARLIER in the month, the maples had blazed on the hillsides, and now, particularly at higher elevations, the trees were bare. The sun still warmed Taylor Park at midday, but the mornings and evenings were cool. On clear days, Vermont fulfilled its promise: the air sparkled; it was not only easy to work, one wanted to work. It would not last, of course—the wind carried a hint of winter. The street people were spending more time indoors now, welcoming not only the noise of places such as Tuner's, but the warmth. Many talked of moving to the Southwest for the winter. Otto thought that there was some sort of hippie circuit between Vermont and New Mexico. And maybe that was a good thing, he thought. Perhaps the onset of winter would diminish the tensions that had gripped the town for months.

As dawn broke on October 24, a stream of police cruisers began to slide to the curb in front of the red-brick city hall building on Main Street. They carried the markings of the Vermont State Police, the Franklin County sheriff's department, the St. Albans Police Department. There were fifteen cars in all, and inside, in the second floor police headquarters, some thirty cops from the three departments stood around the maze of rooms, chatting quietly and drinking coffee. They were waiting to go out on the biggest drug raid ever mounted in Vermont.

There was considerable tension. No one knew what to expect. Many of the cops despised the hippies they would be going after. Earlier that morning, at about 4 A.M., the state police had received a noise complaint concerning one of the main targets, a camp, or cabin, occupied by a woman named Linda Lamb on the Georgia Point Highway, outside of town.

The state trooper who had responded had been worried and had asked for assistance. The trooper and the local cops who came to his aid had quieted the disturbance without much trouble, but the word nevertheless was that the hippies were armed. The source of this warning was Paul Lawrence, the undercover agent. He had submitted an informal, typewritten report on the investigation he had carried out. It listed the drug buys from more than thirty persons and included the warning that eight of these might have guns. Sonny Cross supposedly had a sawed-off shotgun in his shop, another had a 22-caliber pistol with a pearl handle, one man had a gun in his glove compartment. Another had a "snub nosed revolver 357—small 4" barrel," another had syringes in the lining of his belt. "Anyone with an open wound should be careful," Lawrence said in the report, implying that contact with the syringe could transmit disease. The report also listed nine of the people from whom he bought drugs as "REAL NUTS."

This report by Lawrence fueled the speculation and fear on the part of the police that the supposed drug users were prone to violence. This fear was irrational—for the most part, the street people were harmless and petrified of the police. Still, the threat of violence helped to justify the amassing of this large force of policemen to carry out the raid.

To St. Albans Police Sergeant James Thibault, who would lead the raiding party to the Lamb camp, all this meant trouble, and he was worried. A tall, heavyset man of about thirty with close-cropped brown hair, glasses, and a small moustache, Thibault had been the police department's liaison with Lawrence since he had come to work in August. Thibault gave Lawrence the names of the longhairs he thought were dealing drugs and he included pictures when he could. In fact, every person whom the police would arrest this day had been fingered by Thibault. Thibault was a man who clearly despised the hippies. He had been in Tuner's Place looking for suspects in the past, but the prospect of going in there socially filled him with revulsion. "Not if I care about my life," he said later when asked if he ever went in for just a drink.

In the first phase of the raid, the police split into three groups. The first, made up of state troopers and St. Albans police, would raid Ronnie Rich's camp, or summer cottage, on Hathaway Point; they would be led by Sergeant Ronald Hemond of the St. Albans department. The second contingent, headed by Thibault, would go to Linda Lamb's. The third, mostly members of the sheriff's department for Franklin County, would remain in the police station and would transport prisoners once they were arrested. All the cops had pistols and many had shotguns or carbines.

The two fleets of police cars moved out shortly after six o'clock and achieved complete surprise at both objectives. Hemond's group found Rich at home and arrested him without incident; they then searched his camp for an hour. The group under Thibault's command also had no problem. They drove into the yard of Linda Lamb's camp and covered both doors. The cops at the front door were admitted when they knocked; the ones in the rear smashed in the door. They found five people inside, talking quietly or snoozing off the effects of the previous night's party. The two men, Richard Campbell and Ronald Hemingway, were ordered to stand against the wall while they were searched. The three women—Linda Lamb, Dale Susan Goodroe, and Brenda Denton—were ordered to sit in the kitchen while the cops searched the cabin. Lawrence had told them there was a stash of drugs in the camp, but all they found was a little marijuana. Thibault said they found needles, which he said were used for shooting hard drugs. No hard drugs were found. Thibault also said they found an empty pistol on a table. The cops had warrants for two of the people at the camp, but they arrested all five on the basis of the marijuana they found. To Thibault, none of the five seemed surprised by the raid.

The two teams returned to the station about eight o'clock and prepared to go out again. The next two targets were Tuner's Place and Sand Castles, Sonny Cross's place on Lake Street. The Thibault team knocked on the front door of Tuner's and, getting no answer, smashed the door in. They found Otto Kremer in bed in his tiny room off the bar and arrested him. They also arrested Alan Bibeau, who wandered in through the shattered door. Then they searched Tuner's Place, knocking over liquor bottles and ripping out paneling. They found a few marijuana cigarettes behind a radiator; some were butts, others unsmoked. Thibault thought they might have been abandoned by some bar customers when a cop came in. As they left, someone wrote on a blackboard near the door:

"Police one, hippies zero."

At Sand Castles, the same kind of search took place. Sonny Cross, the only one in the place, was arrested and taken to the police station. He and the other suspects were questioned there, then taken to the Franklin County Jail, which is located behind the courthouse on the hill. Later they would be arraigned.

By midmorning, the townspeople were beginning to realize that something big was going on. Kids on their way to school and other passersby gaped at the lines of police cars moving to and from the police station and at the raiding parties gathered around Tuner's and the Sand Castle. Most of the bystanders seemed to approve. "This is great," said one. "We haven't had this kind of excitement for a long time," said another. "It's about time the police cracked down."

After the raids on Tuner's and the Sand Castle, the cops broke up into small units and went after the individuals named in the warrants.

Stan Merriam and another cop found Jane Eaton and Ritchie Eustace in bed in an apartment on Center Street. They broke in quickly and ordered both to get dressed. The couple were more indignant than frightened. "What are you, some kind of peeping tom?" Eustace demanded. "I ain't getting dressed in front of you," Jane said when Merriam handed her her clothes. Both were taken to the police station. At a house in West Enosburg, Clifford Patterson, a local cop, arrested Thomas Kimball and Mike Lotowitz, members of the Graefe band, and Arvis and Steven Pacquette, who owned the house. The state police seized Roland Prior while he was at work in Essex Junction. In all, they arrested twenty-seven people by sunset that day. Jim Levy, a local attorney, was walking down Main Street with Wayne Larry, when Wayne saw what looked like his stepbrother, Gary Burbank, across the street. As they drew closer, they realized it was Gary. He was standing up against his truck and police were searching him. Stan Cummings, of the St. Albans City Council, was walking on

Main Street when he saw a sheriff's car pull up and two men, armed with shotguns, leap out and chase a youth down the street. They collared him and threw him into the back of the police car.

Many of the charges made in the arrests were serious—the sale of sizeable amounts of heroin and cocaine, for example. Other sales were smaller, a few tablets of LSD, for instance, but there was relatively little about speed or marijuana in the charges. There were warrants out for three individuals who had not been picked up by Wednesday evening.

The police dragnet that day cut a wide swath through the St. Albans counterculture. Many of those arrested had been busted previously; most of the others were also known to the police. Ronnie Rich was supposedly the drug kingpin in town; he had been recently arrested by agents of the state and federal governments, who had been after him for three years. Others were younger, like Sonny Cross, who had been arrested earlier for a small sale. Still others, like Gary Burbank and Otto Kremer, had never been arrested before.

To the police, all those arrested looked like obvious targets: they had long hair, and wore hippie clothes, or they hung around at Tuner's or in the park, or they had dealt drugs in the past, or were often seen with people who had dealt drugs. Actually, there were wayward young kids who had been affected by the drug culture. Among them were a few seriously impaired by drug use—their lawyers would call them "space cadets"; they would have been drifters anyway. There were political and social rebels; some of them were well educated, and, in fact, a few of them had relatively well-paying jobs, but they scorned establishment values. Some saw drugs as a route to a higher consciousness, although these were relatively few. And then there were some genuine criminals, like Ronnie Rich, who happened to be working as a speed dealer, but who might have been into some other kind of crime if he did not deal drugs.

As the day wore on, these suspects gathered in holding locations, first the police station, where they gave their names, addresses, and other vital statistics to a police officer, and received the formal notification of charges against them; then to the Franklin County jail, behind the superior court house, then to the district court building on Kingman Street for arraignment; finally, for those who could not make bail, to places like the Burlington and Woodstock correctional centers, for incarceration. Only two people, Gary Burbank and Jane

Eaton, a twenty-year-old bartender from Tuner's Place, could make bail the day they were arrested.

As the suspects waited and talked in the jail and at the police station, they were, for the most part, mystified. Ronnie Rich was furious. He had been dealing drugs, as everyone knew, but it was speed, not heroin. Heroin was ridiculous. It was clear to Otto Kremer that something was wrong. He had been expecting some kind of trouble because of the traffic in soft drugs, but there was no heroin or coke in town, at least none that he had heard of. Other things struck him as strange. He knew, for example, that John Welch, an intelligent man with a good job, had not been a user of hallucinogens, yet he was charged with selling LSD. And as for anyone arresting Gary Burbank, that must be some kind of joke. Gary looked like a hippie, but everyone that knew him knew that was an illusion. Gary was a boy scout, his friends thought. All he cared about was fixing television sets or cars. What really got him excited was talking about auto repair collectives. As for drugs, he smoked marijuana occasionally, but so rarely that he was outside the mainstream of St. Albans street life.

As the suspects talked, more anomalies showed up. Steven Pacquette was charged with selling LSD on August 7, although he was sure he had been in jail in Burlington at the time. Eric Goodroe was another who was puzzled. He had been charged with selling LSD to an undercover agent in a yellow Volkswagen. The story was that the agent had picked him up while he was hitchhiking to see his grandmother in Alburg, a small town on the Canadian border. The agent reported that Eric told him he was working for the city of St. Albans at the time. Goodroe had never worked for the city, and he had no grandmother in Alburg. . . .

The air of unreality that infused the day was heightened for the suspects when they got to the district court to be arraigned by Judge Carl Gregg. They had to wait while one of the local characters sparred with the judge over obtaining free legal counsel against a charge of shooting ducks after dark. When it was the drug suspects' turn, they all pleaded not guilty, some quietly, some loudly and bitterly. "Not guilty to this ridiculous charge," Jack Welch yelled when asked for his plea.

That afternoon Ed Chamberlain, the St. Albans correspondent for the Burlington *Free Press,* came to the police station to do a story on the raid. First, he interviewed Chief Hebert and Paul Lawrence in the chief's office. Lawrence had been there all day; he did not go on any of the raiding parties. Hebert first told Chamberlain that he had been misquoted in previous stories to the effect that there was no drug problem in St. Albans. Hebert said he had told the city council five years earlier that drugs were becoming a problem, but that he had been ignored. The problem had become more serious the previous year, Hebert said, and something had to be done about it—quickly. And Hebert emphasized that Lawrence, whom he made it clear he admired, was largely responsible for the solution.

"I've never seen an area so infested with drugs," Lawrence said to Chamberlain. "Kids selling them in the park and on the streets. And there are lots of people using them, too," he added. Chamberlain did not identify Lawrence in his story, but stated that the narc told him that 90 percent of the people dealing drugs had guns. The raid that day had shattered a heroin and cocaine ring, the unidentified agent said, and both he and Hebert said they were astonished at the quality of the heroin—20 percent pure compared to the normal 3 percent for street sales. "It's so open it's unreal," Lawrence said.

Chamberlain asked Hebert whether that day's raid would solve the drug problem in St. Albans. "I'd like to be able to say this is the answer, but I'm sure it will continue to go on," the chief replied. "But if we can curtail the sales—or the pushers—at least we can really water it down."

Part of the problem, the chief said, was parents who did not recognize the danger signals of drugs, or who did not want to deal with the problem. "Many of the local citizens don't even feel that drugs are a serious problem in our community," Hebert said.

There was no doubt, however, that many of the leading citizens in the town were certain the police were on the right track. Keith Campbell was particularly enthusiastic.

"I'm especially pleased that the raid has taken place and that some of these people, although not all, have been picked up in this drug-peddling situation," he said. "I wish to compliment very much the St. Albans Police Department, the state police and the Franklin County sheriff's department, and all the other agencies that worked together on this project," he said. "It's about time things were done in this fashion."

At the same time, Campbell made it clear he wanted the court to be tough with the hippies. "It's a sad situation that exists . . . whereby these guys are allowed to have their wrists slapped and then are released," he said.

City Councilman Bob Hill was also pleased. "This is what I—what we all—have been looking forward to for a long time," he said. And Cely Gamache said she was particularly shocked about the heroin. She knew there were some drugs in the city, she said, but she had never suspected heroin.

On Thursday morning, the Burlington *Free Press* published a list of those arrested. Name, age, address, charge, plea—the flat, journalistic account carried no hint of the gravity of these charges to the suspects. To some, finding their name in the paper was old hat; it had happened before. To others, their names on that list were epitaphs, graven in stone. It looked like this:

Ronald Rich, 25, Isle La Motte—12 glassine envelopes of heroin valued at $200, Oct. 23. Total bail: $20,000.

Robert [Otto] Kremer, 29, St. Albans—five glassine envelopes of cocaine valued at $150, Sept. 4; five glassine envelopes of heroin valued at $600, Oct. 3; and $350 worth of pethidine (Demerol), Sept. 13. Total bail: $20,000.

Alan Jerry Bibeau, 20, St. Albans—four glassine envelopes of heroin valued at $200, Oct. 11; $250 worth of heroin, six glassine envelopes of heroin valued at $300, Oct. 5; and $25 worth of hashish, Aug. 6. Total bail: $17,500.

Richard R. Campbell, 22, St. Albans—possession of less than half an ounce of marijuana, Oct. 23. Bail: $500.

Steve Aldrich, 17, St. Albans—two tablets of lysergic acid diethylamide (LSD) valued at $16, Oct. 18. Bail: $2,500.

Mark Beauregard, 18, of St. Albans—pethidine (Demerol) valued at $400, Aug. 27. Beauregard pleaded guilty Tuesday to selling $225 worth of methamphetamines to an undercover agent July 21. A pre-sentence investigation was ordered. Total bail: $3,800.

Edward Cross, 20, of St. Albans—five glassine envelopes of cocaine valued at $150, $25 worth of heroin, Aug. 9, $300 worth of methylenedioxyamphetamines

(MDA), Aug. 15 and $400 worth of Demerol, Aug. 27. Total bail: $17,500.

John Dave Dalcourt, 22, St. Albans—$200 worth of heroin, Oct. 23. Bail: $10,000.

Allen Dischaw, 18, Swanton—five tablets of LSD valued at $25, Aug. 21 in Swanton. He was held pending arraignment.

Richard Eustace, 25, of Fairfield—$25 worth of marijuana, Oct. 5. Bail: $2,500.

Eric Goodroe, 17, St. Albans—four tablets of LSD valued at $20, Aug. 17. He was lodged, pending arraignment.

William H. Houghton, 20, St. Albans—$5 worth of LSD, Aug. 21; Bail: $2,500.

Lawrence Lewis King, 23, Swanton—$140 worth of marijuana, Aug. 23. Bail: $3,000.

Linda Lamb, 25, St. Albans—four glassine envelopes of heroin valued at $100, Oct. 19. Bail: $5,000.

Michael Allen Lotowitz, 22, St. Albans—$3 worth of LSD, Oct. 5. Bail: $2,500.

Arvis Robert Pacquette, 25, St. Albans—$25 worth of hashish, Aug. 6. Bail: $2,500.

Steven Roy Pacquette, 22, St. Albans—$30 worth of LSD, Aug. 7. Bail: $2,500.

Terry Lee Pilon, 19, St. Albans—LSD valued at $5, Aug. 21, and $10 worth of hashish, Sept. 24. Total bail: $5,000.

Gary Thomas Rich, 29, Isle La Motte—four glassine envelopes of heroin valued at $200, Oct. 1, and $25 worth of methamphetamines, Oct. 5. Rich is currently being held on $50,000 bail at the Burlington Community Correctional Center on another drug charge.

Steve Robtoy, 16, St. Albans—two tablets of LSD valued at $6, Oct. 18. He was placed in custody of juvenile authorities.

John Welch, 22, St. Albans—one tablet of LSD valued at $3, Sept. 19. Bail: $2,500.

Roland James Prior, 22, St. Albans—$200 worth of heroin, Oct. 23. Bail: $10,000.

Norman Paul Young, 22, Swanton—five tablets of LSD valued at $25, Aug. 21. Bail: $2,500.

Ronald A. Hemingway, 16, Swanton—$25 worth of hashish, Oct. 23. Bail: $2,500.

Brenda Laurie Denton, 17, St. Albans—$100 worth of heroin, Oct. 19. Bail: $5,000.

Dale Susan Goodroe, 19, St. Albans—possession of less than half an ounce of marijuana, Oct. 24. Bail: $500.

Thomas Robert Kimball, 23, Sheldon—hashish valued at $10, Oct. 3, and $3 worth of LSD, Oct. 11. Total bail: $5,000.

Two of those arrested were able to put up bail that day, both of them because their parents were able to come up with the money. They were:

Jane K. Eaton, 20, St. Albans—hashish valued at $7, Sept. 25, and two brown dots of LSD spotted on brown paper and valued at $7, Sept. 12. Released on $5,000 bail.

Gary Paul Burbank, 26, St. Albans—Methamphetamines valued at $25, Sept. 27. Released on $2,500 bail.

Warrants were also issued for Dominic Cusson of St. Albans, Lewis James Tanius, Daniel Leon Thompson, and Lawrence Marvin Young, all of St. Albans, all on a variety of charges. The total for the day was twenty-seven arrested, with four still to be picked up. There was an enormous range in the gravity of the charges. Some had been arrested for selling three dollars' worth of LSD; others had been arrested for the sale of hundreds of dollars' worth of hard drugs like heroin and cocaine.

That night, firemen in St. Albans were swamped with a barrage of false alarms and leaf-burning incidents.

St. Albans—First Doubts

THE OCTOBER 24 RAID HEIGHTENED THE TENSIONS THAT
had gripped St. Albans for months. The street people were bewildered
and afraid—dealers and nondealers, users and nonusers. On the day
of the bust, many had assumed, or hoped, that the charges were
somehow a mistake. In the days that followed, however, as they
talked in their cells and in the bars and in the park, they began to
realize that, mistake or not, the system—that impersonal thing they
had scorned or laughed at or hated for years—was going forward to
prosecute their cases.

No one knew who the narc was; that was one thing that was
frightening, but sooner or later his identity would be exposed;
perhaps the whole thing could be explained then. Yet it was not only
the narc . . . the state's attorney, E. Michael McGinn, had to sign the
warrants for the arrests. Was it possible that he knew the charges
were false? How could he not know they were false? And the judge?
He had approved the affidavits of probable cause, the first legal step
in the arrest of a suspect. If he had approved these charges, saying in
effect he thought that there was enough evidence to justify an arrest,
did that mean that he was involved in some sort of scheme? McGinn
was known to be mean and tough, but would he be involved in

something like that? The judge had always been a tower of rectitude;
yet he clearly disliked the street people. . . .

A week after their arrest, nine of the hippies wrote a letter to the
St. Albans *Messenger,* which the paper printed on the front page. It
was unusual, to say the least—a broadside, from inside a jail, against
the law enforcement community, printed on the front page of the
paper. The letter was addressed to

> Keith Campbell
> George Hebert
> Jim Thibault
> Stan (the man) Merriam
> and none other than Mr. Michael McGinn (and to whom it
> may concern in St. Albans)
> We the innocent 31 to 47 supposed drug dealers would
> like to thank you for wasting our time and money (which
> we don't have much of) sitting here doing nothing [here a
> word is blacked out] behind except thinking of the future.

The letter was signed by Mike Lotowitz, Mark Beauregard, John
Dalcourt, Ronald Rich, Steve Pacquette, Arvis Pacquette, Lawrence
Young, Larry King, and Gary Rich.

The arrests brought no peace of mind to those members of the
establishment who had pressed so hard for the anti-drug campaign.
On October 31, Halloween night, the fire and police departments
were hit by another rash of false alarms and small fires all over town,
an indication that the street people were angry and defiant.

Keith Campbell, meanwhile, was known to keep a gun in the
drawer at his office, and he demanded that a policeman be stationed
there. He also kept a citizen's band radio at his home. His life was in
danger, he told the police.

Around the city, the lines hardened. Cely Gamache and Stan
Cummings, who had tried to stem the tide within the city council, fell
silent. If it had been difficult to argue for moderation in the past, it
was impossible now in the face of what appeared to be an epidemic of
heroin in the city. Chief George Hebert was now seen to be leading a
strong anti-drug effort, rather than just bumbling along.

It was a coup for Hebert to have hired Lawrence. Hebert deeply
admired the young narc, whom he had met when Lawrence was police
chief in Vergennes. They had talked in July, during a police chiefs'
association meeting, about Lawrence's coming to St. Albans. He was
leaving Vergennes—the politicians there did not like tough, fair law

enforcement, he said—and he was looking for work.

No one knows the extent to which Hebert was aware of Lawrence's past. On the surface, Lawrence looked like the perfect man for the job. Hebert had a serious drug problem in his city, and Lawrence had as much experience as any man in the state in the enforcement of the drug laws. Lawrence's resumé showed that—five years on the state police, attended several drug schools, taught at others, assisted police in New York, New Hampshire, and other states in drug investigations. The personnel file he sent along to Hebert bulged with commendatory letters from state's attorneys around Vermont.

It is hard to believe that Hebert had not heard some of the unfavorable rumors about the man; but even if he had, there were those favorable ratings from the state police. Surely a sour cop could not get ratings like that. And Hebert talked to Stan Merriam, the state cop who worked the St. Albans area. Merriam told Hebert that Lawrence was an outstanding cop. Perhaps another police chief would not have hired Paul Lawrence. But Hebert was a man under pressure. Keith Campbell and others were demanding action. The kids seemed to be thumbing their noses at him. Even if there were rumors that Lawrence was flaky, he did not appear that way: he seemed intelligent, steady. It was all good enough for Hebert. He hired Lawrence and, in a very short time, Lawrence gave him precisely the results that Campbell and the other hard-liners were looking for.

In fact, Lawrence's performance suited the public mood perfectly. The hippies arrested were on everybody's target list. He had found more drugs, and more serious drugs, than even Campbell had suspected. Lawrence's remarks about a city awash in drugs, about most of the hippies having guns, firmed the sentiment in favor of the anti-drug campaign.

Despite this hardening of public sentiment, there were doubts about the raid within the establishment and from the day the raid took place. In the St. Albans Police Department, for example, Captain Terry Flanagan, a bear of a man with a pixie grin, an on-and-off antagonist of Chief Hebert, had been dubious from the beginning about the hiring of Lawrence.

Flanagan had neither respect nor affection for the hippies who had been swept up in the raid, but he had a different view of the way the problems should have been handled. Six months earlier, a Massachusetts law enforcement official had recommended that the city hire a couple of college kids who had worked in the past for the Boston Police Department as undercover agents. The kids could work in St. Albans for the summer. This scheme had reached the point where the principal of Bellows Free Academy had agreed to accept the two men as students for the purpose of providing them with a cover. Hebert told Flanagan that this scheme had fallen through; he had not been able to contact the official in Massachusetts by telephone, he said. What he wanted to do instead was to hire Paul Lawrence, the former state trooper and Vergennes police chief.

Flanagan at first demurred. He felt that Hebert simply wanted to find a job for a fellow police chief. Also, Flanagan had heard some disquieting stories about Lawrence, both when he was in the state police and while he was at Vergennes—nothing very solid or specific, just rumors, bits and pieces. Flanagan told Hebert this, and that seemed to quiet the Lawrence talk. But in midsummer, while Flanagan was on vacation, Stan Merriam, state trooper working out of the St. Albans barracks, stopped to see him. It wasn't long before Merriam brought up Lawrence's name and praised him highly. Flanagan respected Merriam's opinions, so he went along with Hebert's desire to hire Lawrence.

When Flanagan returned to work, Hebert said he wanted him to meet Lawrence, so he and the chief drove out to the rest area on the Interstate and met the undercover agent there. Lawrence got in tbe rear seat of Hebert's car and they talked at length about the drug situation in the city. Just before Lawrence was to leave, Hebert took a roll of bills from his pocket, making sure Flanagan could see it, and handed it into the back seat to Lawrence. "You can give me a receipt for it later," Hebert said.

Flanagan did not care much for that method of handling money, and he did not care much for Lawrence personally, something that he felt Lawrence could sense. They seldom talked when Lawrence came to the police station, although at one point Lawrence gave Flanagan a small thermometer to hang on his wall; it was characteristic of Lawrence to cultivate older people with whom he worked, even if they didn't like him. Later, Flanagan warned Merriam that Lawrence ought to provide receipts for the money he was drawing. Flanagan knew there was something like ten thousand dollars in a special drug fund that would be available for buys. Merriam later told Flanagan he had talked to Lawrence and that Lawrence had said he would keep perfect records.

On the day of the bust, which he was warned about only the previous evening because of the secrecy surrounding Lawrence's activities, Flanagan's doubts about Lawrence were renewed. For one thing, he simply did not believe that there was the volume of heroin in town that Lawrence's charges would indicate. For another thing, the circumstances set forth in some of the reports didn't ring right. The most dubious was the report that Ronnie Rich had sold heroin to Lawrence in a car parked near Taylor Park in the middle of the afternoon, and that Rich had then driven down to park in front of the police station. Rich was a serious criminal, not a punk kid, and Flanagan looked out of his second-story window to the busy Main Street below, trying to imagine the scene. "Ronnie Rich would never be crazy enough to do something like that," he concluded.

The doubts outside the police department ran along similar lines. To Richard Gadbois, the young city attorney, the surprising thing was that all of those who were arrested proclaimed their innocence. And in many cases, not only proclaimed it, but shouted it. It is not unheard of for people arrested for a crime to plead not guilty, but in any such group, Gadbois figured, there ought to be at least a couple who would plead guilty to avoid the hassle, especially if the case was solid and would lead to a conviction anyway.

Moreover, many of those who had been busted by Lawrence had been arrested before and had pleaded guilty then, quietly and without any serious protest. Several of those arrests had come as the result of an investigation by Augustino Fernandez, a state police undercover agent, and the comparison between his operation and Lawrence's seemed highly significant to Gadbois and some other observers in the city.

Fernandez had come into town with Dana Goodnow, the head of the state police drug unit, after Diane Voudrien had died, and the two talked briefly with Chief Hebert about what was going on in the town. That was all the contact Fernandez had with local officials before moving into the Thompson Hotel. He registered under the name of Al Ferrara, and immediately went downstairs to Tuner's. Within hours he was offered the opportunity to purchase both marijuana and LSD.

He had never seen such an abundance of drugs, mostly soft stuff and speed. "This place is no challenge," he thought. "It would be a good place to break in a new man."

His primary target, however, was Ronnie Rich, the big speed dealer, and Fernandez could not afford to concentrate on making small buys from the local kids. That would look suspicious—why put heat on yourself with this small stuff? He concentrated on trying for big buys of speed.

Fernandez himself looked like a speed freak. He was tall, well over six feet, and gaunt to the point of emaciation. He had jet black hair hanging to his shoulders, a moustache, and dark brown eyes. He looked more like a hippie than many of the St. Albans street people.

Fernandez spent weeks establishing a connection with Bruce Scofield, one of Rich's henchmen, and toward the end of July, he began to make buys. Scofield's routine was to arrange the buy—the amount and the price—and to get the money from Al, as he knew Fernandez. Then Scofield would leave and return later to tell Fernandez where he could find the drugs. One time it would be in a trash barrel in a service station men's room, another time in a bag in a culvert, yet another time in Fernandez's car, which Scofield used to get the drugs. Fernandez would then go and pick up the drugs.

Scofield thought the fact that he did not personally hand over the drugs would protect him, although it amused Fernandez that Scofield's fingerprints were all over the drug containers. It is instructive, however, that Scofield, by his own lights, was so cautious. Lawrence's victims, by contrast, had apparently pressed drugs on him directly, even when they had only known him for hours, or days.

Fernandez started out buying ounces of speed for about three hundred dollars, then he went for pounds at twenty-five hundred to three thousand dollars. His final buy from Scofield took place at the Burlington Airport, and Scofield was arrested there. The buy soured Fernandez on the whole state police operation; he had wanted to make the buy at St. Albans, but his superiors wanted him to make it in Chittenden County: Pat Leahy was a better prosecutor than Mike McGinn, they said. Fernandez wondered whether they were doing it to help Leahy politically.

In any case, once Fernandez arrested Scofield, he shaved, cleaned up, put on his uniform and returned to St. Albans to make arrests stemming from the dozen or so small buys he had made in the course of his Scofield connection. He headed first for the Sand Castle and found Sonny Cross and some of his friends waiting for him there. They had put two and two together: Scofield had been busted, Al was not around, Al had not been busted, Al must be the narc. Fernandez and Sonny and the others walked across the street to the courthouse for arraignment. He didn't have to handcuff them.

Sonny Cross and the others pleaded guilty before their trials came up. Cross had sold Fernandez ten dollars' worth of speed, and although he pleaded not guilty at arraignment, he never went to trial. He knew that the information in the Fernandez complaint was accurate; the trial would be a waste of time and money. He got a zero-to-three-year sentence, suspended. There were no trials as a result of the small busts Fernandez made that summer.

There were other differences between the Lawrence and Fernandez operations, beyond the fact that the victims of Lawrence were screaming they had been set up. One was the drugs the two men claimed they bought. Fernandez was buying pot, hashish, and speed. Lawrence was buying heroin and cocaine. Fernandez had never seen any heroin in town, although he had once heard that some brown Mexican heroin might become available. He had neither seen nor heard about any cocaine. . . .

There was a final, significant difference. Fernandez, like the rest of the St. Albans establishment, figured that Otto Kremer was selling drugs out of Tuner's Place. As the most conspicuous owner of the city's most conspicuous counterculture hangout, Otto had been a target of establishment wrath for months. Yet Fernandez could get nowhere with Otto. He could not make friends with him, and he could never get into a position where he could try to make a buy from him. Yet Lawrence claimed he had made heroin and cocaine purchases from Kremer that would have been respectable in a large city.

While this sort of discrepancy was enough to excite some suspicion about the overall bust, preparing a defense for individual clients was another matter. None of those arrested were what one could call upstanding citizens. Most were very poor and were badly dressed; several had been arrested previously—some for drugs, some for greater or lesser offenses. Their life-style could best be described as casual: they were hard put to tell where they had been and what they had been doing on a specific day and time in weeks past. One day, to many of the suspects, was pretty much like another.

The essence of the state's case was also a problem for the defense attorneys. The evidence against the raid victims consisted of just two elements—the drugs themselves and the testimony of the undercover agent. The cases, in other words, would come down essentially to whether a jury would believe Paul Lawrence, a policeman, or an individual from the streets. A defense would have to consist of an alibi, or an assault on the credibility of the undercover agent.

At first, it was not easy for the street people to understand that. Even for people who scorned the American system, it was hard to believe that one could be convicted for crimes one did not commit. Nonetheless, the more perceptive of them began to see that it *could* happen, a realization that generated a paralyzing fear.

To Gary Burbank, the whole thing was ridiculous. It was simply a matter of explaining to the jury that he had not sold anything to Paul Lawrence, had, in fact, never met him. The arrest was difficult for his family, obviously, since his mother had to borrow money for his bail, but his initial reaction was that the whole matter was simply a mistake.

To Otto Kremer, the arrest felt at first like an insult. He considered himself a cut above the street people—he aspired to be a bridge between them and the establishment in St. Albans. He had been the wise man, the elder, of the counterculture. Now he was faced with the problem of raising $20,000 for bail and defending himself against very serious charges. His first reaction was to kick over wastebaskets in the local jail. Later, his experience as a radical and his imagination led him to wonder whether the cops transporting him to a jail in Woodstock might assassinate him as part of some insane, right-wing coup. For a week, Otto and Ritchie Eustace were locked in a tiny cell in Woodstock, condemned to fruitless conversations about what was going on. Eventually, Otto's parents and Ron Kaye, a local dentist, put up his bail.

Sonny Cross, the son of a welfare mother, never made bail. He felt at first that the bust was a simple mistake. He had stayed straight since getting busted by Augie Fernandez; at the police station he had laughed and joked with the others. When a girl he knew came in and burst into tears when she read her charges, he confidently reassured her that nothing would come of it. When the cops began to question Sonny, he was scornful at first:

"How tall are you?"

"I don't know."

"How much do you weigh?"

"I forget."

"Here," said the cop, "if you think this is a joke, take a look at this," and he threw Sonny the statement of charges against him. A week later, in Woodstock, he was sure it wasn't a joke. His lawyer, Richard Gadbois, called, and said he could not represent him. Gadbois was the city attorney and he had taken the job with the understanding that he could carry on his own law practice while handling the city's business. Now the city administration had made it plain to him that he would be fired if he continued representing clients arrested in the big raid. Gadbois had to get out.

As the walls of his cell began to close in, Cross began to panic. "What's going on? These guys are really out to get me," he thought. He called his sister and brother-in-law in Brattleboro, and begged them to get him a lawyer. They retained Peter Cleveland, who went to see Cross. At first it seemed to Cross that Cleveland had doubts that Cross was telling him the truth. Cleveland seemed to change his mind after Cross flatly rejected the state's attorney's offer to go easy on him if he would testify against Mark Beauregard and Otto Kremer. Still, in insisting on a trial, Cross was risking the intervening months in jail and an uncertain outcome. Pleading guilty in return for a lenient sentence would have been safer, Cross knew.

In some ways, the charges against the arrestees were a greater wrench to the parents than they were to the young people. The young people had developed a sense of being outsiders, of alienation from the usual sources of power and authority in the community. That was not true, however, of many of their parents. Many parents had had trouble with the children who had drifted into the counterculture, but the parents tended to see these as transitional emotional problems, subject to solution with advancing maturity. These parents faced suddenly both the crisis of serious charges against their children, and the criticism which came from the community at large. Those who believed their children's contentions that they were innocent had to confront, for the first time in their lives, the possibility that the processes of justice were suspect.

The lives of Mr. and Mrs. Norman Kimball of Sheldon, Vermont, were jolted to the point where they felt they would never be the same again. Norman had come home from work that Wednesday bringing the St. Albans *Messenger;* the paper carried the story of

the huge raid, but their son Tommy had been arrested in the afternoon, after the paper had come out, and his name wasn't among
those arrested. The Kimballs knew some of the names, though, and
they found it hard to believe. Otto Kremer, Jane Eaton . . . they didn't
seem like criminals. "I just can't believe it," said Diane Kimball,
their daughter.

When they returned from shopping in the city, their younger
daughter, Nancy, gave them the news. "Big bubba is down to jail," she
said. Shortly thereafter, the girl Tommy had been living with called
them to say that Tommy was innocent. "Don't worry," she said,
"Tommy did not do this." But the Kimballs were nonetheless
heartbroken. The worst thing for Mrs. Kimball was to think of
Tommy spending the night in jail, but there was no way that night to
get bail. So they called their minister, who came to see them, and he
called the legal aid office, only to be told that that office did not deal
with criminal matters. Mrs. Kimball also tried to call Tommy at the
Burlington Correctional Center, but officials there would not let her
talk to him. When could she talk to him? Tuesdays and Thursdays,
they said.

The next day, they called the president of the Enosburg Falls
bank and arranged to mortgage their home in order to raise the bail
money. The president of the bank, Guy Hubbard, arranged the loan
immediately; he knew the family and was concerned. He also wanted
to know whether Norman's mother, Tommy's grandmother, knew
about the arrest. Norman and his wife went to see his mother after
they got the money. She said she would do anything she could to help,
but that it might be a good idea if they let Tommy stay in jail awhile.
"Let him think over what he's done," she said. It was at that point that
the Kimballs realized what a heavy burden the community sentiment was likely to become. Later, they would hear the talk show on
the radio station. "It's about time they got the scum off the street,"
was a common expression.

That afternoon they went to the courthouse in St. Albans to pick
up Tommy after his release on bail. The hardest part for his mother
was seeing him brought into the courtroom in handcuffs. The judge
let him go, with the proviso that he not go out after dark except when
the Graefe band was playing a job. The Kimballs also bailed out Mike
Lotowitz, who could never have raised the money on his own. They
did so despite the cautionary remarks of their lawyer, Robert Cronin.

"How well do you know this guy?" he said of Lotowitz. "You might lose your money."

Although they had a few uncertain moments, the Kimballs believed their son's contention that he was not guilty of the charge brought by the police. It was not that they thought he was perfect, far from it. He had been a problem for them for a long time. They had five children, four of them girls. Tommy was a passive, lazy boy. He would work occasionally haying or sugaring in the spring, but other than that, music seemed to be all he cared about. His life-style was also far different from that of his family. The Kimballs lived in a rambling old frame house in the tiny hamlet of Sheldon, not far from the Canadian border. Norman Kimball worked in a mill and his wife was a housewife. Tommy, on the other hand, lived in the house occupied by the Graefe band, had long hair, was a street person. Diane was particularly critical of his behavior.

In this case, however, Diane was convinced her brother was innocent, a fact that impressed their parents. The crucial factor, however, was the nature of the charge against Tommy. The sales were minor by the standards set by the big raid—ten dollars' worth of hashish and three dollars' worth of LSD. The Kimballs would not have been surprised to hear that Tommy smoked pot. But the acid charge was incredible. Sometime previously Tommy had gone to Boston and had taken LSD while he was there. He had a "bad trip" and told his mother about it when he came home. It had been horrible, he told her. He would never have anything to do with hallucinogens again. He would hate acid for the rest of his life. He would never have sold the stuff, his mother felt.

None of that was likely to help Tommy much. The question was how to defend him. Diane went to St. Albans to collect petitions to the governor and attorney general, calling for an investigation of Lawrence's activities. The Kimballs wrote letters to state officials, but to no avail. Meanwhile, the men at the mill where Norman worked scorned his claims that his son was innocent, and they made it clear they were glad that the raid had taken place. Everyone wanted the scum off the streets, and Tommy, the indication was, was part of the scum.

Within a week of the big raid, city officials tried to close Tuner's Place on the grounds that several drug buys had been made there.

Otto and his partners considered acceding to these efforts, but finally decided to fight. They retained James Levy, a local attorney, and he prepared for an appeal to the state Liquor Control Board.

Levy is a very short, intense man with blond hair and blue eyes. A New Yorker, he had graduated from Columbia University Law School and had been in St. Albans for a few years trying to build a law practice. He was defending some of the suspects arrested in the raid, and he jumped into the Tuner's case eagerly. Levy was different from the other defense lawyers in his rage at what he felt was a monstrous injustice. The other lawyers—Dan Lynch and Joe Cahill particularly—fought the cases as best they could, but Levy did more—he seethed with indignation.

He particularly looked forward to the liquor board proceeding because it would unmask the undercover agent. The great mystery in the city was who he was—no one in the counterculture seemed to know the narc. Moreover, Levy felt that the city's effort to close Tuner's was more than the normal reaction of city officials to a drug bust. Tuner's, Levy thought, was a kind of economic threat to E. Michael McGinn, the local lawyer now serving as the state's attorney.

McGinn, Levy knew, owned a piece of the Tea Company, a dance hall and bar just off Main Street, not far from Tuner's. It was contrary to state regulations for a county prosecutor to own a bar, but that didn't appear to bother McGinn much. Levy knew about the Tea Company because he had been a part owner himself for a time; his dislike for McGinn was one of the reasons he had gotten out.

McGinn was not the owner of record; his shares were in his sister's name. But McGinn was always in there, often tending bar, which created some talk in town. Ed Chamberlain, the local reporter for the Burlington *Free Press,* interviewed McGinn about the issue, and McGinn claimed, in what was an elaborately farcical interview, that bartending was a hobby of his.

In early November, the liquor board held its hearing on the issue of closing Tuner's. Levy, Dan Lynch, Otto Kremer, Gary Burbank, and Jane Eaton, two of Tuner's bartenders, and two of Otto's friends, Brenda Corliss and Tyrone Shaw, traveled to Montpelier together.

The main witness for the city, of course, was Paul Lawrence. And when he came in to testify, his appearance was a shock to the hippies—they still didn't know him. Otto Kremer was particularly stunned: he thought he knew everyone in town, and once he found who the narc was, he could begin trying to solve the riddle of these charges. Yet, here he was, and no one knew him. . . .

Levy questioned Lawrence closely, and he was, as always on a witness stand, cool and impressive. He seemed to know what he was talking about, and he simply claimed he had made the buys he had charged the various suspects with. The first day's session was inconclusive, but for the first time, the defense lawyers had something to go on—Lawrence himself.

Having now learned from Lawrence the locales of his actions, Levy called Peter Langrock, an attorney in Middlebury, from his Main Street office that evening. Langrock had defended a client against Lawrence charges and he had told his client that Lawrence was a bad cop. He sketched Lawrence's career for Levy. The Addison County state's attorney had refused to prosecute Lawrence cases when Lawrence was chief in Vergennes; Lawrence had contradicted himself on the stand in a couple of Brattleboro cases; he had beaten up a kid in Brattleboro. . . .

Levy could scarcely contain himself. He called John Deppman, the state's attorney for Addison County, who confirmed Langrock's tale and told him more: the man had been pressured to resign from the state police; there was a question about expense accounts in Vergennes, and about $1,400 worth of uniforms for a three-man police force. There was a story in law enforcement circles about Lawrence shooting out the window of his own police cruiser while in the state police.

Meanwhile, Otto Kremer had gone up to the home of Ron Kaye, a young dentist who had bailed him out of jail. He told Kaye and his wife about seeing Lawrence for the first time. Kaye called a dentist friend of his in Addison County to ask about the man. Kaye got the same sort of picture that Levy had just received. Kremer called Levy and they traded stories. They were jubilant; Otto could imagine Levy standing on his toes and striding back and forth in his office as they talked. . . . Tomorrow they would go after Lawrence on the stand.

The following day, they returned to Montpelier and Levy questioned Lawrence about the charges. Levy could not shake Lawrence's story, but Kremer and the others testified that buys had not taken place in the bar, and the members of the liquor board seemed impressed. The St. Albans contingent was pleased when they left. Regardless of the outcome of the liquor proceeding, the defense would now have a handle on Paul Lawrence. And he looked vulnerable: his police record in Vermont was a mess—it should be possible to impeach him on the stand.

Right after the liquor hearing, someone put Lawrence's picture up on a bulletin board in Tuner's Place. Within days, everyone in the St. Albans counterculture knew his face. Things were still tense in the city. Many of those arrested were still in jail, unable to provide the bail. But the narc was exposed. It was early November and the grim Vermont winter loomed, but things seemed brighter for the street people.

Mocking Justice

ON NOVEMBER 8, JOE CAHILL, THE PUBLIC DEFENDER FOR Franklin County, hired a private detective, Randolph Brock III, to investigate Paul Lawrence. Several of the defendants arrested in the October raid were indigent — they could not afford a lawyer, and the public defender's office would have to represent them. Cahill was convinced that the charges against them by Paul Lawrence were bogus, and he persuaded the state defender general to pay for the private investigation into Lawrence's background. Impeaching Lawrence would be the only defense many of his clients would have.

Brock, who had a background in military intelligence and law enforcement, ran a private firm in Middlebury called Champlain Security Systems, Inc. He began work on the Lawrence matter immediately.

Meanwhile, the defense attorneys arranged for seventeen of their clients to take polygraph, or lie detector, tests, given by Brock. Brock was an expert and painstaking examiner; he spent an average of two hours with each client, interviewing them first, going over the questions he would ask, then putting them on the machine to answer the questions.

Of the seventeen, eleven were found to be telling the truth, or telling the truth with some qualifications, the qualifications arising from their mental states or from medicine they were taking. (Some of those arrested were drug users at the time.) Five of the tests were inconclusive; nothing could be determined from them. One person was found to be lying, but that was qualified because of the person's psychological background. None was found to be lying outright.

The polygraph tests were not admissible evidence in state courts, but the police and prosecutors nevertheless placed considerable credence in them at the time. The defense attorneys thought they were valuable in this instance: any prosecutor looking at the results Brock got from these seventeen defendants ought to be very curious about the information provided by his police officer. At the very least, he ought to force the officer himself to take a polygraph examination.

Mike McGinn was not interested, however. At least that is what he said. Lawrence had said in a deposition that he would be willing to take a polygraph exam, but McGinn ruled that out. These cases would go to trial, he said. The polygraphs did confirm the belief of the defense attorneys that their clients were innocent. And Brock's first reports were coming in, giving the lawyers the kind of information they would need to attack Lawrence's story, at his deposition, and in the trials that would begin early in 1974.

Brock found that Lawrence had received less than an honorable discharge from the army, after serving only seven months. He had testified under oath previously that he had been discharged for medical reasons; the military records showed he was discharged for "character and behavior" disorders.

Lawrence had worked as police chief of Vergennes, Vermont, for five months in early 1973 and had finally resigned under pressure from the city council. During that period, John Deppman, the prosecutor for Addison County, had soured on Lawrence and had declined to prosecute Lawrence cases unless he, Deppman, approved them in advance. Deppman simply did not trust Lawrence's word.

Brock also talked to a secretary in Deppman's office who said that she spent a day socially with Lawrence, driving to Montreal with him for a drink, and returning to Burlington for dinner. Lawrence had filed an expense voucher with the city of Vergennes for $52.95 for a "drug invest. in Vergennes combined with U.S. Customs."

Brock talked to Jerry Diamond in Windham County and Diamond told him about the trouble they had with Lawrence there.

Brock also obtained a copy of the letter that Diamond's deputy, Garvan Murtha, had written Lieutenant Robert Iverson of the Vermont State Police. Lawrence's stories were constantly changing, Murtha said in his letter to Iverson.

"These discrepancies," Brock said in one of his reports, "which reportedly occurred between depositions, reports, and probable cause hearings included: varying times at which significant events happened; changes of testimony as to how LAWRENCE became acquainted with either defendants or witnesses; changes as to where certain sales took place or the inability to recall where such sales occurred; conflicting statements as to the disposition of the evidence; the ability of LAWRENCE to recall conversations, including exact words precisely compared to the inability to recall physical details, or facts such as where sales took place."

In addition, in four of the seven drug cases Lawrence handled in the Brattleboro area, the quantity of drugs that Lawrence claimed to have bought turned out to be significantly larger than the amount that the New York State Police drug laboratory later tested. The obvious implication was that Lawrence was holding back part of the evidence. The apparent shortage of drugs occurred in every instance where loose drugs were tested. The other cases involved capsules or tablets that were not purchased by weight.

There were disturbing odds and ends confirmed in the reports. Lawrence had been sued and an insurance company had paid a settlement of $2,500 in a police brutality case in Brattleboro. Lawrence had beaten the man up outside a courtroom in Brattleboro. Lawrence had said under oath he had not applied to other police departments before getting a job as chief in Vergennes. The records showed he had applied in Rutland and in Fairfax, Virginia, and there were indications he had applied in Providence, Rhode Island.

In Vergennes, there had been questions raised about his expense vouchers, in addition to the day spent with the secretary from the state's attorney's office. He had ordered $1,364.95 worth of uniforms for himself and two other men. In his resumé he had said the Vergennes force was four men and up to fourteen special officers; actually, there were never more than three, including Lawrence, and never more than four specials. He had misstated the population of the city, apparently to make his job seem more prestigious.

He had testified in depositions that he had never seen a psychiatrist for professional reasons; his military records showed that he had. A tobacco company he worked for after leaving the state police had forced him to resign and had sued him after he said his stock had been stolen from his car. The case had been decided in Lawrence's favor.

Brock also found out about the affair at the Farrell Distributing Company in Rutland, and his sources told him that several members of the state police believed that Lawrence had shot the window out of his own cruiser. Brock also learned that the men who had tried to break into Farrell's that night had watched the affair from nearby, and that they had never fired any shots.

On the other hand, Brock interviewed Major Glenn Davis, the top professional in the state police hierarchy, and was told that Lawrence's transfer to Bethel at the close of his state police career had not been out of the ordinary. The only derogatory thing said was that if Davis had been asked, he would not have recommended that St. Albans hire Lawrence. The man was "obstinate," Davis said, implying that he concluded this from Lawrence's reluctance to move to Bethel from Rutland.

Some of the Brock information was available when the defense attorneys jointly took a deposition from Lawrence in early December. The lawyers—Jim Levy, Dan Lynch, John Easton and Peter Cleveland—got to the courtroom on Kingman Street in the early afternoon. Mike McGinn was there, dressed in hunting clothes and lolling in the judge's chair, his feet on the podium. Lawrence was in a chair to the left of McGinn. Before going into the session, the lawyers had devised a scheme to test Lawrence's ability to identify their clients. Each one had a recent photograph of his client, and pictures of four or five other people. If, as the suspects claimed, they had never met Lawrence, the man might not be able to pick out the right picture.

Peter Cleveland began the questioning, delving into Lawrence's background in police work, his army experience, and methods. Lawrence was cool and self-possessed, as they knew by now he would be. But they ran into trouble when Dan Lynch brought up the issue of the photographic identification. Lawrence said that he could identify the various suspects if he saw a picture of them, but when Lynch produced a handful, McGinn stepped in.

"Don't answer any questions on those," he said quickly. "Just leave them and let him bring them to Judge Gregg."

"Are you able to identify any of those individuals?" Lynch persisted.

"Why don't you just forget them?" McGinn cut in.

"You can't advise him what to *do*. You *can* advise him what to answer," Lynch argued.

"I can advise him whether I want him to answer the question," McGinn said. "He is not going to identify the pictures. He has answered the question. I am saying I am not going to permit any further questions of photographic identification. If you want to go on with another line, okay, otherwise we will end the deposition here."

The lawyers abandoned the photographic issue briefly, but then returned to it and this time Lawrence himself responded:

"My answer to that is I am not here to play any games or lineups or anything else."

"I am aware," McGinn said, "we are about to go out the door in about five seconds if you want to keep going on the photographs."

Having failed to get Lawrence to identify the pictures, but still suspicious about his claims, they asked him to describe Tuner's Place, which he said he had been in several times. McGinn was dubious about that also, but it seemed too obvious a thing to forbid, so they went ahead.

Lawrence proceeded to draw a rough diagram of the bar in so erroneous a fashion that the attorneys immediately wondered if he had ever *been* there, let alone made drug buys there. He knew nothing of the pool table in the rear that was a constant source of attention and interest. He indicated that the bands that played there did so in the rear of the bar, and he said the area in front of the front window, the actual location of the stage and the piano, was open. He said he saw no piano there. As for restrooms, he knew nothing of them, although he presumed they existed; he never used the men's room there, he said. He also had no idea whether the bar was air-conditioned, although he had been working there in August.

When it was Jim Levy's turn to question Lawrence, he returned again to the photographs and on hearing the McGinn threat to end the deposition, Levy called for a recess and went into the clerk's office to call Judge Gregg. Levy wanted the judge to order McGinn to permit the defense attorneys to test Lawrence's ability to identify the suspects. The judge flew into a rage, telling Levy that it was improper for him to call and that Levy appeared to be trying to manipulate his office.

Levy protested that McGinn was threatening a walkout and that the lawyers were unreasonably cramped in their efforts to discover the state's case against their clients. Gregg would not hear of it: he could not make that kind of ruling, he said.

Still, later that afternoon, they tried again. Could Lawrence identify one of the suspects, if he saw him in a picture? "Yes."

"Would you be able to identify her if she were in one picture of several pictures presented . . . you would be able to identify her?"

"I believe so," Lawrence replied.

"How about Terry Pilon . . . could you identify him from a picture?"

"Yes."

"If he were one of several people in a picture, could you identify him from a picture?"

"Yes."

"If Brenda Denton were present in person, could you identify her?"

"Yes."

"If she were with a group of other persons, could you identify her?"

"Yes."

"How about Terry Pilon . . . could you identify him in person?"

"Yes."

"If he were by himself, could you identify him?"

"Yes."

"If he were with several persons, could you identify him?"

"Yes."

"Mr. Lawrence, would you be willing to identify Mr. Pilon if he were present today?"

"No, I have been advised by the state's attorney not to."

"Would you be willing to identify Brenda Denton if she were present today?"

At that point, four men walked into the courtroom; one of them was Terry Pilon.

As soon as McGinn saw the four enter the room, he got to his feet. "Let's go," he said to Lawrence, and the two began to leave.

"Are any of these people . . . can you identify any of these people who have just walked into the room?" Lynch asked Lawrence as he made his way toward the door.

"Will the record show that four males just entered the room; that the witness left the room without making any attempt to identify them, although he did see them. The state's attorney is also leaving the room," Lynch said, "that the state's attorney has advised the witness, Paul Lawrence, not to make any identification."

The deposition was over.

Despite the existence of a sizeable body of evidence that would tend to impeach Lawrence, the deposition and its outcome were ominous for the defense. McGinn's attitude was that Lawrence was telling the truth, that the accused were lying, and that the prosecution was going to drive these cases to conviction, in the face of whatever extenuating information the defense lawyers would offer. The polygraphs, the startling things about Lawrence's background—these the prosecutor's office would not consider at all. Moreover, Judge Gregg's sharp reply to Jim Levy's phone call at the deposition indicated he might be hostile to the defense also.

This would be critical since getting the damaging information about Lawrence into evidence in the trials was by no means guaranteed. Lawrence's performance in Brattleboro, in other locations in his state police career, and in the short period he served in Vergennes was not directly related to the St. Albans cases. Under Vermont's trial procedure, they could be excluded from a trial, if the judge saw fit to do so. It would be an interpretive judgment for Gregg; the defense lawyers would argue that in one-on-one cases, more so-called collateral matters should be allowed into evidence. But Gregg would be within the bounds of procedure to keep them out.

This fact is one of the reasons why sound judgment and a sense of discrimination are required of the prosecutors in our criminal justice system. For most small-time criminal cases the odds lie with the prosecution: policemen are more believable to juries than defendants, particularly defendants whose life-styles are alien to the jurors. Most prosecutors know that in many cases it is they who decide who is guilty and who is innocent: they do this by prosecuting some of the cases the police bring them, and by declining to prosecute others. They judge the weight of the evidence and such questions as the veracity of the police, and many prosecutors say there have been cases that would stand up in court that they refused to press.

No such critical examination was made of Paul Lawrence in St. Albans, His personality and articulate nature seemed to carry him past such tests without a hitch. As far as Chief Hebert was concerned, Lawrence stood on Hebert's version of a pedestal. When the defense attorneys asked Hebert in a deposition what kind of instructions he, Hebert, had given Lawrence on carrying out his undercover work, Hebert said, "It was far from me to tell a man of his experience how to conduct an investigation in the drug field."

More might have been expected, however, of Mike McGinn. The Champlain Security Systems report made it clear that Jerry Diamond in Windham County and John Deppman in Addison County had refused to prosecute Lawrence cases. It was true that Stan Merriam was an admirer of Lawrence, and there were the favorable state police reports, but by late December, much of the disquieting information that lay beneath the smooth Lawrence veneer had come to light. Once the veneer was stripped away, however, one had to be willing to look beneath the surface, and McGinn never gave any sign of being willing to look.

If there was any doubt about the determination of the police and prosecutors to press ahead with their anti-drug campaign, they disappeared on December 16. On that day, the local cops carried out a second major sweep, arresting nine persons on a variety of drug charges. Once again the drugs were hard-core—heroin and cocaine, in many instances.

The sales were all reported by Paul Lawrence; again, there was no corroborating evidence, other than the drugs themselves. And in most cases, the sales took place after Lawrence's picture went up on the bulletin board at Tuner's. This was striking indeed: by early November, every kid in town had heard of Paul Lawrence. Why would they sell drugs to him in those circumstances?

On top of that, there were particular peculiarities. One of those arrested was James Poquette. Poquette had been charged with selling LSD to Paul Lawrence. Joe Cahill went down to the courthouse to talk to Poquette; he would represent him. As they were talking, a local sheriff stuck his head in the door, and said, "Hey, Eric," then he corrected himself, referring to Poquette as Jimmy.

Something clicked in Cahill's mind. There was a superficial

resemblance between Poquette and Eric Goodroe, who had been arrested in the first sweep. So Cahill, remembering the Lawrence report on the Goodroe situation, began to question Poquette. He *did* have a grandmother in Alburg, and he *had* worked for the city of St. Albans, which is what Lawrence had said of Goodroe. Moreover, Poquette had been picked up once, while traveling to his grandmother's home, by a man in a yellow Volkswagen.

Cahill immediately took this information to the prosecutors, and they asked Lawrence about what appeared to be a clear case of mistaken identity. Lawrence denied it flatly. "They're full of shit," he said. The prosecutors accepted Lawrence's story.

The apparent success of the first raid had driven much of the debate in the city council underground. But the liquor board had shocked the local officials by vacating their order to close Tuner's, pending some disposition of the trials in St. Albans, and Keith Campbell and his hard-core supporters, Bob Hill and Bill Bessette, had held a session of the council to discuss it.

Stan Cummings and Cely Gamache had not been invited; nor had Richard Allard, although Allard had been a supporter of the anti-drug effort through the spring and summer months. Cummings and Gamache protested bitterly about what they said was an underhanded procedure, but this issue was essentially peripheral to the question of Lawrence's campaign. They had given up trying to stop that.

The council was now embarked on a relentless course to rid their community of the drug menace, and they began to think beyond Lawrence's activities. Campbell and Bessette drafted a resolution calling on the Vermont legislature to enact the same kind of tough drug laws that had been recently passed in New York State, under the sponsorship of then Governor Nelson Rockefeller.

These draconian statutes called for imposing mandatory sentences as severe as life imprisonment for the selling of illegal drugs—they were said to be the ultimate step in wiping out the drug traffic. Cummings and Gamache voted against the move. "There's such a thing as overkill," Mrs. Gamache grumbled. But that did not deter the majority.

In late November, the council held a session to discuss the resolution, and Gary Burbank, then out on bail, went to the council meeting and asked to address the members. In his quiet, halting fashion,

Burbank pleaded with them not to pass the resolution. He had been essentially unaffected by the deep alienation from the system that marked many of his peers, and he was deeply distressed that not only might a cop frame an innocent person, as Lawrence had in his case, but that society might provide a massive increase in the penalties that might result.

"Can you believe a policeman might frame an innocent person?" Burbank asked Keith Campbell. Campbell said he could. But the council was unmoved, although Bob Hill told Burbank he was sorry for him.

Although the council was committed to a very hard line, another of its members began to entertain doubts about what was happening. It was Richard Allard, a young man, just over thirty, who had until then been nearly as distressed about drugs as Campbell. Two years earlier, he had written a letter to the police warning them that drugs were becoming a problem. He had heard from his brothers that drugs were available in the high school, and he wanted to do something about it. His reaction to the October raid was favorable; it was a job that needed doing, he thought. The money spent on buys was well spent.

But Allard was a different man from Campbell. He lacked the burning hatred for the counterculture that Campbell displayed. Allard had grown up in a blue-collar family, on the west side of town, and he still spent time in some of the city bars. He knew people like Otto Kremer and Jane Eaton, and to him they were not monsters. He still had something approaching an open mind.

Allard was shaken, therefore, when four or five hippies cornered him one late fall evening at the Edgewater, a bar at St. Albans Bay. Allard was there with his wife, and the hippies, including Otto Kremer, asked him if they could talk to him in a back room. He agreed; you could always talk to Allard. His wife was apprehensive to see her husband go into the room alone with the group of youths, and he was gone for a long time.

With Otto doing most of the talking, the group insisted to Allard that they were not guilty and that it was crucial that he do something about getting the city council to realize that. Allard listened, made no commitments, but he began to wonder. And his doubts increased when the second big bust took place in late December. How could

Lawrence make these buys, he asked himself. His face was known, he had testified at the liquor board hearing, he had been deposed by various lawyers, the kids on the street had talked of nothing else for weeks. Even if Lawrence wore disguises, Allard figured, there was no way anyone would forget his face. The man had a very faint cast in one eye, and Allard did not believe that if a person saw him once he could be deceived by him a second time.

Allard began to ponder other questions as well. Why was Lawrence using the New York State Police laboratory instead of the Vermont laboratory? Why was the city not getting back some of the thousands of dollars it was pouring into drug buys? There ought to be restitution to the city, he thought.

Yet, Allard was not willing to buck the tide in the town. There was strong pressure for action against drugs, and placed in that context, his doubts and questions did not seem substantial enough. There were some countercurrents, moreover, that Allard knew about. Kenneth Libby, the police chief in Stowe, said Lawrence was a terrific cop. Stan Merriam thought highly of him. The thing to do was to wait and see what developed.

At the end of December, the city council voted to increase the appropriation for the drug operation from nine thousand to ten thousand dollars. "I want to push these so-called drug pushers out of St. Albans and into prison for many years to come," Campbell told his colleagues.

In mid-December, the defense attorneys felt a short breath of hope. Mike McGinn resigned as state's attorney, and Governor Thomas Salmon nominated Ronald Kilburn, a partner of Dan Lynch, to replace him. Kilburn represented half a dozen or so of the drug suspects, and he knew all about the rash of suspicions about Paul Lawrence. Furthermore, he was thought to be a liberal, unlike McGinn, whom the defense attorneys thought of as a local version of Attila the Hun. Kilburn could be counted on to give Lawrence the sort of scrutiny that he had escaped until then.

At about the same time, Chris O'Shea, the publisher of the Franklin County Newspapers, which published twice-weekly newspapers for St. Albans, Swanton, Enosburg, and Richford, printed the first serious public allegation that Lawrence might not be trustworthy. O'Shea had sent his reporter, Stephen Jackson, to Addison

County to check Lawrence out, and on his return, Jackson had written a story attacking the man's credibility and his record. The story was heavily opinionated, but it touched on the kind of evidence that had already been developed in more detail by Randy Brock. The story ran on page one under a headline that read:

SOME DOUBT RELIABILITY
ON STATE'S STAR WITNESS
IN ST. ALBANS DRUG CASES

The story said that Lawrence had been forced to resign from the Vergennes Police Department "because the local City Council felt he was bilking the tax payers. . . . Many Vergennes citizens and council members were also dissatisfied when they learned their tax dollars were going into Mr. Lawrence's personal, ideological campaign against illegal drugs," the story said.

Opinion on Lawrence was "mixed" in Vergennes, the story said, with some people supporting him because "he had an 'uncanny' way of telling if a person handles drugs or is a pusher." The story went on to say that Hebert wanted to take advantage of that capability to mount "an instant crackdown in a part fantasy, part reality drug situation" in St. Albans.

This was as far as O'Shea felt he could go in dealing with Lawrence, without flouting the laws of libel. Even this much criticism, however, brought a hostile reaction from his readers. One local insurance man told O'Shea that Lawrence was doing a great service to the area, and that it was reprehensible for the newspaper to slander him so.

Whatever the Franklin County newspapers had to say about Lawrence, the voice of the community—the St. Albans *Messenger*—had considerably more influence. The pages of that newspaper provide a picture of at least a portion of community sentiment in the waning days of December, and the first few weeks of 1974.

On December 18, the paper printed an interview with Ron Kilburn, who promised that when he took over the state's attorney's office, there would be "no softening" of the anti-drug campaign. He also said that that campaign would be furthered if only judges would impose the sentences they had available. For example, the sale of marijuana could bring up to five years in prison and a ten-thousand-dollar fine.

"If there was any likelihood that kind of sentence would be imposed, then I'm sure that would stop many people from engaging in that activity," Kilburn said.

The following day, the *Messenger* applauded the Kilburn statement, and went on to say in an editorial that not only were stronger sentences desirable—they should be mandatory. It read in part:

> This newspaper, mind you, is in favor of the strongest possible laws and subsequent law enforcement and court sentences for the deranged individuals who peddle drugs to immature and foolish people young and old. But until such time as action is taken MANDATING heavy sentences as provided under state law, they or even tougher laws will be meaningless. Since there are some addle-headed judges sitting in Vermont who have not seen fit to hand down judgments as provided under the law, then there seems no recourse but to make those sentences MANDATORY.

And if anyone still doubted where the newspaper stood, it printed an editorial written by the paper's owner, William Loeb, in early January that went about as far as it is possible to go. The editorial was headed "Three Cheers for Turkey" and noted that two American women had been arrested in Turkey for smuggling hashish into that country. They were tried and sentenced to be executed, a sentence later commuted to life in prison.

"It must have been quite a shock for those two American girls to realize that not every country in the world has a permissive society whose foolish judges give only slaps on the wrists to drug smugglers and drug users," the editorial said. It added:

> HEARTIEST CONGRATULATIONS TO THE GOVERNMENT OF TURKEY AND TO THE THREE JUDGES INVOLVED IN THE SEN-TENCING. THIS NEWSPAPER THINKS IT IS A SAFE CONCLUSION THAT IT WILL BE A MONTH OF SUNDAYS BEFORE ANY AMERI-CANS TRY ANYMORE SMUGGLING OF HASHISH INTO TURKEY.

First Trials

THE FIRST MAN TO GO TO TRIAL WAS NORMAN YOUNG. HE was charged with selling twenty-five dollars' worth of LSD to Paul Lawrence on August 21, in Swanton, a town just north of St. Albans. Young was twenty-one years old and had had an occasional scrape with the law. At the time of the supposed sale, he was painting a house in Swanton. Lawrence said that he approached him while he was on a ladder, inquired about the prospects for buying the LSD, and that Young had sold it to him. Young was one of those thirty persons picked up in the big raid in October.

The trial would take place in a small courtroom on the second floor of an old white-painted brick building on Kingman Street, a long block west of Main in downtown St. Albans. Across the street is the Cornerstone Restaurant, a hangout for politicians and the professionals who work downtown; the remainder of the neighborhood consists of aging buildings, some residential, some commercial.

The atmosphere of the court building itself is early municipal, but the courtroom, while small, has been renovated and is very modern, almost jarring. The judge's podium and the railings and the other woodwork are a pale blonde, the seats curving around the prosecution and defense area are a bright blue.

Presiding over this court, day in and day out, was Judge Carl Gregg, a tall, imperious man, with gray hair, dark eyebrows, and a square, chiseled face. At times he resembled a younger Ronald Reagan. His manner on the bench was stern, but calm; and his days were filled by a stream of minor criminals and the county's misfortunates. Drunken driving, fighting, heavy drinking, cow stealing, shoplifting, driving snowmobiles on the public highways, jacking deer, the passing of bad checks—these were the crimes that came before the Franklin County District Court.

Each day, before the session began, Gregg made a meandering little speech, something that he was very proud of and which the court employees commended to visitors, about the procedures to be followed, about how defendants should advance promptly to the rail when their names are called; how they should already have the "information" from the state's attorney, outlining the case against them; how they can plead guilty or not guilty, and if they want to plead guilty, that they can describe the circumstances of their misdeed.

Trials commence, and Gregg is firm, but fair. The people who tend to show up in his court regularly call him Judge Grudge, but they concede his sentences are relatively mild; in fact, they are often surprisingly so. He will lecture a shoplifter about the evil of stealing, but the shoplifter, unless he is incorrigible, is likely to get no more than a suspended sentence and a requirement that he report to a parole officer.

Nonetheless, there is a quietly authoritarian ring to his manner on the bench. Most of the people who come before him are guilty. The questions are, how can they pay the fine, how can they stay out of trouble in the future? But, occasionally, someone will be defiant: they'll plead not guilty when the case against them is strong. "Who's your lawyer?" Gregg will ask quickly, with a sudden rasp in his voice.

The lawyers who practice before him—in matters other than those brought by Lawrence—rate him about as good as the ordinary district court judge in Vermont. He tends to favor the prosecution, but then, so do most district court judges. And he will dismiss a charge that manifestly has not been proven; some district court judges will never do that, simply throwing the issue into the lap of the jury.

In the Norman Young trial, Joe Cahill knew that Gregg's attitude and judgment would be critical to his case, more critical even than the jury's attitudes and perceptions. Cahill had to get the derogatory information about Lawrence admitted as evidence. That was virtually the only case he had. Young had admitted being in the place Lawrence said he was, so the issue would be whether the jury believed Lawrence or Young. Gregg would have to decide whether Lawrence's background and performance in other communities would be "collateral" matters, immaterial to the case at issue. Unless Lawrence could be shown to be untrustworthy, the case would be lost. Cahill wrote Gregg a detailed memorandum arguing that federal courts had expanded the boundaries for collateral material in those criminal cases that were one-on-one, where the only evidence against the defendant was the uncorroborated word of the police officer. The reason for this is obvious: in a one-on-one case, a defendant, unless he has an alibi, is helpless unless his accuser can be shown to be untrustworthy. Showing a police officer like Lawrence untrustworthy requires putting him on trial, to an extent.

Cahill argued long and hard in the judge's chambers about this issue, and he lost. Gregg simply would not go along. "It is your client who is on trial here, Mr. Cahill, not Mr. Lawrence," Gregg told him.

Cahill got nowhere either with the man who would prosecute the case, William Keefe. Keefe was the deputy attorney general for Vermont, who had entered the case when McGinn resigned at the end of 1973. The new state's attorney would be Ron Kilburn, but he represented some of the people busted in October, so he had a conflict of interest—he could not prosecute anyone arrested in that raid. The first four or five trials would be prosecuted by Keefe.

Keefe's attitude was identical to that of McGinn. A short bulldog of a man, his method of prosecution was to hammer at the defendant relentlessly, with everything he had. Cahill told him that Young had passed a polygraph examination, but Keefe scoffed at that. "The best polygraph in the world is those twelve people in the jury box," he told Cahill. He also brushed aside all the unfavorable information about Lawrence, although Brock's report indicated that Lawrence had committed perjury, whether that fact was admitted into evidence or not.

Once it was clear to Cahill that the Lawrence information would not be admitted, he advised Young that it was likely that he would be convicted and that he would go to jail. Keefe had offered a plea bargain: if Young would plead guilty, the charge would be reduced from sale of LSD to possession; that would keep Norman out of jail.

"I can't see pleading guilty to something I didn't do," Young insisted. So on a cold day at the end of January 1974, Norman Young went on trial. He refused to cut his hair, which he wore in a ponytail, but he managed to find an old sport jacket, which gave him the appearance of a relatively neat hippie.

Lacking the Lawrence impeachment, the trial was relatively straightforward. Lawrence testified that he had driven to Swanton with Larry Young, Norman's cousin, ostensibly to buy drugs. Norman Young was on a ladder, painting a house. The conversation, according to Lawrence, consisted of Norman's statement: "It's orange sunshine (LSD), and it's five bucks a tab."

Young, according to Lawrence's testimony, came down the ladder, got the drugs and gave them to Lawrence. That was it. Young took the stand to say that he had been painting the house and he remembered someone trying to buy drugs from him, but he said he didn't sell him anything. . . . The jury believed Lawrence. They found Young guilty, and he was sentenced to from four months to three years in jail.

The only untoward thing in the trial was the presence of half a dozen street people in the audience. They muttered and stirred whenever Lawrence said something they considered outrageous; they left only when Cahill pleaded with them. "You're not helping at all," he told them.

They were outside, however, when the jury left the building after the verdict, and some yelled and cursed at the jurors.

As the shouts of the hippies outside the courthouse faded in the cold winter air, a deepening sense of gloom and menace settled over St. Albans. Norman Young was far from the ideal defendant. He had admitted being at the scene of the supposed sale, and he had no alibi. A drifter and an occasional day laborer, he was known to have used drugs in the past. Judge Gregg was within his rights to reject the use of the disturbing information in Lawrence's background. Yet, Norman Young was innocent; his friends knew that, and so did the defense attorneys who represented the more than forty young people who had been arrested on Lawrence's charges.

In early February, the defense lawyers got together to discuss the strategy for the forthcoming trials, and they concluded the outlook was not good. Dave Yarnell and Joe Cahill suggested that one possibility was to contact Kimberley Cheney, the attorney general of Vermont, and ask him to investigate the situation, and to get Lawrence to submit to a polygraph test. Since all the cases were one-on-ones, Lawrence had to be impeached some way, and since Gregg would not permit any such effort to be made before a jury, law enforcement officials, somehow, somewhere, would have to do it.

There did remain, however, a glimmer of hope. The Young case had been a very simple one—a meeting of the two men, a small sale, and that was all. But at the end of February, the case of Sonny Cross would come up for trial and Cross's attorney, Peter Cleveland, thought that he might be able to win.

The Cross case was not simple. He was being tried on five charges, four of which resulted from alleged sales to Paul Lawrence. The fifth charge involved the discovery in early October of a bag of marijuana in a furnace room in back of the Sand Castles, Sonny's arts and crafts shop on Lake Street.

Cleveland had been struck by the similarity of the reports Lawrence wrote on all of his cases—the dialogue was all the same; the reports were full of little details about what the suspect said and about little things that Lawrence did, walking here, mentioning this: all of that would be effective with a jury.

At the same time, the Cross case was filled with obvious discrepancies. The first sale was alleged to have taken place August 9. Lawrence said that he had simply walked into the Sand Castles and that Cross offered to sell him some MDA. The report indicated that Cross had never met Lawrence previously. Cross supposedly sold Lawrence two hits of MDA for twenty-five dollars. But when the MDA was taken to the New York State Police laboratory, it turned out to be three tenths of a gram of heroin.

On August 15, Lawrence said, he returned and bought an ounce of MDA for three hundred dollars. There was nothing in his report about any conversation about the sale of heroin instead of MDA a few days earlier, although Lawrence said that he and Cross had had a glass of red wine. The same report said the first sale had taken place August 10, not August 9. It was the Brattleboro pattern showing up again: the convincing little detail about the glass of wine alongside the error in the time of sale.

On August 27, Lawrence said, he had gone to the shop and bought what he was told was a quarter ounce of cocaine for four hundred dollars. Mark Beauregard was with Cross at the time, and participated in the sale. This time, when the drug was tested at the New York laboratory, it turned out to be Demerol, not cocaine.

Lawrence had the buy from August 27 tested on August 29; yet on September 4, he said he bought one hundred fifty dollars' worth of cocaine from Cross and Otto Kremer at Tuner's Place, and, according to his report, Lawrence never mentioned having been cheated in the previous buy, although cocaine is far more expensive than Demerol.

Lawrence alleged a fourth buy—again a hundred fifty dollars' worth of cocaine—from Kremer and Cross on September 6.

This set of circumstances, so filled with incongruities, should not be credible, even to a redneck jury, which Cleveland expected he would get. Moreover, Cross had an alibi on his first two charges—the buys that occurred in the shop. In one instance, Sonny's sister, Donna, and his brother-in-law, Donald Pasha, said Sonny was with them at the time. On the other, Jill Gondolfi, a friend from Richford, said she was in the shop at the time the sale was supposed to have occurred, and that it had never taken place.

There was no alibi for the second two charges, although one would turn up at the trial, but Cleveland thought the internal mistakes by Lawrence, evident from his reports, plus the alibis, might be enough to get his client off.

On the possession of marijuana charge, Cleveland may have privately thought that the stuff probably did belong to Sonny, but he was prepared to argue that there was more than one access to the furnace room, and that there was thus no way to say to whom the dope belonged. Cleveland spent hours during February preparing for the Cross trial, and he had high hopes for success.

The other attorneys were not nearly so sanguine, although a close observer could see some anti-Lawrence sentiment simmering.

Dick Allard, who served both on the city council and in the Vermont legislature, had called Edward Corcoran, commissioner of the Vermont State Police, in January to ask him about Lawrence. "I'd like to come and see you about it," Allard said.

"Stay right there," Corcoran said quickly. "I'll pull the Lawrence file and come and see you." Corcoran told Allard about the state police view that Lawrence was bad news, untrustworthy. But Lawrence was so slick and tough, he could probably lie his way through a polygraph test, Corcoran said. He confirmed the view that had been growing in Allard's mind for weeks, and Allard took these impressions back to the city council. The council at the time was debating the budget for the forthcoming year, and Chief Hebert was looking for a major increase in his appropriation, a move that drew some significant political opposition.

Hebert had asked for two new police officers, in addition to Lawrence, who was operating on a special drug budget. Keith Campbell, the head of the council's public safety committee, was strongly in favor of this expenditure, but Terry Flanagan, the number-two man in the department, told the council that only one new man was needed.

In addition, Flanagan told Allard that Lawrence himself had "shot his wad," he was too well known to function any longer as an undercover agent. Allard took these bits and pieces of information and wrote out a series of questions that he thought Lawrence should answer. He wanted explanations as to why Lawrence was using the New York laboratory, why so much city money was going out for drug buys—and why none of it ever was recovered—and how Lawrence could keep making buys when he was so well known.

Some of this byplay broke into the St. Albans *Messenger,* although seldom in context. There was a mention in one story of Flanagan's objection to Hebert's budget request; there was also a reference about Flanagan's comment to Allard that Lawrence's usefulness in St. Albans was at an end. He was "burned out." The February 5 edition alluded to "furtive references" to a series of questions that Allard had given to Chief Hebert. The specific nature of the questions was not disclosed. In an editorial, the paper criticized Campbell for the request for a bigger police budget, commenting that "Alderman Campbell seems to have gone wild with spending for the police since his involvement in the local fight against drugs . . ."

These bits and tatters of information were scarcely sufficient to inform the public about what was going on in the city. The reader had no basis on which to judge the issues or to fathom the politics involved. The stories in the newspaper reflected Allard's efforts to undermine Lawrence, without challenging him directly. Allard and Flanagan were attacking Lawrence through the budget process in the council, and for the first time, the hard-line forces there were showing a degree of vulnerability. Even the *Messenger,* with its harsh attitude on drugs, appeared at this time to be either wondering about the validity of the Lawrence charges, or at least finding that pursuing them conflicted with another favored principle—austerity in government. But none of this was clear to the people of the city.

In some circumstances, these efforts might have broken a campaign like the one Lawrence was running. A stronger group of councilmen or a better newspaper might have forced these issues into the open. But it didn't happen there. Lawrence's prsuasiveness, Campbell's implacable drive against the counterculture, the acquiescence of the prosecutor's office, community support—all these kept Lawrence in operation. People like Allard and Flanagan and Stan Cummings could snipe away, and they had some limited success. But glancing blows such as these were not enough to stop the Lawrence campaign.

In mid-February, Levy, Cahill, Dan Lynch, and several other attorneys traveled to Montpelier to see Attorney General Kimberley Cheney. Before they did so, Jim Levy made sure that Bill Keefe got a copy of the Champlain Security report, so that both he and Cheney would be familiar with it. To the attorneys, Cheney was the last hope. Although the American legal system is an adversary one, every lawyer, prosecutor, and judge is an officer of the court and bears a responsibility for the dispensation of justice. The defense lawyers knew that they were making a serious charge, but they were sure they would be taken seriously—such an organized appeal was unprecedented.

The lawyers met with Cheney and Bill Keefe in Cheney's fourth-floor offices in the Pavillion Building in downtown Montpelier. They laid out the case to both men. They went through all the Brock information, then all of the polygraph results. But Cheney was not much impressed. He thought it not uncommon that defense attorneys would claim their clients were innocent. The contents of the Brock report were not that persuasive either, Cheney thought. The stuff didn't look savory, but lots of cops have that kind of thing in their backgrounds. A defense attorney could use it to make Lawrence look bad in front of a jury, Cheney figured, but there was nothing there that proved to Cheney that Lawrence was not to be believed.

As for the admittedly bizarre Farrell Distributing incident, surely the state police would have investigated that, and if they had done so, why had they given Lawrence such good ratings and recommendations?

The only impressive information in Cheney's view was the polygraph tests showing that some of these people were telling the truth when they said they had not sold to Lawrence. Despite his reservations, therefore, Cheney said that he would make an independent judgment about Lawrence's integrity. The lawyers left hopeful that such an investigation would bring an end to Lawrence's depredations.

They never heard from Cheney again. And on February 19, ten persons were arrested in Swanton on drug charges brought by Paul Lawrence.

Sonny Cross was twenty years old, and scared. Norman Young had got a fairly light sentence for selling LSD, but the charges against Cross were for big sales of heavy drugs, heroin and cocaine. The Lawrence charges indicated he was a major dealer.

He told Peter Cleveland that he did not have any "straight clothes" for the trial and Cleveland told him not to worry about it. "You'd just look like a dressed-up hippie," he said.

Sonny was dressed in a T-shirt and jeans when he went to trial before Judge Gregg at the end of February. Lawrence gave his usual plausible performance on the stand, as did Martin Horan, the senior chemist from the New York State Police laboratory. Horan had done the tests on the drugs submitted by Lawrence.

Peter Cleveland went to work hard on Lawrence in cross-examination. He asked him whether a dealer like Cross would know the difference between one drug and another, and Lawrence said he would. Why would Cross mistake heroin for MDA, Cleveland asked. Lawrence did not know.

"What was your cover, your story to Cross?" Cleveland wanted to know. Lawrence said he claimed to be a middleman drug dealer himself—thus the large buys of MDA and coke.

Would Cross know the difference between cocaine and Demerol when he apparently cheated Lawrence on the cocaine sale? Yes, he would, Lawrence said.

"Well, then, why didn't you mention that the second time you made a coke buy from him?" Cleveland demanded. "Wouldn't you blow your cover by not confronting him with the deception?" At that point, Lawrence suddenly reversed himself. Often a dealer like Cross will not know the difference between two drugs, he said.

Cleveland thought he had him. He hammered away at this point, forcing Lawrence each time to reverse himself, destroying the logic of the case against Cross. Either the dealer would or would not know the difference between cocaine, one of the most expensive drugs, and Demerol, which is cheap. If a supposed middleman allowed himself to be cheated as Lawrence had, then how could he maintain his credibility in the drug trade?

Cleveland rammed this point home for nearly forty-five minutes until Judge Gregg stopped him, pointing out, accurately, that the ground had been covered.

On the third charge, Cleveland got a break he had not expected. In questioning Horan about his relationship with Lawrence, he elicited the information that Horan had had two meals, either breakfast and lunch, or lunch and dinner, with Lawrence in Rutland, three hours' drive to the south, on the day when Cross supposedly made a coke sale to Lawrence in St. Albans. Although it was a little tenuous in that Horan couldn't remember which two meals were involved, it appeared to put Lawrence in Rutland at the time of the buy.

At the conclusion of the trial, Judge Gregg granted a motion to dismiss the marijuana charge against Cross. If there was more than one access to the furnace room, and there was no evidence that the dope had been put there by Cross, then that charge should not even go to the jury.

The jury in the Cross trial was out for several hours on the other charges. At first, Cleveland waited with Sonny, then he went across the street to have a drink at the Cornerstone with Bill Keefe. Cleveland was confident, and it appeared to him that Keefe was reconciled to losing. Lawrence had been made to look very foolish in cross-examination, and there was an alibi on three of the four buys. . . .

When the jury came back, they found Cross guilty on the first three buys, the ones for which he had an alibi. They found him not guilty on the charge against which he had no defense.

Judge Gregg sent him to jail for from four months to five years.

Justice Denied

JIM LEVY THOUGHT THE CRIMINAL JUSTICE SYSTEM IN ST.
Albans deserved one more try. If anyone had a chance to be acquitted
by a jury, it was Gary Burbank. Burbank had been a bartender in
Tuner's Place, but everyone who knew him realized that he was not
really a member of the counterculture in the city. A boy scout was
what they called him—even his friends. His background was also
different from those of many of the others who had been arrested
during the Lawrence roundups.

Burbank had graduated from BFA and had served four years in
the United States Navy, much of that time in Vietnam. He had
operated his own business in town, and had a good reputation. He
came from a well-respected family. He had no police record, had, in
fact, never had problems with the police department. Finally, he had
an alibi, and there were potential witnesses—primarily Addison
County State's Attorney John Deppman—who were willing to come
forward to testify that Lawrence's word and his reputation were
suspect.

So Levy prepared for trial. He had three things in his favor,
beyond Gary Burbank's good reputation. The first was the alibi. Otto
Kremer's records showed that Gary had not been on duty at the bar on
the evening when Lawrence said he purchased twenty-five dollars'
worth of methamphetamine, or speed, from him. There was the

Lawrence deposition, which showed that Lawrence knew so little about the layout of the bar as to raise the question of whether he had ever been in there. And there was Deppman.

On the other hand, there was a serious problem with the judge and the prospective jury. Gregg had given short shrift to the previous defendants. Both Sonny Cross and Norman Young had been butchered, Levy felt; neither of their attorneys had been able to introduce evidence such as Lawrence's military records, or other evidence that might have challenged his credibility. Moreover, the judge was using the same pool of jurors for each Lawrence case. There had already been three trials, and several of the prospective jurors had already found defendants guilty, indicating that they believed Lawrence when he said he bought drugs from someone.

Despite the relatively favorable outlook for Burbank, therefore, it was still doubtful that the same jurors would reject Lawrence's word, thereby rendering their previous judgments suspect. So Levy asked for a change of venue. The judge refused to switch to another location. Levy next pressed Gregg for a new jury to hear the case.

"These other drug cases were in many respects similar to the case at bar," Levy said, "and we feel that it would be practically impossible for basically the same group of individuals to fairly judge the demeanor of Paul Lawrence, and conclude that he's not telling the truth, since that would inevitably involve a determination on their part that they might have made a mistake in some of the previous cases. And I don't believe that human nature permits such willingness to admit error."

Bill Keefe objected, of course, and Gregg went along with him.

"Yes, the Court, in order to leaven this jury somewhat, as I've indicated previously, has called six brand-new jurors to be involved in this panel," Gregg said.

However, of the twelve-member jury finally selected, nine had served on at least one previous Lawrence trial; three of the jurors had served on two. Levy, in his initial question, elicited the assurance from each of them that the previous trials would not weigh on his mind—that having found Lawrence credible once, he would not hesitate to disbelieve him in the Burbank trial. Levy had to live with it.

The Burbank trial began at 9:30 A.M. on March 19, 1974. Gary

Burbank and Jim Levy were at the defendant's table in the small, modern district courtroom in the old courthouse on Kingman Street. Bill Keefe was on hand to prosecute the case. In the audience sat some twenty people, including Ron Kilburn, the new state's attorney, and a smattering of lawyers interested in the outcome of the case. There was just a handful of street people; there would be no repetition of the outburst at the Norman Young trial, when a swarm of hippies had harassed the jurors after they found Young guilty.

Also in the audience was Mrs. Burbank, Gary's mother. Levy had wanted her to sit at the counsel's table within the enclosure, but Keefe had objected and Gregg had not allowed it.

The trial opened with statements by the opposing attorneys, Keefe stating that his evidence would show that Lawrence had bought a small amount of speed from Gary Burbank at 6 P.M. on the previous September 27, while Burbank was tending bar at Tuner's Place. In his turn, Levy emphasized that Burbank had never met Lawrence, and he also issued an oblique attack on Lawrence's credibility. The chemist who would testify on the drug in question was a personal friend of Lawrence, and in fact the tests had been made at the New York State Police drug laboratory, rather than at a laboratory in Vermont.

Keefe called Paul Lawrence to the stand as the first witness. He had been there dozens of times, and was quietly self-assured. Keefe led him through an impressive litany of credentials as a drug investigator. A former state trooper, a graduate of the New England State Police narcotics school, a former instructor on drugs at the Vermont State Police Academy, an investigator on loan to the states of New York, New Hampshire, and Massachusetts, chief of police in Vergennes . . .

Lawrence told the jury he had gone into Tuner's at about a quarter to six and had sat down at the bar, ordering a beer. Within a few moments, Gary—he said he knew him then only as Gary—came over and asked if Lawrence wanted to buy some "meth," or speed.

"As best I can recall, he advised me that there was some really good meth that was in town, that it was supposed to be some of the best that had come into town in a long time, and that he was getting twenty-five dollars a—at two different times he changed the wording for the amount. At one time he referred to it as a lid and then another time as a spoon."

"What does the term 'lid' mean? If you know," Keefe asked.

"Mostly lid and spoon are used in sales of powdered narcotics, such as cocaine or methamphetamine, heroin, and any narcotic that would be sold as a powder, and, basically, I don't know if there's any equivalency as far as gram or metric measures for it, but it basically falls into the category of a spoon. It's a small container probably with a gram or less of powdered narcotic . . .

"After agreeing that—I told him I wanted to purchase one spoon, and if the stuff was good that possibly I'd be back at a later date and purchase some more. And he then left the area of the—immediate area of behind the bar and went to a location, a doorway which was along the west wall of the bar, and came back to the bar—"

"Is that the room that you said you saw billiard tables in?" Keefe asked.

"Well, you'd have to cross I believe it is where the billiard tables are and there was a doorway I believe it's in the south—more or less the southwest location of the building."

"And have you ever been in that room?" Keefe asked.

"No, I have not."

Keefe asked Lawrence about the price for the drug and Lawrence then continued his account of the sale.

"Upon returning he came back to the same location of where I was seated at the bar, and handed right across the bar a glassine envelope, handed it to me. I looked at the envelope, I could observe that it had white powder in it, and I placed the envelope in my pocket, and I paid him twenty-five dollars in cash."

After looking at his report, Lawrence said that there was a final bit of conversation in which Burbank had said that "it was really dynamite speed and that it was the best speed that had come into the area in a long time."

In his testimony, Lawrence did his best to slip in references to the volume of drugs or other specific sales. In an opening question, he said he had been told that "Tuner's was a general place where narcotic traffic was flowing." And when asked if he knew Jane Eaton, he mentioned, more or less in passing, that he had bought drugs from her. Levy objected to these questions, and the judge instructed the jury to ignore them; but they nonetheless contributed to the sense of reality that Lawrence was able to convey.

In his cross-examination of Lawrence, Levy elicited the testimony that Lawrence had had no personal contact whatever with Burbank before buying drugs from him. He had seen Burbank, Lawrence said, but he had never talked to him. Still, even simply seeing Burbank was placed in a damaging context:

"At one particular point during—I believe it was during the month of December—we had a surveillance established on a building at which narcotics were being dealt from, and we observed Mr. Burbank at that time operating a vehicle, and also on another surveillance he was observed also," Lawrence said.

On further examination, Lawrence conceded that Burbank had simply been seen driving in the area where someone was being watched, but it was all in the context of the selling of drugs.

Levy chipped away at Lawrence, pointing out that he had said in his deposition that there were just one or two other people in the bar when he made the sale, whereas he had said in direct testimony there were four or five. In the morning session, Lawrence had said he had been in Tuner's Place seven or eight times; in the deposition he had said he was in the bar twenty to twenty-five times.

Lawrence replied that he had thought in the morning he was being asked how many times he had been in the bar to purchase drugs; that would be seven or eight times. If he had been asked how many times he had wandered in or out, it would have been different, many more.

"So you must be really familiar with Tuner's Place, is that a fair statement, as far as the physical aspects of Tuner's Place?" Levy asked.

"Not necessarily."

"Not necessarily—why not?"

"The times that I was in there I was involved in narcotics transactions or just in there looking for someone that might have been around, and I didn't get into the physical aspects of the place at all," Lawrence said.

"Did you ever—how long did you stay on the average of each time you went in there?"

"Short times. I didn't stay in there long at all."

"Well, when you say 'short times,' are we talking one minute, five minutes, an hour, two hours?"

"It would vary from—as long as it took to make a purchase in there."

"How long does it take to make a purchase in Tuner's?"

"Sometimes it was relatively short depending on who was there, and other times I wouldn't be in there ten–fifteen minutes."

Levy then asked Lawrence to go to the blackboard and draw a diagram of Tuner's Place. Lawrence did so, drawing in two pool tables in the rear of the bar. He also indicated where the band played, at least where he saw instruments lined up. Lawrence could not recall whether he had ever heard music played in the bar or not.

At this point, Levy tried to introduce Lawrence's police reports on three other arrests, showing that the language he used in describing the conversation he had with the other three was very similar to that used in describing the Burbank transaction. After a conference in the judge's chambers, Gregg refused to permit the line of questioning.

Levy examined further into Lawrence's use of drug-buy money and ran into trouble again.

"Now let's just suppose for a minute, and again, this is a hypothetical case, no one's making any accusations at this point, just suppose that an experienced narcotics officer wanted to utilize some rather significant amounts of money for his own purposes. Can you think of a control apparatus which could be designed to prevent that officer from getting away with it?" Levy asked.

Keefe angrily objected to the question. "It's totally improper," he said. "What's being implied here is that this officer is stealing," he said.

Gregg cut off the debate and went into chambers with the two attorneys.

"The line of questioning at this point, Mr. Levy, would appear to be—for want of a better expression—cheap shots," he said.

Levy argued that the Burbank defense was that Lawrence had fabricated the incident and that it was proper to inquire into what happened to the thousands of dollars Lawrence had received. Gregg said he would permit him to inquire into the source of the twenty-five dollars that was paid to Burbank, but not about the range of other buys.

Levy then tried to bring in the R. J. Reynolds tobacco case, in which the company had challenged Lawrence about his claim that tobacco stock had been stolen from his automobile. They went back into chambers. "This is another cheap shot," Gregg said.

"Your honor, it's relevant for several reasons," Levy replied. "First off, the issue in this case is credibility, and I think—"

"The issue in this case is not credibility," Gregg cut in. "It's whether or not the respondent did or did not commit the offense that's charged in the information."

Levy agreed, but he argued that "the Vermont Supreme Court and other courts in other jurisdictions have ruled that as far as interrogation into collateral matters goes, this rests in the discretion of the trial court, but with a caveat that in situations where credibility is an issue raised by the defense, that broad leeway be granted . . ."

Gregg would not allow that, but before the three men left the chambers, Levy, in order to avoid another outburst in front of the jury, told Gregg he would like to lay out his remaining questions to get all the rulings at once. One of these, Levy said, was whether he had applied to other police departments before getting the job in Vergennes.

"What has that got to do with it?" Gregg asked.

"Because he has stated under oath that he didn't, and I would like to see his response. If he said yes, then I would bring to his attention a deposition which he gave to Mr. Cahill in which he indicated he had not sought other employment. If he says at this time he didn't, I guess I wouldn't pursue it any further, or I would ask him whether he had dates when he submitted applications to the Providence, Rhode Island, Police Department, the Fairfax, Virginia, Police Department, and one other police department.

"Again, Your Honor, this is—"

"So what?" Keefe asked.

"Well, obviously, if he's stating something today different from what he did at the time of this deposition, I think this relates to his credibility."

Gregg said that the whole matter seemed extensively collateral to the main issue. "What has the police application issue got to do with it?"

"It's the fact that he denied making these applications under oath that has relevance," Levy replied.

"Well, I don't believe that," said Keefe. "He told me he has."

"I don't care what he told you, Bill," Levy said. "I'm saying that he gave a deposition in which he said, 'I did not apply to these other departments,' and I think that again this is relevant because if the man is telling a falsehood on this particular thing, I think a jury could infer his credibility is not worthy of belief . . ."

Gregg continued to question the relevance of the material, but he did say he would permit a question on whether Lawrence had applied to other departments.

"If he says no to that answer, can I ask him whether he gave a deposition on a certain date to Mr. Cahill in which he said—gave a different answer?"

"Mr. Keefe?" the judge asked.

"Well, I don't know—all I know is he's made application to other departments. I don't know when the times are. If the question is asked, I want it to be specific."

Levy then asked whether he could bring in the issue of Lawrence's apparently falsified expense vouchers in Vergennes, and his military background to the extent that Levy would ask whether the discharge Lawrence received was normally a bar to reenlistment in the armed forces.

"No, no, no," Gregg broke in. "No, this is not proper cross-examination," he said. "It doesn't have any bearing or materiality to this case. The matter of his military service has been injected into this case by Mr. Keefe. I certainly feel that you can go—but to go beyond on collateral issues incident to his dismissal or discharge or whatever it is, the court is not going to allow that type of inquiry. It's not material and here again, it's an—I would think it's an effort somehow to involve this man in questionable activities in connection with his army career."

It was 2:22 when they went back to open court. Levy asked Lawrence about his work in Vergennes, but could not get into the expense vouchers. He got Lawrence to talk about his military record and Lawrence said he had got a general discharge under honorable conditions, but Levy could not question him about what that meant. Lawrence said he had left the army because of an operation on his appendix.

Levy then tried to show that Augie Fernandez had taken several weeks to make his first buy when he had come into the city, in sharp contrast to Lawrence, who had made buys immediately. That was shut off also after a conference in the judge's chambers. That was the end of Levy's effort to use the material obtained by Randy Brock. The only thing he had left was the testimony by John Deppman, that Lawrence was a bad cop.

Keefe then brought onto the stand Chief George Hebert, a crucial witness. Levy was prepared to argue that Burbank had not been working the evening that Lawrence said he had made the buy. Moreover, Levy had been unable to find any reports that Hebert had seen Burbank there. Hebert was aging and had thick glasses, and the possibility that he had peered through the front window of Tuner's, through the curtain and the plants, and into the gloom of the bar, and had seen Burbank there, and had only remembered it weeks later, struck Levy as unlikely.

Nonetheless, that is what Hebert said. He also said that he had just told Keefe about the incident that morning, six months after it had occurred.

"Now, at any point prior to your testimony here today, did you indicate to Mr. Keefe that you recalled having seen Gary Burbank on the premises of Tuner's during the afternoons of September 27 and 28?" Levy asked.

"I could have."

"You could have. Now, when could that have been?"

"Well, I don't know. I don't have no idea. I have met with Mr. Keefe from time to time and—"

"So it would have been sometime after our opening remarks this morning?"

"Yes."

"Did Mr. Keefe tell you at that point that the defendant was going to present evidence that he was not working on that date?"

"Not to me . . ."

"But you just happened to volunteer that you could testify that he was there during the afternoon?"

"Well, the case was discussed—that's right."

Levy's first witness was Gary Burbank himself, who told the jury about his background, his service in the navy, his efforts to set up his own business. He spoke quietly, and occasionally haltingly, getting finally, as Levy led him through the questioning, into the work schedule he followed in September of the previous year.

By that time, he and Otto Kremer had worked out a coherent schedule that covered himself, Gary, and Jane Eaton. Gary's job was to open the bar and work until about one, then to come back at 8 P.M. and to work until closing. Was there any possibility, Levy asked, that he would have been in the bar about six on September 27?

"No, I would not have been working."

"Now, is there any possibility that while you might not have been working, you could have been on the premises for some other purpose in the afternoon?"

"It's possible, but I wouldn't make a habit of it. I don't think I was in that day."

"Now, what about September 28? Were you—that's a Friday—Friday, September 28, again were you on this same type of schedule on the twenty-eighth?"

"Yes, I was."

"Now, ordinarily, if someone peers into a place such as Tuner's, would you have ample opportunity to notice this?"

"Hopefully, yuh, I mean you don't normally have someone staring in the door at you."

"Did Chief Hebert ever come in while you were on duty that you're aware of?" Levy asked.

"To be honest, I don't remember Chief Hebert ever stepping in the premises when I was there, ever working or otherwise . . ."

"Now you saw Paul Lawrence this morning—have you ever seen that man before?"

"No."

"Are you positive?"

"I'm absolutely 100 percent positive."

"You realize you're under oath?"

"I'm under oath and I do not recognize that man."

"You've never seen him before?"

"No."

Levy asked Burbank if he had ever dealt drugs and he said no. He also said he had never used drugs except for occasionally smoking marijuana.

They then went into the diagram of the bar, and Burbank said Lawrence's rendition had been way off. The pool table—there was only one—was mislocated. So was the place where the musicians supposedly played, and the restrooms. Finally, no rock bands played there, as Lawrence had said. Mostly it was folk music; rock would have been too loud.

On cross-examination, Keefe savaged Burbank and Levy was helpless to do anything about it.

"Mr. Burbank, is it your testimony that in the past you have possessed marijuana and used it?" he asked.

"Yes."

"On how many occasions?"

"Well, it was a random use. I never have had any particular pattern."

"Been more than ten times?"

"That I what?"

"That you've used marijuana?"

"Oh, yuh."

"More than twenty?"

Levy objected, but Gregg let Keefe continue. Levy had brought out the marijuana matter on direct examination. Keefe could pursue it on cross-examination.

"More than twenty?"

"Well, if I—let's say if I was a casual user and maybe once a week at the most, that would be four times a month."

"Over how long a period of time have you used marijuana at least four times a month?"

"I would say probably since I got out of the service, since 1969 or early '70."

"So that would be at least three years, thirty-six months, four times a month, we're up over one hundred times you've smoked marijuana, is that correct?"

"Um, well—." Burbank was in agony. He had wanted to bring up the marijuana to show that he was totally honest, that he wasn't claiming to be perfect, only that he was sincere in what he said. He had been afraid of the trial, but he could believe finally, they would not believe him if he was perfectly honest and sincere.

"Well, if it's over three years, you would concede that's thirty-six months at least," Keefe pressed him.

"I said four times a month would be a maximum, sir," he replied.

"I see. Well, would you concede that you've probably used marijuana in the neighborhood of one hundred times?"

"That's possible, yes."

"Did you know that's a crime in this state?"

Burbank hesitated.

"So what you're really telling us is that you've committed a crime at least one hundred times, is that correct?"

"Well—"

Levy protested, but Gregg ruled the questioning was admissible. Gary Burbank had committed at least one hundred crimes against the state.

Keefe continued his questioning, eliciting the information that Burbank had said he "assumed" he had not been working the afternoon of the twenty-seventh, and that there had been a picture of Paul Lawrence on the wall of the bar, so that Burbank, if he did not know Lawrence personally, had seen what he looked like.

None of the remaining questioning of Burbank was particularly crucial. What was important was that Lawrence's credibility had gone essentially unchallenged, and Burbank's had been damaged.

The next morning, Levy brought in Otto Kremer to testify on Burbank's behalf. Otto said that Burbank had not worked at the time in question, and he also said that Lawrence's sketch of the bar was inaccurate. As for Lawrence's comment that the Graefe band played there, that was simply impossible, Kremer said. Kremer said that Graefe had thousands of dollars of electronic equipment, and Tuner's had a serious problem with noise. Graefe, he said, "is a heavy rock band and there would have been no way in the world for them to play there."

Keefe, on the other hand, produced a transcript of a liquor board hearing in Montpelier that contained a line by Kremer to the effect that September 4 was the only day he had accurate logs for. Levy challenged that—he was the attorney for Tuner's in the liquor board hearing—but the judge chided him for leading his witness.

"Well, what's sauce for the goose is sauce for the gander, Your Honor," Levy replied.

Gregg was shocked. "I beg your pardon," he said icily.

Levy was risking his legal standing, but he was angry and frustrated. Jane Eaton and Otto Kremer testified they had never seen Paul Lawrence in the bar, that they would have noticed him if he had come in, and that no rock bands like the Graefe had played there. But it turned out that a newspaper photograph of Paul Lawrence had been placed on the bulletin board in the bar following the arrest, and the discussion over this seemed to indicate that people in Tuner's would benefit from a warning about a narc in town.

Of course that was true generally, but it didn't help Gary Burbank much.

It was shortly after eleven o'clock when Levy prepared to call

John Deppman, the Addison County state's attorney to the stand, but Keefe saw him and moved quickly to shut him out. Deppman was prepared to testify to Lawrence's bad reputation in the law enforcement community.

Levy wanted at least to get Deppman to the stand. Levy could then ask him what his name and occupation were, and even if he was not subsequently allowed to testify, the jury would have seen him, and might draw an inference about what he might say. But Gregg took Levy and Keefe into chambers immediately.

Inside, Keefe argued that unless Deppman could testify about the events of August 27, he should not be allowed to take the stand. Levy said Deppman knew the man when Lawrence was chief of Vergennes, that he had talked to many people in Addison County about him, and that he could therefore testify to the man's reputation for truthfulness.

The problem with that was that under Vermont law, testimony on a man's reputation is supposed to be taken only from people in the community where he lives, which in Lawrence's case was in Rutland. Levy argued that the Supreme Court had implied that the subject's business associates might constitute an acceptable "community."

Gregg ruled against him. He said Levy was going through a "set of legal gymnastics" to get the witness on the stand. "The court will not go that far," Gregg ruled.

Levy then tried to bring in Karl Neuse, the city attorney of Vergennes. Gregg ruled that out. Levy then tried to argue that these men should be allowed to testify on Lawrence's reputation in the criminal justice community. That was not allowed. Neither was testimony by Peter Langrock, an attorney who lived in Salisbury, but who could testify about Lawrence's reputation in Rutland.

The only testimony that would be permitted on that line, Gregg said, was testimony by people who lived in Rutland, and who knew of Lawrence's reputation in Rutland. One problem there was that much of Lawrence's career involved activities either undercover or outside Rutland, and if there were people in the town who knew Lawrence and who felt that he was untrustworthy, Levy did not know of them.

Levy had gotten none of his witnesses onto the stand. Levy whispered to Deppman in such a way as to draw another rebuke from the judge, but that was the end of the effort to impeach Paul Lawrence.

Levy then brought on character witnesses who said that Burbank had a good reputation in the community, that he was an honest man. Keefe dealt with them by asking them if they thought a man who had committed one hundred crimes could be "a man of character and integrity."

In his final argument to the jury, Keefe shrugged off the doubts that Levy had tried to instill about the fact that all of Lawrence's buys lacked corroboration. "Perhaps Mr. Levy is suggesting that Officer Lawrence should have a couple of burly uniformed state troopers follow him around, so that they could testify to drug purchases," he said. As for the mistakes in the diagram of Tuner's, Keefe argued that Lawrence was not the tax assessor, or a building inspector; he was in there after drugs. Finally, he said the state had never taken the position that Burbank was "a bad man or an evil man," only that he had sold drugs to Paul Lawrence. He did not refer in his summary to Burbank's one hundred crimes against the state.

At 2:14 P.M., the jury retired to consider the case. They asked to hear the tape recording of Lawrence's early testimony. At 4:25, the jury returned a verdict. Guilty.

When the foreman pronounced the verdict, Mrs. Larry, Gary Burbank's mother, collapsed.

Hope Fades

DORIS BEAULIEU WAS THE ONE BURBANK JUROR WHO
had held out for acquittal; that was why the jury took so long to reach
a verdict. It took them hours to convince her. The evidence is there,
they said, and she believed that. Lawrence sounded convincing to her
. . . there were the drugs, and the police chemist, and all. But she had
nonetheless believed Gary Burbank. It was the way the boy talked.
He was so sincere, she thought. But there was the evidence . . .

As she stood in the jury box and watched as Gary Burbank's
mother collapsed, she thought, "My God, I've hung that boy."

For most of the jurors, however, there was no doubt about the
evidence. Several had sat on as many as three Lawrence cases, and
they believed him. Even Doris Beaulieu thought that the Lawrence
drawing of Tuner's indicated the man had been in there; the jury
apparently got no sense of the discrepancies in the Lawrence stories.
Mrs. Beaulieu had believed Lawrence in the Sonny Cross trial too . . .

Mrs. Beaulieu was a worker on an assembly line at the Union
Carbide plant, and knew little about the drug culture and its mores
and customs. Mrs. Sylva Gagne, whose four children had grown up
before drugs became common, believed Lawrence. So did George
Samson, who thought Lawrence was impressive; he had no doubts
about the man. Jeannine Kittell thought Lawrence was telling the
truth, and there was the laboratory report from New York State—

that looked good. Mary Ellen Decker believed Lawrence. She was on three of the cases, the last of which was the Burbank case, and she was convinced he was guilty. "I thought he must have done it," she said later. "He was a bartender at Tuner's Place."

The Burbank decision spelled the end of resistance for the street people of St. Albans. The information developed over weeks of investigation into Lawrence's background would not be permitted into evidence. Neither Keefe nor Ron Kilburn was willing to take action on the basis of this information. The demonstration of substantial internal inconsistencies in Lawrence's stories had but little impact on juries: given a choice between believing Lawrence and believing the defendants, they believed Lawrence. The judge would not even empanel a wholly new jury to hear the later Lawrence cases. Alibis were not accepted by juries, whether the alibi was the word of a defendant's family or of his friends. The desperate protestations of Gary Burbank could sway but one juror, and then only for a time; his character witnesses did nothing to peel the veneer of plausibility from Lawrence's testimony.

The defense attorneys thus concluded that they had no chance to win, and they advised their clients to accept the plea bargains offered first by Keefe, then by Kilburn. Gary Burbank had been given a suspended sentence, but the others who insisted on going to trial had been given jail terms. If a defendant was willing to plead guilty, the prosecution was prepared to reduce the charges, perhaps from sale of a drug to possession of a drug, or to recommend to the court that a person's sentence be suspended.

That was the logic that persuaded Otto Kremer to plead guilty. Although Otto was supposedly—one could infer from the charges— one of the most important heroin and cocaine dealers in the region, Gregg gave him a suspended sentence on the condition that he leave the state within seventy-two hours.

Exile was an unusual penalty for crimes such as those he was charged with, but Otto accepted it; in fact he was vastly relieved. "Getting out of this place is a hell of a lot better than going to jail," he thought. Actually, his attorney, Dan Lynch, had had to bargain hard with Keefe to keep Otto out of jail. But Keefe wanted guilty pleas, and he finally agreed to the suspended sentence. The one remaining person who insisted on a trial was Gary Campbell, one of the suspects arrested in the first bust. It was sheer courage, Jim Levy said, since Campbell had no defense other than his simple denial of guilt. Of course, Campbell was convicted and Gregg sentenced him to a year in jail, although he was released on bail pending the outcome of his appeal. Levy also appealed Gary Burbank's conviction, despite the fact that Burbank's sentence had been suspended and he would escape going to jail.

Virtually all the defendants from the St. Albans and Swanton arrests began to accept the advice of their attorneys to plead guilty. Some of the people arrested in the spring—Christine Currey was one—intended to go on trial. She came from a wealthy family, and her attorney, John Kissane, was constructing an elaborate, detailed defense. But for the bulk of the defendants, this was impossible. They had no money; for the most part they had no alibi—many had no idea whether they had been at the location described by Lawrence; the judge would do nothing for them, the prosecutor would hear nothing against his narc, the juries kept coming back with guilty verdicts. To insist on a trial in St. Albans in the spring of 1974 was to earn a jail sentence.

By the time that the warm winds off the lake had begun to melt the snow in Taylor Park, the St. Albans atmosphere had congealed into bitterness and fear. More than fifty persons had been arrested on Lawrence's charges, and everyone in the counterculture knew that all Lawrence had to do was see you, and you might get busted. Tuner's, of course, had long since been closed. When young people wanted to drink they went to Benson's, the utterly graceless old railroaders' bar on the west side of town. The town was quiet. Norman Young and Sonny Cross were in jail; Ronnie Rich was headed for a federal prison. Otto Kremer was on the West Coast.

The park was soon to grow green again, but lest anyone forget what had happened, two signs stood atop one another at one corner of the park. The top one said:

> Notice Park
> Closed Between
> 12:30 A.M. and 5 A.M.
> PUNISHABLE BY FINE OR
> IMPRISONMENT

The one below reminded passersby that no alcoholic beverages were allowed.

One of the most discouraging things to the attorneys in St. Albans was the attitude of Ron Kilburn. McGinn, they knew and understood. Keefe, they understood too, without excusing him. Kilburn had appeared to be an enlightened, reasonable man. But he no longer wanted to hear anything about Lawrence. The man's cases were solid, he said when asked. It was clear that if there was to be a return to justice, the system would have to purge itself. In other words, Kilburn would have to move against Lawrence, and Kilburn refused to do that. It is hard to avoid making the judgment that Kilburn's judgment or courage was thrown into question by this failure. He was aware of the evidence that had been gathered about Lawrence; his acceptance of Lawrence's unsupported word about the drug cases would be inexcusable. If he did, in fact, suspect that Lawrence was lying, his failure to move against him was equally damning. In any case, Kilburn's failures permitted Paul Lawrence to continue his depredations against the city's counterculture.

In the city council, Dick Allard continued his efforts to derail Lawrence quietly, without kicking up a storm. In early March, the municipal elections had been held and a man named Joe Montcalm had taken over the mayor's office from Ken Kaye.

The practice in St. Albans is for the mayor to name the chairmen of the city council committees, and one of Montcalm's first moves was to replace Keith Campbell by Allard as head of the public safety committee, the body which oversees the police department. Allard also took over as president of the city council, although Bob Hill, one of Campbell's allies, challenged him for the post.

Campbell was angry about being replaced. He had done a very good job, he told his colleagues, and he wanted to continue. "There are problems I want to see through," Campbell said. But Montcalm would not be moved.

Allard then brought his list of questions about Lawrence into the open, and announced that the council would hear Lawrence in a regular meeting. When Lawrence came in, Allard asked all the questions—and Lawrence answered them all. He continued to make buys, he said, because he used disguises. He used the New York State laboratory rather than the Vermont laboratory because it was more convenient to his own home in Rutland. And so on. Allard was chagrined—Lawrence was indeed very persuasive.

Lawrence was cool and composed during his session with the council, but to Allard, Hebert appeared to be deeply agitated. Allard could see that his hands were shaking. Hebert was an old man. He had been a member of the St. Albans Police Department since the early 1940s, and to some he seemed unable to cope with the drug problem. Moreover, he had been under fierce pressure from people like Keith Campbell to act forcefully. By now he was under pressure from within his own department; Captain Flanagan had publicly opposed his policies. Finally, Hebert was aware that Lawrence, who had solved his problem when he came on the scene the previous fall, was now a figure of controversy in the community.

Pressures such as these would have whipsawed a better man than Hebert. Nonetheless, there was some speculation that there might be another reason for Hebert to be nervous; perhaps he knew that there was something wrong with Lawrence's operation. The suspects and the families of many of them were convinced this was the case. How could he not know, they wondered. But it was all speculation . . . all that Allard knew was that Hebert was very nervous.

Despite his efforts, Allard was unable to move the council away from its support for Lawrence. On April 8, the city council discussed the issue of hiring a new narcotics agent, since Lawrence was so well known. They also talked about trading him to another community in return for the other city's narc. They decided against it.

"This agent is still effectual in his work and is well aware of the dangers involved and is willing to accept risks and accept this assignment," the minutes for that council meeting said. "Possible exchange of agents with other communities was not favorably considered as other 9 [sic] are unknown and is [sic] doubtful if could produce results experienced by this city."

Lawrence was not only willing to accept the St. Albans work; he was branching out. He made a couple of busts in Stowe; and the school board for the Missisquoi Valley Union High School, which is located in Swanton, had made a secret authorization of four thousand dollars for Lawrence to make buys in their area.

Lawrence was also maneuvering that spring to be named head of a proposed metropolitan enforcement group, a strike force of drug agents from federal, state, and local agencies. Lawrence was the most famous narc in the state; he claimed to have made hundreds of successful drug arrests. And the enormous success he had had in St. Albans lent him something of the aura of infallibility.

He also had increasing success in manipulating the press. Whenever he planned a bust, he made sure to contact his favorite reporters, particularly Mike Donoghue of the Burlington *Free Press,* so that they could be present.

In the spring, a group of law enforcement officials met in Williston to discuss the formation of such a group, and some of them were committed to naming Lawrence as commander of the group. This scheme foundered on the objections of Pat Leahy, the state's attorney for Chittenden County. "No way," he said when Lawrence's name came up.

If Lawrence was named head of such a group, then the state's attorney in Chittenden County, the most populous in the state, would not prosecute their cases, he said. Leahy had heard of Lawrence's reputation in law enforcement circles. He could not understand why any state's attorney would prosecute Lawrence cases.

Despite this setback, the spring of 1974 was a good one for Paul Lawrence. There was a bust on March 28 and six more people were arrested on the basis of his charges. Most of these buys were sizeable amounts of heroin, although one of them involved a gram of opium, a rare drug in Vermont. On April 22, he made a speed buy in St. Albans; on the twenty-sixth, another speed buy; on May 9, he made a buy of speed in Essex Junction. He made another eleven buys in May, a very rapid pace. Most of the buys were in St. Albans, but the sites also included Johnson, Stowe, and Burlington.

11

Kevin Bradley's Story

KEVIN BRADLEY WAS AWED BY PAUL LAWRENCE. BRADLEY was twenty-one years old and had been a cop for just two months when Captain Richard Beaulieu told him and Harry Miles and Dave Demag that Lawrence would be coming to Burlington to work with them. Lawrence was the top narc in the state—"Supercop," he was often called. The Burlington detectives, who had been experiencing difficulties making drug buys, had heard that Lawrence was making seven, eight, ten buys a week in Franklin County. Bradley wanted a chance to work with him.

Bradley had met Lawrence for the first time in mid-March of 1974 when he and Walt Dorfner, a Vermont State Police undercover agent, were driving from St. Johnsbury, where they were working, to Burlington. It was after midnight when Dorfner pulled into the parking lot of the Old Board, a well-known night spot and restaurant off Route 7 in South Burlington. They went in for a drink and as they moved toward the bar, Dorfner introduced Bradley to three people—a woman, whose name Bradley no longer can recall, Mike Donoghue, the police reporter for the Burlington *Free Press,* and Paul Lawrence. Bradley did not find out until later that Lawrence was a policeman.

The two men met again on April 1, when they attended a drug school in Waterville, Maine, sponsored by the Maine State Police. Three other cops from Vermont were there, the others attending were from Maine. All of the out-of-staters stayed at the school, except for Lawrence, who stayed at a nearby motel. Lawrence introduced himself to Bradley one morning before class, and Bradley was impressed. Lawrence was easygoing, and modest for a man of his reputation. He had an easy flow of small talk, and Bradley felt immediately at ease with him.

One morning, Lawrence mentioned to Bradley that he had made a heroin buy the previous evening. Lawrence told him he had met two girls at a nearby bar frequented by men from the school, and that he had driven them home. They had talked some about drugs at the bar, Lawrence said, and he had made the buy in the car, outside the house where the girls lived. The drug was wrapped in aluminum foil, Lawrence said.

It was the first heroin buy by a policeman in Maine's history.

Lawrence had made the buy on a night when Bradley and his roommate, Kevin Scully of the Burlington Police Department, had stayed home; usually, they and many of the other cops went to the same bar. Lawrence also told the Maine State Police officials about his heroin buy, and that night virtually the whole class of fifty or so men staked out the bar to watch Lawrence try to make another buy. There were cops at the bar, cops scattered among the tables, cops in the parking lot, and more cops spread around the general area. "They stood out like a sore thumb," Bradley said later and, probably not surprisingly, no one showed up. But Lawrence later made a second buy from the two girls, and when he graduated, his classmates gave him an enthusiastic round of applause.

Later that spring, Captain Richard Beaulieu, head of the detective division of the Burlington Police Department, and Harold Miles, the head of the drug division, decided they needed a new undercover agent in town. Dave Demag and Miles himself, Burlington's undercover men, were both "burned"—the drug users in the area knew them. Demag was a detective in his early twenties; he came from nearby Winooski and many young people knew him—disguises were no longer effective. Miles, a man in his thirties, had been working undercover for some time and was widely known also.

What they needed was a trade. They would go to another city

where they were not known, and that city's police department would send a narc to Burlington. Miles decided to try to get Paul Lawrence from St. Albans. Lawrence was by far the most effective narc in the state. Miles had known Lawrence when the St. Albans man had been a patrolman in Burlington, and Miles didn't like him much. Miles thought Lawrence was the kind of cop who would hang around outside bars so he could arrest people for public drunkenness, thereby padding his arrest record. Nevertheless, Lawrence had a remarkable record in St. Albans, and he was getting an unbroken string of convictions. Miles had also heard some of the rumors about Lawrence's escapades while he was with the state police and in Vergennes, but they were just stories and there were always stories about tough cops. Burlington could use a narc who could make a lot of good cases, fast. So Miles talked to the St. Albans department, and that department agreed on the trade. Miles and Demag would work St. Albans; Lawrence would come to Burlington.

The St. Albans City Council had specifically opposed such a policy, and no one has ever explained why Chief Hebert agreed to it. Perhaps he was worried about Lawrence for some reason. Possibly he felt Lawrence must be getting burned in St. Albans. Even Hebert must have wondered how Lawrence could keep making buys after months of notoriety and public identification. In any case, the trade made excellent sense in professional terms—there would be new narcs working in both towns.

Bradley knew nothing of all this. All he knew was that Lawrence was the top narc in the state and he was very pleased that he would get a chance to work with him. The police job in Burlington was something Bradley had wanted for a long time, but he had not been able to make any buys as a narcotics agent. He had undergone on-the-job training with Walt Dorfner for a short time in the St. Johnsbury area, across the state from Burlington. The two, scruffy and unkempt, hung around the bars, claiming they were part of a construction crew working on an interstate highway and trying to buy drugs. No one was interested.

In the several weeks he had been with the Burlington unit, he also failed to make buys and that was a sore point with him. Bradley was anything but a fanatic, but the number of buys one has made are the credentials a narc holds with his fellow undercover men. "How many buys has he made?" is the way they rate one another. Bradley hoped very much that he would learn the trade from Lawrence.

Dave Demag felt the same way about Lawrence, respectful and a little awed. Demag had made some buys, but his record was nothing like Lawrence's. What he would have liked to do was to work with Lawrence in some town where neither of them was known; then he could both learn from Lawrence and at the same time test his own abilities. He was disappointed, therefore, when Miles insisted that he had to go to St. Albans. Bradley would work with Lawrence as a team.

It was not until mid-May that Lawrence arrived. He had been cleaning up some cases in St. Albans, and when he came into town, he came with a flourish. The morning after Lawrence was to work for the first time, Bradley came to work and heard that Lawrence had made a buy on Church Street, the city's retail center, the previous evening. That was surprising, but the alleged seller was more of a shock. He was a short, slight, black man with a hawklike face and burning black eyes. He often wore a black cape, and was known to some as "Spaceman." He was a common sight on the streets of downtown, and he was a vision to frighten little children. But Bradley and Demag considered him a burned-out hulk. He was so spacey, Bradley said later, that you could look in one ear and out the other. The "Spaceman" was an obvious target for any narc and, in fact, both Bradley and Demag had tried to buy from him. They had got nowhere. Bradley had arranged to buy some speed from him once in City Hall Park, but the man had not showed up at the agreed-upon time, and when Bradley saw him later, the Spaceman did not know him.

Bradley recalled how he had felt when Lawrence had made the heroin buy in Maine. He's got the luck of the Irish, Bradley thought, and he felt a little let down. Bradley wanted very much to make an independent buy, to make his own mark.

Later that day, Bradley and Lawrence met in the second-floor office of the drug division and set up their routine, exchanging phone numbers and so on. Bradley lived at 62 North Union Street, a tiny apartment in an area popular with college students. Lawrence lived at 500 Pine Street, in a more expensive apartment building. They arranged to meet at the station in the late afternoon, then they would cruise around in Lawrence's car—Lawrence always wanted to use his car, a blue 1974 Ford Mustang, which he said was a St. Albans police car. The two men would cruise the streets, then work the bars, particularly those in the north end of the city.

Lawrence did little to alter his appearance when he was out working. He had shoulder-length hair and a moustache. It struck Bradley that he looked remarkably like a heavyset Sonny Bono, the entertainer. Bradley and Lawrence would each wear loose-fitting shirts so they could each carry a concealed pistol. Working closely, Bradley again found Lawrence a pleasant companion. He was a good storyteller, and he wasn't the hero of most of them. He did not brag about his numerous exploits and he said little of his state police days.

Moreover, Lawrence showed no particular zeal to prosecute the "heads," as the police called suspected drug users. "What a scumbag," he'd say occasionally, but he was no redneck, Bradley thought. In fact, the narcs themselves got some of that treatment from their fellow officers in uniform. The other cops called the narcs longhairs and other things less complimentary. It gave the narcs an ironic empathy with their prey. It seemed to Bradley that Lawrence's attitude was matter-of-fact: if you get 'em, you get 'em, if you don't, you don't. "Nothing made you think he had a hard-on for these people," Bradley said later.

But in the first three weeks they worked together, Bradley never saw Lawrence make a buy. They always seemed to come when Paul was going to or from work, or when Kevin had a day off. Kevin would meet him at four, and Lawrence would have made a buy at one. "Damn it, Paul, you've got to wait till I'm around," Bradley told him jokingly, but underneath, he was getting upset—"Hell, I wasn't there again." At the same time, Bradley had no chance to make any buys himself—he had let his own contacts lapse in order to concentrate on learning from Lawrence. After three months on the job, he still had not made a buy on his own.

By late May, Lawrence had made more than half a dozen buys, some of which had been seen by Bradley, and Bradley was beginning to wonder whether something was wrong. There were several grounds for suspicion, but all of them very vague. Bradley had accompanied Dave Demag to St. Albans on one occasion, and they had met a pair of hippies when they pulled up to Taylor Park. "Where's the action?" the narcs inquired. "We'd like to get some good dope."

"If you're into drugs, you better get the hell out of town," one of the youths replied. "There's a crazy narc named Lawrence in town, and he'll bust you if he even thinks you're doing drugs."

Demag heard this often in St. Albans; no one would even talk about drugs to him, even though he was able to converse easily with kids from the counterculture in the bars. On one occasion, he had attended one of their parties late at night in a remote wooded area. But no one would talk about drugs. Neither Bradley nor Demag took the warning about Lawrence very seriously, however. Druggies were always proclaiming their innocence. Still, there was that, and Bradley could not fathom how Lawrence could make so many buys without his witnessing any at all. Although they talked about it occasionally, Demag was less troubled. As far as he was concerned, if someone was in jail, he was guilty. If Lawrence said he bought drugs from someone, he bought them.

On June 4, though, Bradley's suspicions were allayed. He and Paul were working the Millard Fillmore, a hippie bar north of the main business district. It was a hangout for longhairs, perhaps the most popular watering spot for the counterculture in Burlington. The two narcs went there often; the place was full of targets. On June 4, Bradley was sitting at a table, talking to a young acquaintance, and Paul was drinking at the bar, a few feet away. With Bradley watching, a man named Geno and a companion suddenly left the bar and went downstairs toward the men's room. A moment later, Lawrence followed.

A few moments elapsed, then the two men and Lawrence returned to the bar. Lawrence hesitated briefly, then walked to Bradley's table. "Let's get out of here," he said.

As they got into the car, Paul said he had bought a "spoon of speed" from Geno in the men's room. He had seen that Geno was dealing, and had asked into the action. Lawrence pulled away from the curb and headed down South Winooski Avenue, then turned into Bank Street. He pulled to the curb by Center's Department Store, took the drug out and showed it to Bradley. It was white powder in aluminum foil, tucked behind the matches in a Millard Fillmore matchbook cover. It cost twenty-five dollars, Lawrence said.

Bradley was both impressed and reassured. The previous day he had seen Geno reach into a bowl on the bar at the Fillmore and stuff a fistful of matchcovers into his pocket. His suspicions had been the result of an overactive imagination, he thought. Lawrence would not have noticed Geno picking up the matches; yet using the matchcovers to deal undoubtedly was Geno's normal mode of operations. Lawrence was straight after all. Bradley had still not seen a buy, but there were undoubtedly reasons for it. He was, after all, still green.

A week later, Bradley said he was going to take a day off to go to Stowe to see his brother, who had come up from New York. Paul said he would try to make a buy on June 10 from Durrell Pacquette; it would be an informant-buy, Lawrence said; he probably could not bring Kevin with him anyway. Pacquette had been a narc target for some time. He seemed to be a typical longhair, working in a menial job at a place called Buzzy's Variety Store in a rundown area north of the business district. It was near B. J.'s Deli, where Donald Mercier, Lawrence's informant, worked.

Paul had indicated that he knew Pacquette well, that he was familiar with his car, and knew, for example, that Pacquette was driving without a license. The next day, Bradley joined Lawrence and Demag for a drive to Albany, where they would submit some drug evidence to the drug laboratory of the New York State Police. In the car, Paul told Kevin he had bought a spoon of speed from Durrell Pacquette the day before.

This is how Lawrence's written report recorded the event:

> On June 10, 1974, at approximately 1415 hours this officer while working undercover on illicit drug activity in the City of Burlington, Vermont, proceeded to meet with the accused in the parking lot of Buzzy's Variety Store.
>
> After speaking with the accused about purchasing a quantity of methamphetamine he advised me to come to his vehicle which was parked near the south end of the parking lot facing the building.
>
> At this time the vehicle was identified as a red colored Volkswagen sedan bearing Vermont Registration #7857G. A check with D.M.V. [Department of Motor Vehicles] revealed that the vehicle was a 1968 V.W. sedan registered to the accused.
>
> Upon entering the vehicle from the passenger side, the accused produced the alleged drug from the glove box and handed it to this officer, stating the price was "$25.00 a spoon." I then proceeded to give the accused $25.00 in cash, consisting of a twenty dollar bill and a five dollar bill.
>
> The accused also advised this officer that he did not have his operator's license, but that he was driving anyway. The accused then advised that he was leaving to go to Burlington Beach and that if I wanted any more speed he

would probably be around later. At this time the accused left the area in his vehicle.

Paul had been in Burlington less than a month and he had already made more than ten buys, a much faster pace than the local department had ever maintained.

It was warm and clear early on Friday, June 12, but by four, when Paul Lawrence swung to the curb in front of Kevin Bradley's apartment on North Union Street, clouds had moved in over Lake Champlain and a cool breeze was blowing. It didn't affect Kevin's mood. He was still anxious about not having made a buy on his own, but his suspicions about Lawrence had been dispelled. Seeing Geno take those matchbooks probably had kept him from making a fool of himself.

Lawrence swung the car into the traffic, turned left on Peal and headed for Battery Park. "Let's check that out first," Paul said, "then we'll try City Hall."

"Okay," Bradley said. "Anything going on?"

"Not much," Lawrence replied. "But there may be some heads in the park. Tonight we can go back to the Fillmore—I can try to make another buy from Geno; there's lots of speed in town."

Lawrence drove slowly through the rush-hour traffic, scanning both sides of the street. At Battery Street, he turned right and began a slow transit of Battery Park, a green cameo on a bluff overlooking Lake Champlain and the Adirondack Mountains to the west. It was a popular hangout for young people. It was shaded by huge elms; a lunch cart on one corner dispensed cheap hot dogs, and there always seemed to be a breeze off the lake.

"Not much there," Lawrence said.

"Nah, it's probably too cool," Bradley replied. "Let's try City Hall."

Lawrence nodded and turned the Mustang back onto Battery Street, drove down the hill and turned up Main. Near the top of the hill, they came to City Hall Park. Roughly a block square, the park is a grassy oasis in downtown Burlington. It's popular with young people, local lawyers, and stockbrokers and secretaries, who often spend their lunch hours there in warm weather. Lawrence made many of his buys there; it was one of his favorite hunting grounds.

One reason for that was the presence of the Vermont Transit bus station across the street, on the corner of Main and St. Paul streets. The station was a center of activity for most of the day and night. Buses move in and out from Montreal, New York, and Boston, as well as from towns in Vermont. Many of the bus passengers were students at the University of Vermont; others were young transients coming into the state. Next door was the Huntington Hotel, a clean but undistinguished establishment.

Lawrence drove slowly up Main, looking over his left shoulder into the park, but there were few people there—a disheveled wino, lying on the grass near the water fountain, a pair of teen-agers sitting on the City Hall steps, a well-dressed man sitting on a bench in the northwest corner of the park.

"Nobody here, either," Lawrence said. "Too bad, I almost made a buy here on my way to work."

Bradley was relieved he hadn't. His suspicions had been laid to rest, but he still badly wanted to see Lawrence in action. So far, he had seen nothing unusual about Paul's technique. He had no particularly effective line of chatter with prospective drug sellers; he seemed not much different from Bradley himself. You see somebody and say, "Hey, what's going on, we'd like to get some good dope." But when they were together, Lawrence wasn't doing any better than Bradley.

Lawrence turned onto Church Street now, eyeing the entrance to Hannibul's, a college bar, and B. T. McGuire's, a second-floor bar and restaurant that caters to both college students and a somewhat older crowd. It was early for any real action there.

"We've got to check B. T.'s one of these days," Lawrence said. "I've heard a guy there is dealing."

"Yeah," Bradley said.

Lawrence turned left on College, and passed the park again slowly. The well-dressed man had gone, but the wino and the kids were still there. A blank. Lawrence swung to the right and threaded his way through a number of back streets toward North Winooski Avenue. He said he wanted to go to Buzzy's Variety Store; he had an informant there.

When they pulled up in front of the store, Donald Mercier, the brother-in-law of Lawrence's girlfriend, came out to talk to them. Weeks earlier he had given Lawrence the names of thirty-five persons he thought were dealing drugs. Lawrence would stop by the store where Mercier worked to talk about them occasionally. One of the names on the list had been that of Durrell Pacquette.

Lawrence introduced Mercier to Kevin, then he and Mercier chatted briefly.

At that point, Bradley saw a red Volkswagen pull into the curb on the other side of the street. A chunky young man got out and walked toward the Mustang. He passed in front of the car and went into Buzzy's Variety Store.

"Who's that?" Lawrence asked Mercier.

"That's Durrell Pacquette," Mercier said.

"That's funny," Lawrence said quickly. "The last time I saw him he had a ponytail."

"He never had a ponytail," Mercier said, puzzled.

Lawrence ended the conversation quickly and pulled out into the traffic. He seemed uneasy for a few moments, fumbling for a couple of explanations that Bradley could scarcely recall later. But it lasted only a short period. Lawrence resumed his normal manner.

Bradley said nothing, but he felt sick. Lawrence had given his partners the clear indication he knew Pacquette well; they were "tight," he had indicated. The remainder of the evening was uneventful and Bradley was relieved when Lawrence dropped him off at his apartment.

When he went to bed, he couldn't sleep. If that's the way they do business here, I want no part of it, he thought. He would have to do something, and there was no way he could tell what the response would be. Lawrence was the best-known cop in the state, and by far the most successful narc ever to operate here. Bradley knew Frank Murray, the deputy state's attorney, personally, and he had great respect not only for his professional ability, but for his integrity. But he could not be so sure about his colleagues on the Burlington Police Department. His relationships with Harry Miles, Dave Demag, and the Captain, Dick Beaulieu, while pleasant, were essentially professional. He had only three months' experience. Maybe they would tell him not to worry about it. If they did, he would have to quit his job.

Quitting would be awful. Since he had been a college student at the seminary in New York, he had wanted to be a cop. The tightly knit society of Irish families in Brooklyn had been supplying cops to the city police force for generations. Bradley was different from most of them, however. For one thing, he was a college graduate, with a degree in psychology. For another, he was absolutely straight, easygoing, but with a rigid sense of honesty and integrity. He had tried for months to get the job. He had worked in a boys' camp in Stowe, run by a priest, and at a children's home in Burlington, before getting the police job. Frank Murray, who had been introduced to him at the Newman Center of the University of Vermont, had told him how to go about it. The job was a plum—Burlington had the largest and most professional municipal force in Vermont. There also had never been any doubt in his mind about the serious nature of the job. A month after his graduation from college, one of his best friends, a New York City cop, had been shot to death trying to stop a holdup in a bar. Kevin returned to the city for the funeral, but it did not change his resolve. He would be a cop.

But nothing could change the fact that Paul Lawrence was sour, he thought. Bradley would move even if he had to give up his job. The next morning Bradley called Demag and said he wanted to talk to him. When they met at Demag's apartment, he went over all his suspicions about the unwitnessed buys, then capped it with a description of Lawrence's failure to recognize Pacquette just two days after reporting a buy from him.

"Oh, shit," said Demag.

Bradley was vastly relieved by Demag's response. It was clear Demag felt the way he did. But Demag was cautious. Lawrence had been accused of this before, he said. The thing to do was to get something concrete before you said anything. Kevin was working daily with Lawrence; he should watch him closely, take precise notes. At the same time, Demag would begin checking on Lawrence's buys to see if there was anything suspicious about the circumstances. By investigating carefully, they could clear up the Lawrence issue once and for all. If he was guilty, they'd get him; if he was not, they would put the steady flow of rumors about Lawrence to rest. Bradley agreed, although he was surprised that there were widespread rumors about Lawrence's veracity. Was he the only one who had not known about them?

Demag also indicated he had complete faith in the integrity of Miles and Captain Beaulieu. But he wanted to keep the investigation to themselves until they had more to go on. He was not convinced Lawrence was faking buys. He thought privately, a reservation he did not share with Bradley, that Lawrence might have been testing his informant. And Demag had no desire to make a fool of himself. It was hard for Demag to believe that a cop would do what Bradley was suggesting. That was the kind of thing that only happened in big cities. This, after all, was just Burlington . . .

But by the end of the week, Bradley was frustrated. Nothing much was happening and he was becoming obsessed by the issue. Demag wasn't getting anywhere either. "Dave, we'd better go to Harry and the captain," Bradley said. Demag agreed.

On June 14, Marcellus Parsons, also known as Div, a television reporter for Station WCAX in Burlington, called Deputy State's Attorney Frank Murray and said he wanted to talk to him. Parsons often called Murray or his boss, State's Attorney Patrick Leahy, to probe for information or to check something out. Today was different—he was deeply troubled.

Over a period of several weeks in the spring, he had received an unusual series of anonymous phone calls about an undercover narcotics agent from St. Albans. "There's something terribly wrong in St. Albans," the callers would say. "Corruption. From the state's attorney on down. Lawrence is railroading people—this isn't called Railroad City for nothing. You ought to look into it." Some of the callers would say they had sold drugs before, but never to Lawrence. The callers were defensive, though, and they wouldn't provide much information, other than to curse Lawrence. "You're the establishment media," someone would say, "and you fuckers probably agree with what Lawrence is doing."

The calls were uncommon in Parsons' experience. He was the anchorman for the 11 P.M. news, and he often got calls from people, but they were usually easier to figure out. Some were from the state prison in Windsor, for example—prisoners unhappy about the administration. There were also calls to be expected on major public issues, but nothing like the stuff on Lawrence. What made it more troubling was that Parsons had already heard some vague stories about Lawrence.

He had picked them up from Lt. Jimmy Scott at the Burlington Police Department. The previous year, the twenty-eight-year-old Parsons had spent a lot of time hanging around the police department. He cared little for the liquid life of Burlington's bars and he was courting a young woman at the television station who worked daytime hours. She was asleep after midnight, so Div would hang around the police station in the early morning hours, making an occasional sandwich in the first-floor squad room, and dropping in on Scott to chat.

Scott and the other cops liked Parsons, and they soon included him in the endless round of storytelling common to all police stations. Burlington had its share of cop yarns.

There was Red Dubois, a cop who was terrified of dead bodies. He found one one night behind the Old Veterans' Club and pulled half the police alarms in town, yelling in terror the whole time. There was Benny Winterbottom, a cop who could not ride a motorcycle. He had tried to ride one on Church Street one day, jammed the accelerator open and rocketed across the street and halfway up the side of a truck before crashing to the street. And then there was Paul Lawrence, who had come on the force in the late 1960s as a patrolman. He had been the prototype of the tough cop, clearing the bums and winos out of city hall with some well-placed threats to break legs. Lawrence had so impressed Police Chief Arthur J. Caron that Lawrence had never had to work nights, even though he was a rookie. Caron had offered him the chance to get off the street and into a cruiser, but Lawrence had declined. The other cops thought he liked clearing the streets of winos.

Parsons had also heard about Lawrence from his friend, John Gladding, who did a lot of police reporting for WCAX. Gladding had told him in the early seventies about a state trooper named Lawrence who reportedly had shot out the window of his own cruiser while investigating a robbery in Rutland.

There were other stories about Lawrence, but Parsons thought little of them. At the time, Lawrence was merely part of the pantheon of strange cops and weird doings, probably much embellished.

The calls from St. Albans along with the web of unusual stories he had heard about Lawrence excited Parsons. There is probably a terrific story here, he thought, and he badly wanted to break it. But he was not sure how to go about it.

On two occasions during the spring he drove to St. Albans and wandered about the town, speaking to no one. He was even a little scared; he was enough of a child of the television age to wonder whether a bunch of crooked cops might harm him. On the other hand, he had no way to deal with the scruffy young people he found hanging around town. He walked around Taylor Park, hoping that someone would come up to him and say, "Have we got a story for you!"

No one did, of course, and Parsons thought it would be useless to try to approach the kids in the park. It would take at least six months to look as bad as they did, Parsons thought.

When he came back to Burlington, Parsons sounded out Beaulieu about Lawrence, but Beaulieu told him there was nothing to his suspicions. Nonetheless, Parsons learned that Lawrence had come to Burlington, and he also learned that a black private investigator was looking into Lawrence's activities and background. Parsons wanted very much to get this story—he was afraid someone else in the press would beat him to it—but he had come to a dead end. On June 14, he called Frank Murray. "Frank, I'd like to come over and talk to you," he said. Murray told him to come ahead.

When Parsons arrived at Murray's third-floor office, he sat on the couch at the end of the room and got right to the point. Did Murray know a guy named Lawrence? Parsons said that friends at the police station had said he was a "bad actor" and that he was now investigating drug traffic in Burlington. Jimmy Scott, a lieutenant, had a lot of stories about the man, Parsons said. He also asked Murray if he knew about the private investigator.

Murray had only a vague recollection of Lawrence. He told Parsons that Lawrence had been arrested by the Shelburne, Vermont, police for speeding through their town, which lies astride Route 7 south of Burlington. Murray had received calls about the case from William Keefe, the assistant attorney general who prosecuted criminal cases, and George Hebert, the police chief in St. Albans. Finally—it was during the early spring, Murray thought— Lawrence himself came into the office to ask Murray not to prosecute. He had been chasing a Mercedes-Benz in Shelburne, he told Murray; it had been legitimate police business. Murray had not pressed the case.

Parsons told Murray what he knew about Lawrence, then related some of the stories he had heard from Jimmy Scott. Lawrence had a mean streak; he apparently liked bullying the drunks in town when he had been a patrolman. There was also a story that Lawrence had, while in Burlington, been harassed by a young man on the street, and that he had then called the youth's draft board and impersonated him, badgering the board and telling off the members. The draft board, or so the story went, not surprisingly saw to it that the youth was called to active duty. And Lawrence, on the day the youth was to leave for induction, went to the bus station to bid him good-bye.

Murray realized that there was no way to tell if this string of tales was significant or pointless. But he was impressed with Parsons and he had long trusted Scott. Scott had never lied to him, and he had always winked when someone else did. "I was getting a picture of a guy," he said later.

Although he had never run across a thoroughly bad cop, Murray did not find it hard to believe that Lawrence might be operating illegally. A boyish-looking man in his late twenties, Murray had a sharp intelligence edged with a sense of impatience with the police. Sloppy police work was endemic in Vermont. The pay for police is low, there is relatively little sophisticated crime, and the level of professionalism on police forces is commensurately low. Murray was annoyed at poor police work, and the cops knew it; they thought him somewhat cold.

Moreover, Murray had a deeply idealistic sense about law enforcement. He was a Philadelphia native, and was brought up in the same sort of Irish-Catholic milieu that had sent Kevin Bradley to the Burlington police. He had worked his way through college working nights as a clerk in an FBI office, at a time when a rocklike integrity was thought to be the hallmark of the federal bureau. At the same time, Murray had been deeply affected by disclosures about the Nixon administration in the Watergate case. There can be nothing worse than the corruption of law enforcement, Murray had concluded from watching Watergate, and while he had never suspected that anything untoward might happen in Burlington, he would always in the future be sensitive to any sign of it.

Murray told Parsons he would look into the Lawrence issue. And on Monday he went to see Dick Beaulieu. He found him at the foot of the stairway leading to the detective division and asked him about Lawrence, including whether Beaulieu knew of a private investigator watching Lawrence.

Beaulieu told him that Lawrence was investigating drugs in Burlington, in an exchange program with St. Albans; that Lawrence had promised him twenty-five "busts" and that he (Lawrence) had already made ten. There was no problem with the cases, Beaulieu said. Kevin Bradley had witnessed all the sales. And Beaulieu went further: "Look," he said, "when you're in this kind of business . . . the same thing happens with this guy Miles . . . people say all kinds of things about these guys. Their lives are spent in bars, it's tough business, and the people they're dealing with are going to make up a lot of things about them. You can't believe what these people are telling you."

Murray didn't press the point. For one thing, Kevin Bradley was solid, as far as Murray was concerned. If he had witnessed the buys, they must be all right. He returned to his office.

When he got there, Murray found Bill Keefe using his office to work on a case. Murray had heard that Keefe had some contact with Lawrence in Franklin County, so he asked him about Lawrence. Keefe told him that he had confronted Lawrence with the allegations against him, and that Lawrence had explained them. One of the charges was that Lawrence had used city time in Vergennes for dalliance with women. Keefe said Lawrence had conceded he liked women, but that otherwise there was no substance to the charges.

Keefe said he had talked to Stanley Merriam, a state trooper in St. Albans, and that Merriam thought highly of Lawrence. Keefe also said he thought Lawrence was very tough. On one occasion, Keefe said, Lawrence was working undercover on a college campus in the southern part of the state and there was a bar near campus that had Lawrence's picture pasted on the wall, the message being that the man was a narc. And Lawrence could be found talking to the bartender about drug traffic, with the picture staring down at him. The idea was that Lawrence had a lot of moxie.

"I left no stone unturned," Keefe said of his investigation into the Lawrence charges. Murray got the impression that Keefe thought well of the man.

Nevertheless, he decided he would talk to Kevin Bradley privately. The next morning he called Bradley, woke him up, and asked if he could come over and talk to him. Bradley said he could, and Murray walked over to 62 North Union, arriving shortly before noon. They sat at the kitchen table, chatted briefly, then Murray told Bradley he had heard some reports that Paul Lawrence might not be operating legitimately. Bradley was surprised that Murray had contacted him about it at that time. "I was just about to call you," he said.

The most important issue at stake, Murray told him, was the integrity and reputation of the law enforcement community. He told Bradley about his conversation with Beaulieu to the effect that Lawrence had guaranteed to make twenty-five buys and that he had made ten thus far, and that Bradley had witnessed them.

"I haven't seen any of them," Bradley said.

He went on to detail all the suspicions about Lawrence that had accumulated over several weeks: the fact that he never got to see the buys; the fact that Lawrence had made buys almost immediately from people who had never agreed to sell to narcs before; and the incident in which Lawrence had apparently not known Pacquette. Demag and he suspected Lawrence of "salting," the practice of alleging that drugs have been bought from a known dealer when in fact no buy has been made. The drugs would come from previous buys in which only part of the evidence had been turned in.

Murray was sure now that Lawrence was bad. But he did not want to upstage Beaulieu. Murray was sure Beaulieu simply did not know that Bradley had not witnessed the buys. "Listen," Murray said, "you take this information to your chief. If nothing is done about it, get back to me."

The next morning when he got into the office, Murray got a call from Beaulieu. "I think Lawrence is bad," he said. "My men suspect him of framing people."

The Trap

ON A WARM AFTERNOON IN LATE JUNE, THE DRUG UNIT OF
the Burlington Police Department—Miles, Bradley, and Demag—
their superiors, Beaulieu and Lieutenant Wayne Liberty, and Deputy State's Attorney Frank Murray met to discuss what to do about
Paul Lawrence.

Lawrence had been operating in Vermont in a questionable
manner for eight years, and for the first time a local law enforcement
community was moving to stop him. The prosecutors in other counties, the hierarchy of the state police, local police departments—all
had either failed to move decisively, or had actively abetted him.
Burlington would be different.

There was, surprisingly, no hesitation about setting out to trap a
fellow police officer. Murray, for one, was sure that the policemen
were committed to bringing Lawrence to justice. The motivation,
however, varied somewhat. To Murray, what Lawrence apparently
was doing seemed monstrous—a miscarriage of justice. He saw it,
and despised it, in its social and political context—Lawrence was a
threat to society and a potential lever against the entire law-
enforcement community.

For Beaulieu, a major consideration seemed to be that Lawrence, by faking buys, was stealing money from him. "I was irritated, only to the degree that a fellow police officer was taking money to do a job," Beaulieu said later. "I take care of the books . . . I'm audited . . . I'm not going to be ripped off by Paul Lawrence or anybody else," he said.

During the period when the drug unit was watching Lawrence, Beaulieu continued to fret about Lawrence drawing large sums for his alleged drug buys. "You better get this guy good," Beaulieu groused to Demag one day. "He's cleaning me out."

Beaulieu seemed not to doubt that Lawrence was worth going after. Demag noted that when he and Bradley told him their suspicions, "he didn't hem and haw a bit." "Here's what we're going to do," he said. Something similar had happened to Beaulieu previously. In the 1960s, when he had been a detective, Beaulieu had helped to catch a group of patrolmen on the Burlington department who were breaking into stores. The surveillance lasted three months. One of the targets, who eventually went to prison with the other members of the gang, was a friend of Beaulieu's; the man and his wife used to come to Beaulieu's home regularly to play cards. It was hard to nail a friend like that, Beaulieu said later, but he did not sound as if he had grieved excessively over it.

When Lawrence had met with Beaulieu to discuss his working in Burlington, it had been the St. Albans man who had suggested that he could make twenty-five cases within a two-month period. "Jesus, Paul, that's a lot of cases," Beaulieu remembered saying. But Lawrence said it would be no trouble. In fact, he offered to bet Beaulieu that he could do it. Beaulieu said to go ahead, and then he left the operation to Miles, as was his normal practice.

At the meeting in June, the primary issue was how to carry out a close surveillance of Lawrence, and whether to trap him with a decoy. Murray thought a decoy would work, and he had two to suggest. They were undercover agents for the New York State Police and they had recently trapped a Burlington area businessman who wanted his establishment "torched," or burned for the insurance money. Murray had been impressed by their intelligence and their ability. "Let's get them," he suggested.

This idea was later dropped. Beaulieu called Murray to say that Lawrence had close friends at the New York State Police drug laboratory in Albany. He might get a phone call.

The alternative to a decoy was surveillance, and Beaulieu decided they should try it. They tried close surveillance, in which the members of the drug division would follow Lawrence's car. That didn't work because Lawrence was able to recognize the cars of his fellow officers. They also tried check-point surveillance—having people around town radio in when they spotted Lawrence in a specific area. That didn't work well either. The detectives kept losing their man. During this period, the detectives met regularly with Beaulieu in the cellar recreation room of his home in North Burlington. And at one of those sessions, they decided surveillance wasn't working.

They decided then to go to a decoy, and Miles had a candidate. It was his nephew, a seventeen-year-old youth named Thomas Lauzon, who lived in Colchester. He had helped the police in the past and he was a "straight" kid, although he looked like many of his peers— long, dark hair, a moustache, and usually clad in blue jeans. He was indistinguishable from the dozens of young hippies and drifters that Lawrence had been sweeping off the streets for nearly a year.

Beaulieu checked out the idea with Pat Leahy, who approved it. Leahy was campaigning heavily for the United States Senate, and Beaulieu had not been able to talk to him about the Lawrence matter until June 22. Leahy had been upset—what was Lawrence doing in Burlington, he wanted to know. He would have nothing to do with any cases brought by Lawrence. Leahy said his office would do any-thing to help in the investigation, and that if Beaulieu needed help, he should talk to Frank Murray. Murray had gone out of town to visit his ailing father when the detectives decided to use Lauzon as a decoy, but Leahy okayed it. They would go ahead.

On July 3, Bradley and Dave Demag drove to Colchester and picked up Tom Lauzon. They took him to the police station and fashioned a police record for him. He would be Tom Phelps, a known drug dealer. They took his picture and put it in a brown envelope. Then Bradley and Demag took him to City Hall Park, and told him to sit there. If anyone asks you about drugs, you can talk about them, but say you don't have any, they told him. Other than that, they told Lauzon nothing about the investigation. Nothing happened that day; after two hours or so, the detectives took Lauzon home.

On July 4, Demag picked up Lauzon about noon and put him in the park for about three hours. Meanwhile, they tried to locate Law-rence to feed him the story about Phelps, but couldn't find him. Late in the afternoon, however, they spotted Lawrence's car in front of his apartment. Demag took Lauzon to the park again. Then he joined the other detectives at the station, where they waited for Lawrence to show up for work. When Lawrence arrived at the second-floor offices of the drug unit, the other officers began to set him up.

Miles said that he and Bradley would work the northern part of the city, while Demag would watch a house on Park Street, which the unit thought was the site of drug transactions. Lawrence would work the two parks—Battery and City Hall. The secret arrangement was that Bradley and Miles would follow Lawrence, and Demag would remain in the downtown area. And when Lawrence left the room, they activated the second part of the plan.

One of the men yelled to him as he left, asking him whether he had heard about Tom Phelps. Lawrence came back into the room and they told him that Phelps, who had been arrested previously by a Burlington undercover agent, was back in town, and had been spotted in City Hall Park. They showed him the picture of Lauzon, alias Phelps. At that point, however, they almost blew the whole caper.

When Demag went downstairs, he found Lawrence asking a secretary for a master file on Phelps and she was protesting that it didn't exist. Demag quickly grabbed Lawrence's arm and said, "Don't worry about it—it's that goddam Miles. He's always taking the files out and not bringing them back. Don't say anything—he's going to get his ass chewed for this."

Later, when Demag was showing Lawrence the fake file on Phelps, Detective Don Baker, looking over his shoulder, inquired: "Who's that?" He knew that the Phelps picture had never been in his files before. "Don't worry about it," Demag said, and went on talking to Lawrence. These gaffes in the trap attempt never scared Lawrence off.

At 8:30 Demag got a call on the radio from Lawrence, asking him to come to the City Hall Park to identify a subject from whom he had just made a buy. "The kid is sitting on the bench north of the water fountain," Lawrence said. "He's got on blue jeans and tennis shoes."

"That's Phelps," Demag told him.

"Ten four," Lawrence said.

For Dave Demag, the call from Lawrence came as a serious blow. He had come on the force four years previously, at the age of twenty, and as far as he was concerned, there simply could be no such thing as a bad cop in Burlington. When he had talked to Bradley about Lawrence, he had private doubts that Lawrence was actually bad, although he had considerable respect for Bradley.

Bad cops could be found only in big cities, Demag thought. You read about them in books—that probably was the reason Bradley was so suspicious. There could be an explanation for the problems with Lawrence's buys, even the Pacquette case. Maybe Lawrence was simply testing his informant when he appeared not to know Pacquette. Testing your informant was often a good idea.

Nor had Demag's experiences in St. Albans shaken his faith that Lawrence was legitimate, although he had become depressed in St. Albans by his failure to entice anyone into even talking about drugs. Even more strongly, Demag had a personal reason to be suspicious of Lawrence, and had rejected it. Demag's older brother had been arrested years before by Lawrence for a drug sale, and had gone to jail for it. The older Demag had told his younger brother that he was innocent, but Dave, although he was close to his brother, didn't believe him. He knew that his brother had been in trouble off and on, and if he was in jail for selling drugs, then he must be guilty.

Lawrence's move on Phelps upset Demag's world.

"You guys ain't going to believe this," he told Bradley and Miles, "but he called me over to identify Phelps."

Shortly after identifying Phelps, Demag met Lawrence in the parking lot of the Memorial Building. Lawrence said he had bought a quaalude from one suspect when he entered the park, and that he had asked the man where he could get some speed. The guy on the bench can do some speed, Lawrence said he was told. The guy looked like Phelps, and when he inquired, Lawrence said, Phelps offered to sell him some for twenty-five dollars, adding that he had just arrived back in town. Lawrence showed Demag the drug—a glassine package of white powder.

At nine, Demag went to the park and picked up Lauzon. "What happened?" he asked. Lauzon said that a black man had asked him for a match, and that a blond-haired man with a construction hat had asked him for change to make a telephone call. He also remembered seeing the blue Mustang they had followed earlier. The driver had a large leather hat. He knew nothing else.

Demag was doubly surprised. It had been hard enough to believe that Paul Lawrence would actually frame someone. It had never occurred to him that Lawrence would not even approach his victims.

The next day, they placed Lauzon in the park again around noon, then Bradley and Demag went to the Huntington Hotel, which overlooks the park, to watch him. They got in position by ten o'clock, but at one o'clock, Lawrence had called into the station to say that he had made another buy from Phelps. Speed. Lawrence went into the station, and Miles had him sign the picture as evidence that it was Phelps he had bought from.

When Frank Murray got back to the city, he was told of the Lauzon buys, and while they confirmed the suspicions of himself and Beaulieu and the others, it had some holes—the fact that Lauzon was related to Miles, for example. Another was that neither Lauzon nor Lawrence had been under direct surveillance at the time the alleged buys were made. What they needed was a professional decoy.

Murray took his problem to Leahy, who told him to call Eugene Gold, the district attorney in Brooklyn, New York. Leahy knew Gold from meetings of the National District Attorney's Association. Murray called and talked to a Gold aide. "Do you want a black one or a white one," the aide asked. It didn't matter, as long as he was a professional, Murray replied.

In late June and early July, the Burlington detectives made every effort to keep the Lawrence investigation secret, even from other members of the department. Mike Spernak, the detective who had fingerprinted Lauzon, didn't know Lauzon-Phelps was a decoy. Nonetheless, some cracks had clearly developed in the security. Beaulieu knew that Div Parsons had figured out that something was going on, and that it probably involved Lawrence. And on July 5, Beaulieu found that the word had slipped beyond his department.

On that day, Beaulieu got a call from George Ellwood, the police chief in Shelburne, who wanted to have lunch with him. When they met, Ellwood asked him some general questions about Lawrence; he's fishing around, Beaulieu thought.

Beaulieu told him that Burlington was working on Lawrence, and that Ellwood should stay away from the man. "Are you going to put the make on Lawrence?" Ellwood asked. That was a possibility, Beaulieu replied, but Ellwood should simply forget the conversation. Ellwood agreed, commenting that if Lawrence was ripping Burlington off, he hoped they would catch him. Beaulieu was not concerned about Ellwood tipping off Lawrence, but it was nevertheless clear that they did not have unlimited time for an investigation.

That feeling was reinforced on the ninth of the month when Beaulieu got a call from Kim Cheney, the Vermont attorney general, who wanted to know whether Burlington was maintaining a surveillance on Lawrence. Beaulieu was cautious. What was Cheney doing? The attorney general said that the state police had been ordered to investigate Lawrence, and that they were trailing him. Beaulieu was annoyed. If the state police were trailing Lawrence, then they must be trailing his men too. Someone could get hurt that way, Beaulieu told Cheney. Cheney replied that Beaulieu would have to talk to Major Glenn Davis, the number-two man in the state police, and Bill Keefe of his own office, who was in charge of the Lawrence investigation there. "Have you got a good case against Lawrence?" Cheney asked in conclusion. Beaulieu said they did.

When he got off the phone with Cheney, Beaulieu tried to get in touch with Glenn Davis, but was told he was "out of town for a few days." Beaulieu was suspicious: he knew Davis would not lie to him, but he might be avoiding him. So he called Keefe in the attorney general's office. Keefe knew why he was calling, but he was coy. He said he knew the state police were looking into Lawrence's activities, but he said he knew none of the details—what kind of an investigation it was, for example, or how far it had progressed.

Beaulieu told him that Burlington had "made" two cases on Lawrence and that he intended to make another with an outside police officer. At that point, Keefe told him that Major Davis was bringing in an outside police officer of his own, and that the man might already be in Burlington. That angered Beaulieu. He would talk to Pat Leahy, he said, and he ended the conversation.

When Leahy heard from Beaulieu, he instructed him not to permit the detective bureau to give any more information to the attorney general's office without clearing through him or Frank Murray. That evening, Keefe called Beaulieu at home and demanded to know what sort of operation Burlington was carrying on against Lawrence. "You'll have to talk to Pat Leahy," Beaulieu told him, and it was Keefe's turn to be upset. He was from the attorney general's office, Keefe said, and Pat Leahy was not going to tell him whom he could talk to. Keefe added that he would call Leahy, but that he wanted to meet with Beaulieu and Lieutenant Liberty the next day. Beaulieu told him he could contact anyone he wished, but that he was not releasing any information without clearing it with Leahy.

Privately, Beaulieu was disgusted. For years other law-enforcement agencies had had opportunities to stop Lawrence. Now

Burlington was doing it—doing the dirty work, was the way Beaulieu looked at it—and now these other agencies wanted to get on the bandwagon. The hell with them, he thought.

On July 10, late in the evening, Ron Williamson, a Vermont state trooper assigned to the state's attorney's office, went to the Burlington airport to pick up Michael Schwartz, the undercover agent from Brooklyn. Two rooms had been reserved for him at the Colonial Motor Inn on Shelburne Road. When Williamson and Schwartz arrived there, Demag and Miles and Bradley, who were waiting for them, thought that they had blown the operation.

Schwartz didn't look like a drug pusher. He looked, in fact, like a Jewish stockbroker. When he walked into the motel room, the cops there looked past him, expecting the decoy to be behind him. He was very short, balding, with short hair and expensive clothing. This guy must be a businessman, Demag thought. And, as it turned out, Schwartz didn't have any conventionally grubby clothes. The casual clothing he had with him would amount to sartorial splendor in the counterculture. The best he could do for a disguise was to forego shaving for a day. The cops also gave him a loose-fitting shirt so he could conceal a tape recorder.

There was nothing to do, however, but to go ahead. At six o'clock the next morning, they took Schwartz to the police station, and fixed him up with mug shots and a phony police record. He would be known as "The Rabbi," a well-known heroin dealer.

When they finished at the station, the whole crew went to Henry's Diner for breakfast, then on to the Huntington Hotel. They all went up to Room 223, which overlooks City Hall Park and St. Paul Street. To the immediate right of the hotel, and not visible from the hotel window, is the Vermont Transit Company bus station. Shortly before ten, Demag and Williamson stripped and searched Schwartz and placed him in the park, watching him all the way. Then they did the same for Lauzon, who had joined the group.

At eleven, Demag and Miles were in the drug division, with Lawrence, who had come to work and who was typing reports. Williamson and Bradley were at the hotel. They put the plan into action:

Demag went to the garage and met Sergeant Donny Davis, who was supposed to set Lawrence up. "Wait ten minutes," Demag told him, "then come up."

Davis waited, mounted the stairs, and burst into the juvenile room, obviously excited.

"I've got a hell of a tip for you guys," he said. "The Rabbi's back in town.

"I made a heroin buy from him in '70. His name is Mike Schwartz. He comes into town from New York on a bus for a few days, deals in the park and leaves. I saw him in town this morning at the bus station."

"I'll get the picture from the files," Miles said.

He went out and got it. "Take a look at this guy, Paul," he said.

Lawrence looked at the picture, kept typing. Shortly thereafter, Bradley, who had been relieved at the hotel, came into the room, and Lawrence asked him if he was working.

"No, I'm going to Stowe," Bradley said.

"I've been trying to get in touch with you," Lawrence said. He showed him the Schwartz picture. "Ever seen this guy?" he asked.

"No," Bradley said.

"Donny Davis said he saw him," Lawrence said. "We'll have to try to make a buy from this fellow."

Bradley said he would wait until he got his paycheck, then he intended to go to Stowe. In the meantime, he wandered into the adjoining recreation room to play pool. At 12:10, he saw Lawrence leave.

At 12:25, Schwartz, who had been sitting in the park, moving from bench to bench and occasionally sitting on the grass, noticed a blue Mustang with white plates moving slowly south on St. Paul Street. The driver made eye contact with him, staring hard.

Schwartz went immediately to a phone and called the Huntington.

"I think I just saw him," he said.

Shortly before one, Bradley and Miles were playing pool when Lawrence came up the back stairs.

"Where were you guys?" he asked matter-of-factly. "Didn't you hear me trying to get you on the radio?"

"No," Bradley said.

"I just made a heroin buy from the Rabbi in the park," Lawrence said. "Got a spoon of heroin from him. Thirty bucks." He added that he had got some speed from a guy on a motorcycle.

Lawrence reached into his pocket and showed them the drugs.

The heroin from the Rabbi was in a small packet. The speed was in two pink capsules.

Bradley shot again, then watched as Miles and Lawrence went into the drug unit office. Paul was talking to Miles about the buy, holding the picture of Schwartz in his hand. He turned to acknowledge Bradley's presence in the doorway.

"He looks exactly the same now," Lawrence said, referring to the photo.

Miles told him to start typing the reports, and Lawrence complied. He was still at it when Charlie Guyette, a detective from the juvenile division, came into the office at two o'clock.

"Hey, Charlie, I just made a buy," Lawrence said. "I just made a heroin buy off the Rabbi," he said, pointing to the picture.

Later that afternoon, Donny Davis met Lawrence in the alley next to the police station. He told him about the buy, also.

"I'm sure it was him," Lawrence said. "He fit the description exactly.

"And he was easy to buy from," Lawrence said. "The guy's an asshole."

The only question then facing the Burlington cops was when to arrest Lawrence. They had two moderately good cases with Lauzon as a decoy, and the Schwartz buy was apparently incontrovertible. However, they wanted one more buy from Schwartz.

On the morning of the twelfth, Lawrence came into the station early to work on his reports; but at nine, he said he didn't feel like working any more, it was too hot—he wanted to go swimming. Miles thought he seemed a little nervous. Moreover, Div Parsons had called the station with the query: "Are you going to arrest someone with the initials, P. L.?" Parsons cleary wanted his camera crew on hand, and if he was that wise, maybe Lawrence was too. The cops were also worried about Mike Donoghue; they knew he and Lawrence were friends and that Mike might let something slip if he knew about the investigation.

Beaulieu went over to Pat Leahy's office to talk to Leahy and Murray. They decided to arrest Lawrence without further delay. The one case with Schwartz would have to do.

Miles, Bradley, and Demag finally located Lawrence at his father's home in Shelburne. His car was parked outside. After waiting for a while to see if he would leave so they would not have to arrest him there, they drove into the driveway.

Lawrence's father came out first. "Who are you guys?" he asked. At that point, Lawrence came out of the back yard where he had been sunbathing; his mother and his girlfriend, Sue Stearns, were with him. "Hey, Dad, I want you to meet these guys," he said.

It was Miles who told him he was under arrest. They let him go into the house to get a shirt and sandals for the ride to the police station and the courthouse.

The elder Lawrence had been a security guard at the University of Vermont; Demag had known him then. Demag took him aside; Mr. Lawrence was stunned. "Why?" he kept saying. "What's going on?"

"It seems like some of Paul's buys haven't been too good," Demag told him.

On the ride back to Burlington, Lawrence rode in the back seat with Bradley; Miles and Demag rode up front. Later, Lawrence would say that when he had been arrested, Miles had held a cocked pistol to his head in the car.

During the ride, Lawrence insisted that there was something wrong. The warrant must be a mistake.

"Cool it, Paul, I don't want to hear it," Miles said brusquely.

For Bradley, the arrest was a sharp letdown. Until then, he had been caught up in the cat-and-mouse aspects of the trap effort. Now he simply felt bad—they had arrested a fellow cop. Demag didn't have that problem. The Lauzon buy had been the critical point for him. Lawrence was just another guy who had committed a crime.

Just prior to his arraignment in the courthouse in the county building on Pearl Street, Lawrence, Bradley, and Demag waited alone in the tiny lawyer's room off the main courtroom.

"Geez, Kevin, you can't believe this," Lawrence said. Then he turned to Demag. "Dave, you can't believe this?"

"If I wasn't 100-percent sure you were guilty, I wouldn't be here," Demag said.

"Okay," Lawrence said, and fell silent.

When they went into the courtroom for the arraignment, Lawrence pleaded not guilty to all the charges.

Untying the Knot

THE ARREST OF PAUL LAWRENCE REVERBERATED through St. Albans and through the law-enforcement community in Vermont. Lawrence had filed one hundred six drug charges between the time he came to St. Albans in August of 1973 and the time he was arrested in July of 1974. If those arrests were bad, then the community and the state faced a law-enforcement scandal of enormous proportions.

The sheer numbers involved, the quick and apparently efficient way that the Chittenden County state's attorney's office and the Burlington police set Lawrence up, and the breathtaking boldness Lawrence had shown in fabricating the Phelps and Rabbi buys raised most upsetting questions.

How could a campaign like this have gone on for so long in St. Albans without the cooperation, or at least the acquiescence of the police and prosecutors there? What role had the local judge played? Were all the Lawrence cases bad, or only some? In the wake of the arrest, local attorneys had said publicly that Attorney General Cheney's office had been given the full details on Lawrence's background, and that Cheney had refused to act. How was that possible? How much damage would have been wreaked on the victims of false drug charges? And how would such a scandal stain the image of law enforcement in Vermont?

Lawrence had worked several years for the Vermont State Police, and during that time had made many drug buys. The state police were the best-organized and most professional department in the state. How could they have overlooked his military record, his brutality, his bizarre behavior? The commonly accepted story about Lawrence as "Supercop" included the supposed fact that he had arrested six hundred to seven hundred persons. The possibility that this many persons in a tiny state like Vermont might have been framed was staggering.

On the day of the Lawrence arrest, St. Albans seemed stunned, according to stories in the local press. That evening, the city council met and agreed that no city official, other than the city attorney, ought to comment on the matter. There were rumors about, nevertheless. One of them was that Mike McGinn, the former state's attorney and the man who signed the warrants for the first and second raids, had raced to Burlington to talk to Lawrence. McGinn has never talked and no one knows whether that was true. But the implications for law-enforcement officials were unmistakable. Ron Kilburn, the prosecutor for the latest wave of arrests, was shocked. He had known for months that Lawrence was under heavy fire from the defense attorneys—the arrests in Burlington cast his judgment in a very bad light. Bill Keefe, the prosecutor of defendants from the first two raids, likewise looked very bad—all the charges he had laughed off now loomed over his career.

Probably the most seriously affected, and in some ways the least culpable, was Kim Cheney. After the Lawrence arrest, Cheney called the affair a black day in law-enforcement history, and he said that any person who had been charged on the basis of evidence presented by Lawrence ought to be let go. But no mere statement could remove the pressure from him.

Cheney, a young Republican with a bright political future, was then running for reelection as Attorney General against Jerry Diamond, the shrewd, young conservative Democrat. Both men were running hard that summer, and the Lawrence affair immediately began to whipsaw Cheney. On the one hand, the fact that Cheney had failed to adequately investigate Lawrence himself made him look at best shortsighted and at worst derelict in his duty; on the other hand, his statements about letting the Lawrence victims go hurt him with conservatives, who argued that Lawrence had not yet been convicted of anything, and that the druggies who had been arrested should be prosecuted. Having failed to move quickly enough in the past, he was now criticized for being hasty.

The defense attorneys in St. Albans wanted the governor to carry out a special investigation of the Lawrence affair, whereas Cheney wanted to see the investigation through himself. Shortly after the Lawrence arrest, Cheney went to St. Albans to meet with the local bar association, and during that session, he pleaded with them not to insist on a special investigation. "If you do," he said, "I won't get elected."

The defense attorneys were not sympathetic, and the Franklin County bar passed a resolution calling for an independent investigation. The investigation should cover all aspects of the case, the performance of police, prosecutors, judiciary, and defense counsel. Judge Gregg was so incensed by what he considered a slur on his integrity that he resigned from the bar association.

Initially, however, Governor Salmon declined to launch the requested resolution and Cheney tried to go forward with his own investigation. Ron Kilburn and Bill Keefe convened an inquest, a secret inquiry into the case. But pressure for an independent public look at the matter continued to grow. Jim Levy gave the Champlain Security report to the newspapers, and the publication of this information was devastating. There was considerable cynicism about people like Kilburn and Keefe investigating themselves. It did not help to have the Watergate investigation going on at the same time; the parallels were obvious.

For several weeks, Cheney held out. In August he wrote to Levy warning him that the release of the Champlain Security report might violate the canons of professional ethics. He also assured him that although Keefe would remain part of the investigation team, the probe would be carried out fully. "There will be no coverup in this case," he wrote.

Finally, however, Cheney concluded there was no way to carry on. No investigation by Kilburn and Keefe was credible. Cheney acceded to the request and asked the governor to appoint a special prosecutor to handle the Paul Lawrence affair.

Cheney was very bitter. He had been assured by Keefe that the investigation he had ordered Keefe to make in February had been carried out and that the defense attorneys were satisfied with it. That obviously had not been the case, and Cheney felt that he had been betrayed. A group of the suspects had taken lie detector tests, and all had flunked, Keefe said. That had been that.

In May, Cheney had sent a hand-scrawled note to Jim Levy asking him to support him in his campaign, as Levy had done two years previously. He asked Levy to circulate a petition for filing signatures and to line up a speaking date for him at the local Rotary Club. "I'd also appreciate any thoughts on who may be willing to assist in my campaigm this year," he wrote.

Cheney got a blistering letter in return.

"Apparently you have ignored all our initiatives and swept the situation safely under the rug," Levy wrote. "As a consequence, manifest injustice has been committed. Innocent persons have been convicted by juries, unaware of all the facts surrounding these cases, and other defendants have 'copped' pleas to avoid harsh sentences. In all, approximately sixty-three individuals have been subjected to prosecution, or perhaps more aptly persecution, on the strength of uncorroborated allegations made by an undercover agent who can only be characterized as a pathological liar.

"The incredibly callous response by your office to the St. Albans drug dilemma has caused me considerable anxiety and personal embarrassment," the letter continued. "As an officer of the court responsible for the perpetration of unwarranted suffering, I am ashamed by the legal system which is capable of spawning such widespread injustice. As an individual, I am repulsed by the moral insensitivity of those officials in positions of authority who have it in their power to right the wrongs which have been committed but, for various reasons, have chosen to take the easy path of non-involvement."

Cheney was badly shaken by the letter. He immediately called Levy on the telephone, and Levy repeated his sentiments, in even more caustic terms. He would never support Cheney for any office, Levy said. He also told Cheney he was disgusted with Bill Keefe, who had prosecuted the first four cases in St. Albans. The behavior of the prosecutors was irresponsible, he said.

Cheney was upset by more than the prospective loss of a political supporter in St. Albans. He took pride in his performance as attorney general; he was a Republican, but a liberal one. He had been a sponsor of such enlightened measures as legislation to open government records to the press and public; and in the area of law enforcement itself his concern for the rights of the accused made him the liberal candidate in his race against the Democrat, Jerry Diamond. Moreover, Cheney had been a local prosecutor, in Washington County, and he knew very well that the local prosecutor must keep justice as well as his conviction record in mind. He was aware that the police can make both good and bad cases, and that the decision as to guilt or innocence of a defendant often depends on whether the state's attorney decides to prosecute.

The Levy call persuaded Cheney that something was deeply wrong in St. Albans. He had been told by Ron Kilburn that the cases Lawrence had made were good, and Cheney considered Kilburn to be beyond reproach—well-intentioned and intelligent. But Kilburn could be wrong. And Cheney was now disenchanted with Keefe. Keefe had given him the impression that the defense bar in St. Albans was satisfied with what Keefe had said was a full investigation of the Lawrence matter. The Levy comments were so scorching that it was clear that not only was this not true, but the lawyers were more convinced than ever that Lawrence was a fraud.

Cheney's first action was to go to Keefe and demand that he supply him with a written memorandum on the investigation he had carried out. Keefe submitted a memorandum dated June 11 and an examination of this document illustrates both the extent to which Lawrence had established enormous influence over Keefe and Kilburn, and the extent to which public officials, through stupidity or lack of courage, can nurture injustice.

Keefe said at the outset that he and Kilburn had gone over the Champlain Security report item by item with Lawrence himself, and the memorandum noted that "we were both satisfied with his version of the events that are mentioned in the report." That in itself is a striking statement. The "investigation" consisted of simply the questioning of Lawrence, rather than an independent effort to determine if the man was reliable. The Champlain Security report made it clear that Lawrence's cases were filled with perjury—he had lied under oath about his military record and about such questions as whether or not he had applied for police jobs between the time he left the state police in 1971 and the time he took the Vergennes police chief post in early 1973.

Keefe was aware that there were problems with Lawrence's background. He had been a party to the discussions in Judge Gregg's chambers earlier that year on whether such information ought to be admitted into evidence. Nothing in the report indicated that Keefe even pressed Lawrence hard on this, let alone checked it out independently. Furthermore, Keefe brushed aside the warnings issued by Jerry Diamond about Lawrence's veracity.

Diamond was no rube, and he was also the last person likely to be sympathetic to drug dealers. He was very much the hard-liner on crime, but he was also shrewd, and he had allowed Lawrence to make less than ten cases before he closed him out of Windham County prosecutions. The charges that Diamond's deputy, Gar Murtha, had passed on to the state police were of a very serious nature— Lawrence's stories were always changing, and Murtha also raised the issue of how Lawrence might be keeping a portion of the drugs he was supposedly buying. In a situation where most convictions rest on the word of the undercover agent, there could be no more serious allegations than these.

Yet, Keefe waved them away. The allegations, Keefe said in his memorandum to Cheney, were very vague. "In fact," he wrote, "they are so vague that Lawrence is unable to respond to them. I, at one time, talked with Jerry Diamond about his experiences with Lawrence and although Jerry Diamond is no great fan of Paul Lawrence, he did admit to me right here in this office one day that with one exception every case Paul Lawrence worked on in that county resulted in either a verdict of guilty or a plea of guilty."

The kindest thing one can say about these comments is that they are disingenuous. The "one exception" Keefe refers to is the case where Lawrence's testimony in two trials is contradictory. And the fact is that the remaining handful of cases that Diamond prosecuted successfully were one-on-ones, which would be suspect if the narc was suspect. Which was precisely the point Diamond had been making. To argue that Diamond had "admitted" the convictions had been obtained was silly.

Keefe went on to say that it was not uncommon for drug sellers to cheat on the amount of drugs they sold to a narc, or the strength of the drug, if sold in pill form. That of course might well have been true; but it is also true that the classic way for a narc to get drugs to plant on victims in what the law-enforcement people call "salting" cases, is for the narc to keep some drugs from actual buys. The issue was not whether such discrepancies were possible, but whether they pointed to dishonesty on Lawrence's part.

The story about Lawrence shooting out the window of his cruiser at the Farrell Distributing Company in Rutland was not mentioned by Keefe directly in the report, but he did say that the implication in the report that Lawrence had not been able to get a job at the local police department in Rutland because of bad reports by state police commanders simply was not true.

"I have copies of Lawrence's resumé and in that are his official efficiency reports prepared by his commanders. While he was with the Vermont State Police and without exception, he got an extremely high rating in most categories. These reports were signed by Lt. John Poljacik, who was his commanding officer most of the time he was with the Vermont State Police. I have discussed Paul Lawrence with Officer Poljacik and Officer Poljacik gave him very high marks as a State Police Officer," Keefe wrote.

Like the discussion of the Jerry Diamond allegations, this report is hard to understand. Many law-enforcement officials around the state knew about the Farrell Distributing incident and it would have been easy to find out about it, if an investigator was inclined to inquire. In addition, the informal practice of the Vermont State Police to deal with disciplinary problems by transferring the individual was known to knowledgeable persons in the state; Keefe should have known it too. Moreover, if he was working from the resumé, he would have had to look no further than the top of the resumé, where Lawrence said he had an honorable discharge from the army, to know that at least part of the information was falsified.

Keefe also said that the report from Champlain Security had noted that Glenn Davis of the state police had said that Lawrence "had the knack and ability to be a competent and productive undercover agent, and that he was just that while he was with the Vermont State Police." Keefe did not mention in his memorandum that Davis had also told the Champlain Security investigator that he would not have recommended that St. Albans hire Lawrence, nor apparently did Keefe consider asking Davis why not.

Keefe's method in this seems clear: he looks for what is positive in the Lawrence record and ignores the rest. Such an "investigation" of course was bound to be a whitewash. Everyone knew that Lawrence was capable and articulate and that many people were impressed with him. The point was: was Lawrence, despite these favorable attributes, inherently untrustworthy?

Keefe did question Lawrence about the allegations concerning his background and his personal behavior, and in his memorandum, Keefe said he was satisfied with the answers. It was clear from the memorandum that in so doing, Keefe overlooked, or chose to ignore, evidence that once again Lawrence was lying.

On the matter of his military records, Lawrence admitted he was a lousy soldier, that he had gone AWOL twice with a friend from Rhode Island. He also said that he had seen several doctors while in the service and that one of them could have been a psychiatrist, although none had represented himself as such. As to why he left, Lawrence said he had done so because of complications due to an appendix operation. In these responses, Lawrence was clearly putting the best face on the facts, but even so the information was readily impeachable. The Champlain report, and Lawrence's military records, indicated he was discharged for character and behavior disorders; the military records likewise showed that Lawrence had had no complications from the appendix operation.

Keefe saw no significance in the allegations that Lawrence cheated occasionally on his expense account while in Vergennes, or that he had an occasional dalliance with a secretary. Lawrence, Keefe wrote, had admitted he was "no angel." In the case of the most serious allegation, that he had spent a whole day with the secretary and had then written it off as a drug investigation, Keefe accepted at face value Lawrence's long, fanciful story about how, despite the fact that it looked as if he had spent the day having fun, he was really investigating whether the secretary was involved in the drug traffic.

This story was vintage Paul Lawrence. The woman had given Lawrence a substance that turned out to be cocaine, he told Keefe. Her brother had been in an automobile accident, and she wanted to find out if he was still on drugs. The cocaine had come from him. The accident had taken place in Connecticut, but when he had called to check it out, he could not find the woman's brother. He thereupon decided that perhaps the woman herself was involved . . .

Keefe recounted this nonsense in his memo and accepted it, apparently, at face value. Yet, it was precisely the kind of story that Lawrence had been spinning for years. It had twists and turns, changes of plot, sudden surprises. What it had in common with other

Lawrence stories was that it was almost impossible to check out. If no brother existed, well, the woman had lied. She wanted to find out about a drug she had obtained from one of her connections or sources. If the woman ridiculed this story—if the woman was to say that Lawrence took her out for the day and then took her to bed, which is what she told Randy Brock—then she was simply lying to protect herself.

All this went right past Bill Keefe. The memo described not an investigation, but an apologia, worded in the most defensive terms, and it was not surprising, for if the defense attorneys in St. Albans were right, Paul Lawrence was a charlatan on a grand scale. And Bill Keefe would be a fool.

The one solid bit of evidence that Keefe had to base his judgment on, evidence that did not rely on something said by Paul Lawrence, was the lie detector tests given to four defendants from St. Albans. That was one of the things that Cheney had called for when he assured the defense lawyers in February that his office would make an independent determination as to Lawrence's credibility. "Get the best polygraph man you can find," Cheney had told Keefe.

Keefe had thereupon procured the services of a lie detector operator from New York City, he had tested four defendants, and he said they were all lying. The defense lawyers were first shocked, then outraged. The tests given by Randy Brock had shown that, with one exception, none of the seventeen defendants he had tested were lying. The tests taken by the New York man were shown to Brock, and he said that they were clearly not performed competently. He also told them that Keefe's polygraph man was so inept that if the State of Vermont licensed such operators, he could not practice in that state.

The problem with these four polygraphs was that they ranged over the behavior of the four defendants generally, rather than limiting the questioning to whether or not the person had sold drugs to Paul Lawrence. Most of the defendants used drugs to at least some extent. Even Gary Burbank, the "cleanest" of the St. Albans defendants, had admitted that he smoked marijuana. The defendants, when asked about buying or using drugs on other occasions, were evasive. And when they weren't, the operator concluded that since they had admitted using drugs on other occasions, they must be lying about their statements in response to questions about the supposed Lawrence transaction.

It is possible, of course, that the polygraph operator retained by

Keefe was right and that Brock was wrong. That does not appear to be likely, particularly in light of what was learned subsequently about Lawrence. And an exchange of letters between Cheney and Brock concerning the tests puts the New York operator in a bad light.

In a letter to Jim Levy on June 13, Cheney demonstrated his lack of understanding of polygraph technique. Cheney cited two defendants who had been cleared by Brock and who the New York operator said were lying. In one case, Cheney said, the suspect had admitted selling drugs previous to his arrest on the Lawrence charges; in the second, the suspect admitted being in Taylor Park when Lawrence said he was. These findings seemed to "verify the findings of the instrument," Cheney wrote to Levy.

Levy passed this information on to Brock, and on July 12 Brock wrote to Cheney, putting forth in detail his position on the tests in the St. Albans cases.

In the first place, he wrote, the New York man was not an "acceptable" polygraph expert. He had not graduated from an accredited polygraph school and was not a member of the American Polygraph Association. A polygraph licensing bill had been introduced in the previous session of the Vermont legislature, and if it had been law at the time, the New York man could not have qualified to make examinations in Vermont.

As for the tests made on the St. Albans suspects, Brock wrote that the New York examiner had erroneously based his conclusions on the suspects' admissions that they had sold drugs in the past and that they might have been in the location Lawrence said they were.

That was not the real issue, Brock wrote. The issue was whether they had sold drugs to Paul Lawrence. Brock said he had talked to the New York examiner, in the presence of Bill Keefe, and that the examiner had admitted that his charts on one suspect were consistent with those obtained by Brock on the same suspect. Brock had concluded the man was telling the truth; the New York examiner concluded he was lying.

Brock said that the man had stated that, based upon the charts alone, he would not be able to form an opinion of "Deception Indicated." He went on to say that there were times when a polygraphist had to "throw that machine right out the window." The New York man told Brock his decision was based on the previous drug sales and on the suspect's admission that he might have been in the park at the time Lawrence said he was. "I consider this approach most unprofessional," Brock wrote.

Brock also said the New York man's questioning of the suspects about the specific sales to Lawrence were unprofessional. "It is totally improper to ask such questions as 'Do you know for certain who sold orange sunshine and chocolate chip acid to Paul Lawrence on October 18, 1973?' when the crucial question is whether *any* sale even occurred at all."

Despite these problems with the New Yorker's polygraph results, Keefe indicated to Cheney in the spring not only that he, Keefe, was satisfied with the tests, but that the St. Albans defense attorneys were also satisfied. Actually, the opposite was true: the attorneys believed that the tests were a sham. But enlightenment in the form of the Brock letter came too late for Cheney. Pat Leahy's office and the Burlington police had moved decisively against Lawrence by that time, leaving Cheney looking foolish.

So, in late August, after the denouement of the Lawrence arrest and the wave of criticism of his performance, and the growing certainty that an investigation carried out by Bill Keefe and Ron Kilburn would not be credible, Cheney gave in. The governor should appoint an independent authority to study the Lawrence cases.

Governor Salmon agreed, but the governor then did his own bit to undermine the credibility of law enforcement in the state. He spent weeks looking for the right man to do the job—to be the special prosecutor—and when he found him, the announcement was made with great fanfare. The man would be a Rutland attorney who could not possibly be biased or prejudiced.

Before the end of that day, Phil Chapman, the reporter for the St. Albans *Messenger,* was writing a story saying that the new special prosecutor was a member of the firm where Paul Lawrence's wife was working as a secretary. Moreover, this attorney had represented the insurance company in the brutality case that Paul Lawrence had lost in Brattleboro.

Governor Salmon withdrew the appointment and named Robert Gensberg to act as special prosecutor. Gensberg, a slight, dark-haired man in his late twenties, was well regarded by his fellow lawyers in Vermont. He was intelligent and clearly honest. He would take the job.

When Bob Gensberg drove into St. Albans in late September, he had no clear idea how to carry out his assignment. He was to look into the allegations that the Lawrence cases were fraudulent; to study the performance of law enforcement generally; and if the cases were fraudulent, he was to figure out how Lawrence had been able to operate so long. To help him, he had been assigned two state troopers—Buddy Rouse and Lloyd Howard.

When they arrived in St. Albans, they were given office space on the third floor of the courthouse building, and they went immediately to work. First, they went over the information that Kilburn and Keefe had turned up in their inquest. Kilburn said that as far as he was concerned, the inquest had turned up some definite problems, and that, based on the Burlington charges, he would not be surprised if Lawrence had made some bad cases. At that point, they had discovered the records showing that the charges against Steven Pacquette had taken place when Pacquette was in jail in Burlington. They had also found that a sale by a man named Tony Badamo had allegedly taken place while Badamo was with his parole officer. They had also heard that a deputy sheriff had claimed that Lawrence had planted drugs in the home of one of the people seized in a raid. That allegation was never proved.

On the Pacquette issue, Sergeant Thibault of the St. Albans police had said he saw the man in the park when Lawrence claimed to have made the buy—the day the records showed he was in jail in Burlington—but the Thibault report had been originally dated in October, and the supposed identification of Pacquette in the park was supposed to have taken place in August. The October date had been x-ed out and August written in. This raised the suspicion that Thibault might have been trying to help Lawrence out of a jam.

Gensberg's investigators, meanwhile, had been looking into Lawrence's financial records and into his telephone records. There was a striking number of calls to the Albany, New York, area, most of which were made to people who worked at the New York State Police laboratory. These calls, combined with the fact that Lawrence had all of his drug tests made at the New York State Police lab in Albany, was a source of some suspicion—Lawrence, if he was making bad buys, had to be getting the drugs from somewhere. "Why don't you go to Albany, Buddy, and tell those people we think they've got a problem with their lab?" Gensberg said.

It was in early October that Buddy Rouse went to Albany and talked to Peter Liverzani, the captain of detectives for the New York State Police and the man in charge of the laboratory. Rouse told

Liverzani about Lawrence and said that the Vermont people suspected the Albany laboratory of being the source of illicit drugs.

That evening, Gensberg got a call at his home outside St. Johnsbury. It was Buddy Rouse. "Bob," he said, "that guy was really bent out of shape. I think he's going to be up here tomorrow."

The next morning, Liverzani and Richard Scholer, his senior investigator, were in Gensberg's office in St. Albans. They sat down and went over all the information that Gensberg had developed. Liverzani suggested gently that Gensberg might not be too clear on how he should proceed. Gensberg, almost gratefully, agreed.

"Get me all the arrest reports on Lawrence's cases," Liverzani said. For the next few hours, the men assembled the reports and began to construct a chart showing the name of the defendant, the date of the alleged buy, the location of the buy, the amount of drugs that the seller had claimed, the price, the laboratory report number, the date that the material had gone to the lab, the person who had taken it, the amount of the drug the laboratory measured, the date it was returned, and who did the test at the laboratory.

After a short period of studying this chart, Liverzani delivered a flat verdict: "There is something radically wrong here," he said. No knowledgeable drug man would accept this sort of information, he said. The prices were all wrong—some buys were as much as ten times the ordinary street price; some of the amounts were absurdly small—in one case, the amount of heroin sold would not have affected someone who injected it into a vein, even if that person had never used heroin before. The heroin was mixed with weird things, like talc and cocoa. In some instances, Lawrence bought a substance identified as one thing which turned out to be another, something that had an entirely different appearance. No street-wise person would do that, Liverzani said.

Over the next couple of days, and in an investigation that finally ran to several weeks, the New York State Police officers and Gensberg and his men went over the drug buys and circumstances with a fine-tooth comb. When they were through, they were positive that Paul Lawrence was a fraud.

In the first place, Lawrence's methods were in sharp contrast to those of other undercover narcotics agents. Usually when an agent comes into a town, he will be introduced to the drug community by an informant and make himself known for some time before trying to buy drugs. For instance, Gensberg and Liverzani noted that Augie Fernandez had come into St. Albans in June and had not made his first buy until July 26. Lawrence, on the other hand, made his first drug buy on August 6, the first day he got to town. By the fifteenth of August, he had claimed his first heroin buy.

Moreover, Lawrence made few barbiturate buys, even though that was the major drug in the community. Augie Fernandez had noted that speed, or methamphetamine, was the most common drug in town, and that there was some hashish and LSD also, but no heroin that he had ever seen, even though he had tried to buy it.

They also had serious doubts that there were enough people or enough money in St. Albans and Franklin County to support the kind of heroin traffic that Lawrence's arrests would indicate. Studies had shown that a heroin seller in the northeastern United States supports an average of about thirty users. Since Lawrence reported a total of twenty-two heroin buys from fourteen sellers in the area, this would indicate that there were over four hundred heroin users in St. Albans and Swanton alone.

"If there were such a large number of heroin users in these communities," Gensberg reported, "there would be obvious indicators of this. Burglary and larceny rates would be abnormally high, especially of pharmacies. There would be an epidemic of shoplifting on a huge scale. There would be an abnormally large incidence of serum hepatitis resulting from the use of unclean hypodermic needles. Heroin users, at one time or another, would be seen 'nodding' in public, heroin overdoses would be reported at local hospitals. Our investigation revealed that none of these indicators existed."

As for the price of the heroin, Lawrence claimed to have paid a total of $1,675 for the first seven heroin buys. This amounted to $1,213 per gram, and, assuming an average of as little as 250 milligrams to a street dose, it meant that Lawrence was paying more than $300 per street dose. This, said Gensberg and Liverzani, was "an absurdly high figure." The normal price of a street dose of heroin is $10 to $15.

While it was a matter of only a short time for an experienced drug agent like Liverzani to tell that the street buys Lawrence had claimed were absurdly inflated, the question of where the drugs came from was much harder to answer. Most of the tests at the laboratory had been made by Martin Horan, a senior chemist. It was clear from testimony in several trials that Horan and Lawrence were friends;

they had lunch or dinner together often, and they had gone goose hunting and ice fishing together. Both Gensberg and Liverzani, after questioning Horan, concluded that he had done nothing wrong. But they still suspected the New York laboratory was involved somehow.

From Pat Leahy and Frank Murray in Burlington they had gotten some important information. The search of Lawrence's apartment on the day of his arrest had turned up a briefcase, hidden in a closet between the bedroom and the bathroom, that contained several empty vials and a small plastic container that had "99% heroin" written on it in grease pencil. The vial contained a residue of white powder that turned out to be heroin of less than 20 percent purity. One of the vials said "speed" and one, "cocaine."

Liverzani examined the vials and said that they were the type of vials used in the New York laboratory. They took the heroin vial back to the laboratory and had it examined by a handwriting expert. He said that the writing was that of Martin Horan, Lawrence's friend. The detectives also determined that the speed and coke vials came from the New York laboratory. Armed with this information, the investigators interviewed nineteen chemists and former chemists at the laboratory, the last of whom was Horan. He acknowledged providing Lawrence with small quantities of drugs for display or training purposes when Lawrence was the police chief in Vergennes. The kit contained small amounts of heroin, LSD, speed, a small amount of opium, a small sample of cocaine, and small samples of PCP, an animal tranquilizer, MDA, and marijuana.

The members of the Vergennes Police Department were interviewed, and they said they never saw such a drug display kit, nor had they had any training that included a display of drugs.

A comparison of the contents of the drug display kit with the chart containing Lawrence's buys turned up some interesting information. On March 12, 1974, Lawrence had reported making an opium buy in St. Albans; it was one chunk that weighed .62 grams, just over the estimated half-gram sample Horan said he gave Lawrence. Opium is rarely bought on the street in chunk form, Liverzani said. And it was the only opium buy ever recorded in Vermont.

Lawrence got one PCP tablet from Horan, according to the chemist. On August 21, 1973, shortly after he arrived in St. Albans, he bought one tablet of what he said was STP. It turned out on analysis to be PCP.

Even more interesting was what Gensberg and Liverzani called buy #53, the purchase of a tab of LSD for six dollars from a man named Leon Bennett in Swanton. Bennett denied making the sale, and the case was typical Lawrence: one-on-one, no corroboration. Gensberg and Liverzani were interested in the drug itself. Although LSD is common, the five-sided tablet Lawrence bought was unusual.

The first time that Liverzani, an experienced drug officer, and Horan, who had conducted thousands of tests, had seen the five-sided tablets was in the early 1970s when police found them while searching a residence in western New York State. Horan preserved a small number of these tablets, although he could not remember how many, and he forwarded some of them to the federal Bureau of Narcotics and Dangerous Drugs. They told him that the LSD had been manufactured in Texas. Horan could not remember whether the LSD tablet he gave Lawrence was pentagonal or not, but the only time he ever saw one, other than the first time, was buy #53, from Leon Bennett.

Although all this seemed to fit the pattern, the key to the Lawrence operation, the investigators thought, was the series of heroin buys. So they began a second chart listing those, and discovered what turned out to be a puzzling but ultimately rewarding detective story.

The heroin buys came in series that showed certain clear patterns. The first series contained seven buys, the first of which was allegedly from Sonny Cross on August 9, shortly after Paul Lawrence arrived in town. Lawrence reported buying two "hits" of MDA from Cross for twenty-five dollars. The drugs were taken to the laboratory and Martin Horan determined that the substance was not MDA but heroin, amounting to 0.3 grams. The test was returned on August 29.

On October 3, Lawrence reported buying twelve bags of heroin from Ronnie Rich and Otto Kremer for $600. On October 24, he said he bought six bags of heroin from Alan Bibeau for $300. On October 11, he said he bought four bags of heroin from Alan Bibeau and Gary Rich for $200. On the eighteenth, five bags from Alan Bibeau for $250, on the nineteenth, four bags from Linda Lamb and Brenda Denton for $100, and on the twenty-third, four bags from Ronnie Rich, Roland Prior, and John Dalcourt for $200.

Each of the doses contained in these bags was tiny, below what a street user would buy. The average street dose is about .3 to .5 grams. The weight of each bag averaged less than one-tenth of that amount. Moreover, the total weight of drugs of each sale after the first one became progressively smaller.

It looked to Liverzani and Gensberg as if Lawrence had got hold of a substance he could not identify, submitted it as an MDA buy, found it was heroin, then divided it up for later buys, using progressively smaller doses to make the supply go farther. The source of the supply for this series could have been the display kit.

The investigators then charted the remaining twenty-four heroin buys and studied the series they seemed to fall into. The first two buys in the new group took place November 13 and November 16 in St. Albans. Each buy was erroneously labeled: they were supposed to be single bags of mescaline, although the prices were very high, $400 and $200 respectively. When they were analyzed, they turned out to be heroin cut with cocoa. The substance therefore had a brownish color, and Liverzani said that mescaline is white and that no knowledgeable undercover agent would buy mescaline that looked like cocoa. In addition, mescaline is normally sold in capsule form, rather than loose. Lawrence took the samples to the laboratory himself and asked for quick action on the analysis. He got back the answer—heroin and cocoa—on November 26.

The investigators figured Lawrence had got hold of another batch of drugs and wanted to find out what it was. A little over a week later, he began a second series of heroin buys. On December 3, he said he made a buy of one quarter-ounce of heroin from Jeffrey Underwood in St. Albans for $450. On the eleventh, he said he bought one bag of heroin from James Poquette for $500. These were truly impressive amounts of heroin.

The first buy consisted of 3.7 grams of heroin cut with talc; the heroin was 16 percent, way over the normal street purity. The second buy was 7.7 grams, with a heroin content of 20.2 percent. Both were a striking departure: big buys, with purity ratios almost never found on the street. Beyond that, the fact that they were cut with talc was puzzling. Liverzani tried to cook it, to liquefy it as one must do before injecting it. It lumped and frothed—impossible to inject.

The chart next showed a series of eight heroin buys between January 18, 1974, and March 26, 1975, followed by a break in heroin buys until May 13. These buys, like the other Lawrence cases, were entirely uncorroborated. The amounts of heroin were huge: up to 16 grams in weight, and purity as high as 67 percent. The first three buys in the series, all made in Swanton in the late winter, were multigram amounts with percentages of 14.9, 11.7, and 19.8 respectively. This sort of purity is normally found only in wholesale lots of an ounce or greater. Buy number 66 was an absurdity in St. Albans. It purported to be a buy from a woman named Mary Martin, three decks of heroin for $175.

Heroin of this purity is never sold on the street, Liverzani told Gensberg. This buy would have had to come directly from a laboratory or high-level supply point, many levels above the normal street deal. The prices of this heroin also had no rational relationship to the first heroin buys. The prices were essentially the same for tiny amounts of weak heroin and for huge amounts of enormously strong heroin.

Gensberg felt that it might be possible to analyze these eight buys, and one that Lawrence made in Waterville, Maine, to see if they came from the same source. If they did, it would be a strong indication that Lawrence had obtained a supply of heroin of high quality, then cut it with various substances and broken it up into samples that could be passed off as individual drug buys.

The prospect of this grew out of the fact that heroin will have a characteristic "signature" based on the circumstances of its manufacture. The process begins with the opium poppy refined into morphine, which is acetylated to produce diacetylmorphine, or heroin. In the process, the heroin picks up trace impurities from the vessel it's produced in. Also, some of the morphine is not fully acetylated and becomes monoacetylmorphine, while the overall sample will contain some pure morphine.

For a given batch of heroin, the ratio of morphine to monoacetylmorphine to diacetylmorphine remains constant. Once this pure heroin is produced, it is cut for street use with diluting agents, such as quinine, mannose, glucose, sucrose, dextrose, and mannitol, and occasionally starch. A given batch thus has a second constant ratio of heroin to the diluting agent.

The first step in the analysis was to submit a total of eleven Lawrence heroin buys to the Drug Enforcement Administration laboratory in New York. They also submitted the powder found in the vial in Lawrence's apartment during the search by the Burlington Police Department.

Of the eleven samples, nine plus the powder found in the vial had common characteristics. All had heroin, starch, and mannitol. An interesting element was that the presence of mannitol appeared to increase with the increasing percentage of heroin in a given sample. However, the drug enforcement laboratory informed Gensberg that there was no analytic test that would tell the *amount* of mannitol in a given mixture.

While these tests were being run, the New York State Police made an intensive search of all the heroin they might have on hand at the laboratory for testing and standardization purposes. Liverzani located a sizeable batch that had been seized in 1971 in a search in the Hudson Valley. This heroin had been cut with mannitol and had been at the laboratory at times when Lawrence was there.

Samples from the two bags were sent to the DEA laboratory in New York and one of them fit the same heroin-mannitol pattern that marked the nine Lawrence buys, as well as the buy in Waterville, Maine. The problem then was to see whether the heroin-mannitol ratio was the same. There appeared at first to be no way to do that. Gensberg contacted mannitol manufacturers in the United States and their methods of quantitative analysis were effective only for mannitol mixtures of 90 percent or greater purity.

At the DEA laboratory, officials said they had neither the time nor the equipment to develop a test for mannitol amounts. Further, DEA could not check for the ratios of impurities in given samples, or the ratio of morphine to heroin in given samples. All such tests would require a major effort, including the breaking of new ground in the area of quantitative analysis.

The Vermont State Police laboratory was eager to try, but could not because of a conflict of interest—Lawrence had been a member of the force. So Harold Linde of the state police laboratory suggested that Gensberg talk to Martin Kuehne, a professor of chemistry at the University of Vermont. Kuehne was intrigued by the problem, and he and a graduate student worked out a method to test the volume of mannitol in a given mixture.

Gensberg then submitted twenty-seven samples to him for analysis. These included four samples from the New York State laboratory, one was the Maine buy, and one was the vial found in Lawrence's apartment. The accuracy of the test was said to be plus or minus 5 percent, and, within that probable error, seventeen of the samples showed heroin mannitol ratios of 85 percent to 15 percent. (In eight cases, other chemicals obscured the mannitol tests and no conclusions could be drawn. In the remaining two samples, which came from the New York State laboratory, the heroin-mannitol ratio was 60–25, and included some quinine.)

If three or four heroin samples contained a common heroin-mannitol ratio, no conclusion could be drawn, Gensberg said, but as the number of samples increases, the likelihood of a common source increases. With seventeen, the indication of a common source was very strong.

Gensberg was willing to concede that it was possible, in one geographic area, for there to be a common supplier for all the sellers, but he pointed out that the buys took place over a seven-month period. And it did not explain how the Maine buy and two of the four samples from the New York State Police laboratory fit the pattern so precisely.

Gensberg's conclusion was that Lawrence had stolen a sizeable portion of one of the stashes at the New York laboratory, had cut it with some material of his own, and used the drugs to frame people.

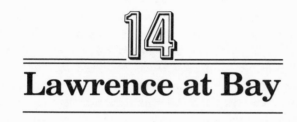

Lawrence at Bay

PAUL LAWRENCE WENT ON TRIAL IN BURLINGTON AT THE end of January 1975. A veteran of dozens of trials, the accuser of hundreds of young people on drug charges, the cool, unflappable witness, Lawrence was playing a new role—defendant. He had been able to sway many juries, but never before had there been so much at stake for him. If he did not sway this one, he would lose his career and his freedom.

Lawrence was accused of two crimes, false swearing and false information in the Rabbi case. The false information was the affidavit of probable cause that he had made out, in which he said he had bought thirty dollars' worth of heroin from the Rabbi. The false swearing consisted of his oath, made before Detective Harold Miles, that the information in the affidavit was true.

Lawrence was represented by Jack Welch, a flamboyant young lawyer from Rutland. Welch, a friendly, affable man, was given to flashy clothes and bombastic oratory. He also had political ambitions. During the previous summer, Welch had sought the Democratic nomination for the congressional seat from Vermont, and there was some speculation that Welch had agreed to represent Lawrence in order to get his name before the public in Chittenden County, the home of the bulk of Vermont's Democrats. Whatever his motive in representing Lawrence, his political campaign failed. He was beaten in the September primary.

Frank Murray was now the state's attorney and he would prosecute the case, assisted by his chief deputy, Jack Bergeron. Murray had taken over as state's attorney when Pat Leahy resigned after he was elected to the United States Senate.

The judge was Edward Costello. He would preside over the case in the brightly lit, modern courtroom in the new state office building on Pearl Street. A good crowd was on hand for the proceedings: lawyers who had confronted Lawrence in drug cases around the state, hippies who wanted to see the Burlington drug unit exposed as a result of its members going on the witness stand, some families of young people arrested in St. Albans, a full complement of reporters. Irene Wielawski was there to cover the trial for the Burlington *Free Press,* Div Parsons for WCAX, Robert Kaplan for the Rutland *Herald,* James Kevlin for the *Vermont Sunday News.*

Frank Murray was keyed up for the case. He was convinced that Lawrence was guilty, and he believed it was desperately important that the jury find him so: the integrity of the criminal justice system was at stake. Murray had slaved over the case, working late into the night for weeks. For, despite the mass of evidence that Lawrence was a corrupt cop, the Rabbi case was by no means as airtight as the prosecution would have liked.

When the police and the state's attorney's office had set up Lawrence, they had hoped he would make two buys from the Rabbi. That would eliminate any possibility of mistake, and would wipe out the prospect that Lawrence might claim that he had bought drugs from someone he *thought* was the Rabbi. But on the morning that Lawrence was to have made the second buy, he had abruptly changed his routine. He had seemed nervous when he was in the office in the morning, and instead of going out to try to make the second buy, he had said abruptly that he was not going to work that day—that he was going swimming.

Leahy and Murray were overseeing the case closely, and they were in the state's attorney's office that day, receiving reports from the police. No one could say whether Lawrence had been tipped off, but there were indications that Div Parsons knew something was afoot, and if he knew, others might also. So Leahy had told the police to arrest Lawrence immediately, without waiting for the second buy.

There were other problems, as well. The search of Lawrence's car, which turned out to have a store of loose drugs in the glove compartment, was carried out without a search warrant. It was thus not certain those drugs could be used as evidence. Moreover, and incredibly, Harold Miles had lost the picture of the Rabbi that Lawrence had signed, and the tape cassette on which he had made his report of the Rabbi buy. This sort of thing drove Murray to distraction.

Murray had studied Lawrence's background and methods, and he knew the man could be a spellbinder in front of a jury. Lawrence had devastated defendants in his drug cases, slipping in damaging bits and pieces of information, describing conversations and situations in so convincing a way that juries had been persuaded he was telling the truth, even when there were contradictions in the stories. Murray determined, therefore, to make Lawrence stick to yes-and-no answers—he would try to keep him from making speeches.

Murray's biggest single problem was to limit the damage he would suffer from having Harold Miles as one of his major witnesses. That fall, Miles had shot a man to death in an alley after a burglary. The man, a Puerto Rican from Rhode Island, clearly had been fleeing from a crime, but the fact that he had been shot while surrounded by armed cops generated some feeling in the community that a grand jury should have been convened. Pat Leahy had not done that—the shooting was an accident, he said—but that incident, combined with the fact that Miles had lost some of the Lawrence evidence, might persuade the jury he was unreliable. And Miles was the man to whom Lawrence had made his sworn statements about the Rabbi.

In his opening statement to the jury, Welch tried to set the case up as one of Miles's word against Lawrence's. "In a word, the nuts and bolts of this case is very simply that according to Detective Miles on one occasion Paul lied to him or a couple of other occasions Paul lied to him. . . . It is Paul versus Miles in terms of whom are you going to believe," he said.

Welch also made it clear that he would try for a defense of mistaken identity. Paul said he made a buy of heroin from a man with a growth of beard at the bus station, across the street from City Hall Park. The man had a purple flight bag. He said on his return to the police station that he had made a buy from the Rabbi, but it had simply been a mistake. The buy, he would contend, had actually taken place, but from someone other than the Rabbi.

Murray called Miles as his first witness, but he asked him only a few questions aimed at establishing that Lawrence had typed out an affidavit on the Rabbi buy, and that Miles had notarized his signature on it. This testimony was essential to prove the false swearing and false information. But after that Murray concluded his questioning of Miles. In the back of the room, Bill Sorrell, one of Murray's assistants, was watching the proceedings and he thought Welch slumped a little in his seat when Miles came off the stand so fast.

Murray was sure Miles was telling the truth and that his problem was simply that he was a hot-headed man and a poor administrator. Fortunately for his case, several other cops had witnessed Lawrence's activities after the buy. Kevin Bradley had seen him look at the Rabbi picture. Charlie Guyette could recount how Lawrence came up to him and bragged about making the Rabbi buy. Donny Davis and Dave Demag had been involved—most of the detectives had been involved in the case in one way or another.

And if Miles was a liability, these others were not. Bradley, for example, was a witness made in a prosecutor's heaven—soft-spoken, intelligent, obviously honest. Michael Schwartz, the Rabbi himself, was a magnificent witness, in a way no one could have predicted. Short, well-dressed, half bald, he looked a world removed from the street scene. In fact, as far as the cops were concerned, he looked like no one else in Vermont. It would be hard for any jury to believe that Lawrence could have made a mistake about his identity.

Once he established the Rabbi buy, Murray brought in four other cases on which Lawrence had not been charged, but which looked like the same kind of frame-up he had prepared for the Rabbi. Normally, these would not have been admitted into evidence, but there is a rule in judicial procedure that such cases can be brought in to show intent on the part of a defendant—to show that the case at issue was not a mistake, that it was part of a pattern. Murray knew that he was running the risk of overtrying the case, but he felt it was crucial to establish that Lawrence was indeed a corrupt cop.

The four cases were those of Christine Currey, who testified about her day with Lawrence and its outcome; Durrell Pacquette, the young man whom Lawrence had not recognized, thus exciting Bradley's suspicions; Tom Lauzon, the first decoy the police had set up in the park; and the parole officers for Tony Badamo, who testified he had been with them when he supposedly had made a sale to Paul Lawrence. The common thread in these cases was the attempt by Lawrence to frame a defendant and the fact that circumstances peculiar to each case tended to prove that. In Christine's case, the jury was simply asked to believe her testimony; in the Lauzon case, there was the testimony of the police that they had planted the youth in the park; Badamo was a case where the man had a clear alibi. The Pacquette case gave Bradley a chance to recount how Lawrence had failed to recognize the man.

In his cross-examination, Welch tried to chip away at these four collateral cases. He attacked Christine Currey's version of her day with Lawrence; he tried to show that Badamo might have left his parole officers long enough to have made the Lawrence sale; that Lauzon and Pacquette were unreliable.

Murray thought at the time that this strategy probably made sense during Welch's preparation. The people Lawrence had arrested in the past had done poorly in court—they were far less persuasive than Lawrence himself. But Murray could tell that the strategy had failed in this case. Badamo did not testify himself and his parole officers did well on the stand. Lauzon and Pacquette, though not so impressive as the parole officers, did well enough. And Christine Currey turned out to be a great witness. Welch described her as a coke sniffer from Buffalo, but she looked like anything but a criminal. Young, beautiful, stunningly dressed, obviously well-educated and intelligent, sincere, she seemed to damage Lawrence's image badly.

The trial was a contentious one, marked by numerous conferences at the bench between the opposing attorneys. These conferences, recorded by the stenographer but out of the hearing of the jury, involved the kind of questions that would be allowed in questioning the various witnesses. Murray raised numerous objections to Welch's lines of questioning, most of which Judge Costello upheld. The reporters took to counting the number of objections made each day, and the numbers soared. Moreover, the proceedings were enlivened by Lawrence's attempt to attend the bench conferences himself. This Costello would not allow, but it lent a madcap air to the trial.

The trial was a difficult and exhausting test for Jack Welch. He was trying the case alone, whereas Murray had help from Jack Bergeron, and he could call on the other lawyers in his office. Welch also had a difficult client; it seemed to the prosecutors that Lawrence's constant whispered bits of advice during Welch's cross-examination distracted Welch. And the case itself was very complex: Welch had to deal with the four collateral cases, plus the main case against his client.

Lawrence himself arrived at the trial each day conservatively dressed—he looked like a bank executive—smoking a pipe, and carrying a briefcase and file folders. He was impassive during the trial, never showing any emotion during the testimony of witnesses against him. During the recesses, he was friendly to the people in the hallways, including the prosecutors.

He also seemed confident he would be acquitted. He told the reporters that there were "some things that will come out" that would help him. When pressed, he would say that he had been getting close to something, that someone wanted him out of the way. And when pressed further, he would say that it involved Leahy, that his trial was political.

In the audience each day were Lawrence's mother and his girlfriend, Sue Stearns. He had been seeing Miss Stearns since the breakup of his marriage to Carole Lawrence. His father came once, but did not return. Mrs. Lawrence, like her son, showed no emotion during the trial. But she lobbied the local press in order to help her son. She went in to see the editor of the *Free Press*, trying to influence the coverage of Paul's case. She also tried to play the reporters off one against the other, telling one reporter that he was the only one treating her son fairly, and then telling others the same thing.

Although Welch chipped away at the state's supplementary cases, trying to show that none of them was solid, that they did not show a pattern of behavior on Lawrence's part, the heart of his case was the claim of mistaken identity. Paul, he claimed, had actually made a buy on the day in question. But it had been from a man at the bus station, across the street from the park. The man had been tall, bearded, and carrying a purple flight bag, Lawrence claimed. That this effort was possible was due to a gap in the Rabbi case—the police had the Rabbi under surveillance at the time of the buy, but they did not have anyone watching Lawrence. It was impossible to prove that he had *not* made a buy at the bus station. The issue was: would the jury believe that Lawrence could have been mistaken that it was the Rabbi from whom he made the claimed buy? The Miles evidence was not crucial to the case, therefore, despite Welch's claim at the outset. All Miles said was that Lawrence had signed the affidavit of probable cause, and Lawrence admitted that.

The mistaken identity claim foundered on the evidence acquired during the searches of Lawrence's car and apartment, which were carried out the day of his arrest. These searches were vital to the case, and they also provided a basis for Lawrence's subsequent appeal.

The police had searched Lawrence's car in the early afternoon of July 12. They had done so without a search warrant, on the grounds that the search was incidental to an arrest, and that the police had "probable cause" to believe that the drugs Lawrence had supposedly bought from the Rabbi were in the car. To have left the car in the driveway of Lawrence's parents' home would have been to run the risk that someone might move the car, or remove evidence from it.

Shortly thereafter, the police obtained a search warrant for Lawrence's apartment, arguing to the judge that Lawrence's normal procedure in drug cases was to take the evidence to his apartment. The problem was that the police had not been able to find Lawrence at his apartment when they first went looking for him. There was no way to tell, therefore, if the drugs were in the car or the apartment. The police wanted to search both.

The search of the car had not turned up the Rabbi drugs, but several foil-wrapped packages of heroin were found in the glove compartment, unmarked as evidence. It looked like a store of drugs Lawrence could use to frame people. The search of the apartment turned up the drugs bought from the Rabbi, along with a file folder that had one of the prints of the Rabbi picture stapled to it.

Before the trial began, Welch moved to suppress the evidence found in the car and in the apartment. The search of the car should not have been carried out, he said, because there was no search warrant. The apartment evidence should be suppressed because the search was a general fishing expedition—Welch claimed they tore the apartment apart—rather than a search for a specific object.

Costello never explained his ruling, but he allowed the drugs from the car to be admitted into evidence, and he suppressed the evidence obtained from the apartment. This included not only the Rabbi drugs and the file folder, but the empty drug vials that had proved so instructive to Bob Gensberg.

Despite this ruling, once Lawrence testified he had not been given a picture of the Rabbi, Murray moved to place the file folder and the Rabbi picture into evidence. The justification for this was the rule that otherwise inadmissible evidence can be used when the exclusionary rule is being used as a cloak for perjury. The introduction of the file folder apparently killed the mistaken-identity defense. And the trial record also shows that Welch's own assessment of his client had been shaken by the folder.

In a bench conference (these conferences are recorded, but cannot be heard by the jury) in which Welch protested the use of the file folder and picture, Welch said he had not known about this evidence. Murray jumped on this statement, since Vermont law calls for a prosecutor to reveal the substance of his case to the defense.

"We showed you a picture of Schwartz stapled inside a manila folder," Murray said. "I remember asking you, 'How can your client say he didn't buy from this guy Schwartz, he didn't think this guy was Schwartz when in fact he has his picture stapled inside his manila folder!' You don't recall that? And you looked at me and said, 'I'm so tired of this case, so confused about this thing I don't know what to think.' It was right in my office."

In the seventh day of the trial, the two opposing lawyers gave their summaries to the jury. Murray ran through his case, rejecting the objections Welch had raised against the state witnesses. He bored in hard on the heart of the case—that Lawrence had been given a picture of the Rabbi, and had gone out and made the buy, then had come back and told his colleagues about it. "Look at that picture," Murray said. "You don't see any pictures of look-alikes of Michael Schwartz, and there aren't any. Michael Schwartz only comes by once in a lifetime, you know."

The other detectives testified that, when he came back from the buy, Lawrence told them he had just made a buy from the Rabbi, and that he looked just the same as he did in the picture. There was no doubt about it, Murray said. Lawrence was guilty and the jury ought to find him so.

"I hope that you realize the significance of this case and the responsibility that is yours," Murray concluded. "It is significant for the defendant and it is most significant for the state. Abuse of power such as this cannot be taken lightly. True, Michael Schwartz was not victimized. True, Thomas Lauzon was not victimized. But I think you can understand how important it is when abuse of power such as this manifests itself.

"It is the entire community, ladies and gentlemen, that is victimized."

In his summation to the jury, Welch ranged over the cases that Murray had brought in, trying to discredit them. Christine Currey

was simply a coke sniffer from Buffalo. Tony Badamo was "weird"—
he was also a convicted drug seller and an expert at concocting alibis.
That was what he had done in the Lawrence case. He had been
hitchhiking and had been picked up by Lawrence. They had arranged
a heroin buy. Badamo had raced back home and gotten into his
pajamas to wait for Brown, his probation officer. Shortly after they
got to Brown's office, Badamo slipped out to make the heroin buy . . .

Murray, on rebuttal, made the point that there was no way
Badamo could have known Lawrence was going to pick him up while
he was hitchhiking, and that in any case, why would he make such an
effort to construct an alibi unless he knew the man he was selling to
was a narcotics agent?

Welch ran through the whole case and he concluded: "Let me ask
you this, you know, have you ever seen—have you ever seen such a
motley collection of X-rated people in your life as the state has
brought in here?" How could anyone accept the word of the state's
witnesses, compared to Paul Lawrence, Welch demanded.

"You know, ladies and gentlemen, you know, those people have
violated the sanctity of the halls of this courtroom with their testimony, you know, testifying as they have, you know, liking you to
perhaps think that maybe they deserve the key to the city or something when the only reason they are in court here, ladies and gentlemen, the only reason is to come into the court to save their own skins.

"They got motive to testify," Welch said, "to save their own skins
even if it means by doing so they have to frame my client and send
him on a one-way ride to Palookasville—terrific, you know.

"That don't wash. Those people are lying. It's as clear, you know,
as apple pie in June those people are lying . . .

"You know, it's a funny thing when you stop to think about it.
That here's a man who's made during the course of his career some six
hundred buys, putting the likes of this scum out of commission,
taking them off the streets, putting them behind bars, preventing
these people, without any consciences, from profiting upon the misery
of ordinary people—and this is where it don't make sense—after
they get through testifying they walk out from that stand, down to
the wall, out the door, free as birds, you know, to sort of do their own
thing.

"While the man who busted them all, all their kind like them,
what's he got for all this trouble? He gets himself a one-way ticket,
here to the combat zone."

The judge cut Welch off at this point, but it is noteworthy that the argument by Welch marshaled the kind of attitude that prevailed in some quarters in St. Albans—that Lawrence was trying to get the scum off the street. And while Welch did not claim that gave Lawrence the right to frame people, he did his best to give the jury the impression that they ought to choose between an upright citizen like Lawrence, and the longhaired scum he tried to get off the streets.

"Ladies and gentlemen," he said further on, "there are men and there are men. And there are some men, ladies and gentlemen, like prophets walking in the wilderness, their eyes and visions sort of span the centuries. I am talking about unorthodox men, people who do things in a different way. The catalysts of social change in this country.

"These are the very sorts of men that very readily arouse the ire and suspicions in the minds and hearts of conventional people. Narcotics is a dirty business," Welch said, "requires unorthodox people doing things with an unorthodox group of people without any conscience . . ."

This peroration by Welch was the closest thing to a justification for Lawrence that any of his supporters ever advanced. Welch did not concede that Lawrence framed people, but his reference to "unorthodox men" who do things in a "different way" sounded like a plea for a jury to permit Lawrence to operate outside the law. If narcotics is a dirty business, as Welch said, and is run by people who have no conscience, then should not Paul Lawrence, like a prophet in the wilderness, be allowed to deal with them in his own way?

The argument carried no weight in Burlington. The jury deliberated two and one half hours, and found Lawrence guilty on both counts. Judge Costello sentenced him to from four to eight years in prison.

Jack Welch said he would appeal the case to the Vermont Supreme Court.

One month later, Irene Wielawski left her apartment in Winooski well before 8 A.M. for the forty-minute drive to St. Albans. Today she would begin wrapping up the first, and in some ways, the most important story of her newspaper career—the story of Paul Lawrence. The previous afternoon she had learned that Robert Gensberg, the special prosecutor appointed to investigate Lawrence's activities in Franklin County, would be bringing Lawrence in for arraignment in Franklin County Court. The arraignment would be at nine, she had learned, and there would be several charges, but no one could say just how many, or what they would be. "You've only seen the tip of the iceberg," Gensberg had hinted earlier, but she could not get in touch with him. So she was leaving home early; she would find out the details before the court convened.

As she headed north on Interstate 89, she recalled the first time she had seen Lawrence. It was at his trial in Burlington the previous fall, and she remembered that he had not fit her preconceptions at all. He was impassive and cool, detached even, although he faced serious charges and a strong body of evidence pointing to his guilt. And it was difficult for her to deal with him. For one thing, she did not know how newspaper reporters were supposed to act toward defendants in a criminal trial. For another, while not an extensive drug user, she was a child of her generation, and she despised narcs on principle.

Still, Lawrence had been very nice to her. He had introduced himself during an early recess. "It's nice to meet you, Irene," he had said. "Where do you come from?" he continued. "You haven't been here very long."

She was surprised at the time. Even at that point, she had written several stories about him in the Burlington *Free Press,* and while she thought they were fair and accurate, there could be no question that they portrayed Lawrence in a highly unfavorable light. She was also suspicious of him: he seemed a little too nice, too relaxed, too smooth, too charming.

She had also not known what to make of his air of quiet optimism, despite the progress of his trial. There were things not yet disclosed that would work in his favor, he had hinted to her. One day she had asked him what his surprises were. They involved Leahy, he had indicated. Leahy had a stake in this—Lawrence was getting close to some things. Lawrence had also arrested the brother of one of the Burlington cops who had set him up. But nothing had ever come of his assertions. She hadn't believed what he said, but she had wondered.

As she pulled off the Interstate and headed into St. Albans, she hoped that the trial in St. Albans would be shorter and clearer. The Burlington trial had been wild, what with Welch's histrionics and Murray's efforts to keep the trial under control. As she drove into town, she noted that Taylor Park, the hippie hangout that had driven the St. Albans establishment to distraction, was empty, still covered by snow. She parked her car across the street, then climbed the hill to the red brick courthouse, pushed through the heavy oak doors, and went to the second floor courtroom.

It was the first time she had been there. Empty and still, its heavy mahogany woodwork gleaming in the pale light, the courtroom conveyed a sense of justice, retribution even. After four months on the legal beat, she had become a connoisseur of courtrooms. This one she liked. She was sitting on the antique benches at the rear of the courtroom when Paul Lawrence came into the room alone.

"Hi, Irene, how are you?" Lawrence said warmly. "How have you been?"

"Hello, Paul, how have you been?" she replied.

"Good, I've been reading your stuff," he said. "I really enjoy it."

How could he enjoy it, she wondered.

He was effusive; his manner seemed to her almost a verbal embrace. She also noticed that he was well dressed as he had been in Burlington: a conservatively tailored, expensive suit, a pastel shirt, an expensive tie. He has good taste, she thought, and she was surprised to find it in a cop. She was uneasy; it was hard to make small talk.

"What have you been doing?" she asked.

"Reading, relaxing, working on my case," he replied.

Still uneasy and out of things to talk about, she mentioned that she liked the St. Albans courthouse. It had a sense of dignity, of timelessness, she said. And things like the old, curved wooden benches were collectors' items.

"That's one of the nice things about Vermont," she continued awkwardly. "I bought a beautiful old desk from a farmer in Milton," she said. "Cheap. I love it."

"I know what you mean," Lawrence said. "In fact, that's my hobby — going to auctions. I went to one in southern Vermont a few weeks ago. Got an old chest for five dollars."

He's making it up, she thought. He's picked right up on my conversation . . . the old benches . . . the desk she got from a farmer . . . and reconstructed it in his own terms without being quite specific. He didn't say where in southern Vermont, or when.

"Hey, Paul," she said after an awkward pause, "by the way, do you know the number of charges you're going to be arraigned on?"

"Just one," he said.

"One — are you sure?" she said. "I heard it was going to be several."

"Yup, just one," he said firmly.

"I can't imagine that," she said. "Everything I've heard has been multiple charges."

Her manner said she did not believe him.

But Lawrence insisted. "Well, it's one," he said. "I know they thought earlier there would be extra charges, but Gensberg said today it would be one. He couldn't make the other charges stick. He called today and said the complaint has been amended. He called me and my lawyer this morning."

A moment later, the other participants began to enter the courtroom—Gensberg, Jack Welch, Lawrence's attorney, who had been making a call in the hallway, the clerk, the judge. With Lawrence standing before the bar, the clerk began reading the complaint.

"Count One—Perjury, lying in the trial of Norman Young, on Jan. 29, 1974, when he said he was discharged from the army because of an appendectomy complication, when in fact he had been discharged for unsuitability due to 'character and behavior' disorders.

"Count Two—False swearing. For making the same false claim in a deposition prior to the Norman Young trial.

"Count Three—False information, for lying about the alleged purchase of LSD from Steven Pacquette in Taylor Park.

"Count Four—Misuse of police funds, by obtaining money from Chief Hebert to make the Pacquette buy, and then converting the money to his own use.

"Count Five—Misuse of police funds, by obtaining four hundred fifty dollars from Chief Hebert to make a heroin buy from Tony Badamo, failing to make the buy, and converting the money to his own use.

"Count Six—False swearing, lying about the alleged sale of heroin to Badamo."

Lawrence pleaded not guilty to each charge, then they all rose to leave. Irene went quickly to Gensberg. Had he called Welch or Lawrence that morning? He laughed. "No," he said.

As they all left the courtroom, Lawrence looked at her casually.

Later that spring, Lawrence was tried in St. Albans on the first two counts of the Gensberg indictment—perjury and false swearing in the Norman Young case, first in a deposition before the trial and then in the trial itself. Gensberg intended to try Lawrence on the other four counts later in the year.

The trial in St. Albans was over quickly. There were no histrionics, battles over objections, or stem-winding orations by Welch. The charges were that Lawrence had lied under oath about why he left the military. Gensberg introduced the military records to show that Lawrence had been forced out of the army for character and behavior disorders. Gensberg located the personnel officer who had handled the Lawrence case at Fort Dix, and the former officer testified there was no doubt that the discharge was based on those reasons. He also testified there was no doubt that Lawrence understood what was happening to him.

Lawrence was convicted and sentenced to from zero to ten years in prison, the sentence to run concurrent with the one he had received in Burlington.

Jack Welch appealed that case to the Vermont Supreme Court also. The St. Albans conviction was quickly affirmed. The Burlington case was much more difficult, however, and a decision was not handed down until June of 1977. Welch argued in the Burlington case that his client had not received a fair trial, and he put forward several grounds. These included the claim that the four non-Rabbi cases should not have been used against his client, and the court's refusal to move the trial to another county, but the most important issue was thought to be the question of whether or not the searches of Lawrence's car and apartment were justified.

The results of the car search, which Costello had admitted into evidence, had "bombed" his client, Welch argued. The unlabeled drugs made his client look very bad in the eyes of the jury. The judge was wrong to admit this evidence because there was no search warrant, Welch said. But there was more to it than that.

The police had argued, on the same afternoon after they searched the car, that they had probable cause to believe the Rabbi drugs were in Lawrence's apartment. They had been granted a search warrant on that premise and had searched the apartment later in the afternoon, Welch said — it was impossible to have probable cause to search two places at once.

Probable cause, Welch contended, means a 51 percent probability, meaning that the state could not claim it for two places at the same time.

Michael Goldsmith, a young attorney in Murray's office, argued the case for the state. A graduate of Cornell Law School, Goldsmith had clerked for a federal judge in Burlington, and he had an outstanding reputation as a legal researcher and brief writer.

Murray's budget would not permit him to hire Goldsmith, so he borrowed three thousand dollars to hire him temporarily to work on the Lawrence appeal and on a handful of other cases. Goldsmith had spent weeks researching and writing the state's brief for the Lawrence appeal.

He was confident that the grounds put forward by Welch were not valid, with the possible exception of the issue of the search of the car. That could be a problem, he thought. He could not find any precedent for search of two locations at the same time, but he did find dicta—legal language in a case—to the effect that such a procedure was justified if the police had reason to believe that the fruits of a crime were in one of two locations.

It was like the child's game, Goldsmith argued, in which someone has something of value in one of his closed hands. He holds both hands in front of him and offers someone the chance to pick one hand or the other. Asking the police to do this when searching for contraband simply was not reasonable, the court had said.

Still, Murray and Goldsmith were worried. For some reason, the decision was taking a long time. The case was argued orally before the state's high court on February 17, and a decision was due to come down in early April. It did not come, and as April wore into May, the two men became increasingly concerned. They knew that the case was complex, and in writing his brief, Goldsmith had cited dozens of cases to support his arguments. Looking up every one of those cases would take a long time.

On June 7, the Vermont Supreme Court upheld Lawrence's appeal from his conviction in the Rabbi case. The decision, written by Associate Justice William C. Hill, declared that Lawrence had not had a fair trial because the prosecution had been allowed to introduce into evidence Lawrence's allegedly false efforts to frame four other people—Christine Currey, Tony Badamo, Durrell Pacquette, and the police decoy, Thomas Lauzon, known to Lawrence as Phelps.

The ruling was striking for two reasons. The first one was that the state's high court avoided ruling on what the defense and the prosecution thought would be the major issue at stake, the possible breach of Lawrence's fourth amendment rights in the search of his car at the time of his arrest. Second, the reasoning behind the opinion on the use of the four "prior similar acts" appeared to be tortured beyond all recognition.

The performance of the state's highest court was thus consistent with the remainder of the state court system that had dealt with the Lawrence affair—poor. And poor, moreover, in such a way that it seemed at the time that the Lawrence affair might never be fully resolved. The Supreme Court opinion raised the possibility that Lawrence supporters might ultimately argue that he had never framed anyone at all.

Justice Hill's opinion had noted at the outset that the general rule of evidence is that the prosecution cannot introduce proof of a distinct, independent offense, even though it might be the same kind of crime for which the defendant is being tried. The fact that a man held up a bank on one occasion should not be used as evidence that he did so on another. The prosecution should not be allowed to poison the minds of the jury.

At the same time, however, there are several exceptions to this rule. Hill pointed out that under Vermont law, "Testimony is admissible to show motive, interest, knowledge, a plan or purpose, or preparation, leading up to or connecting the respondent with the commission of the offense. . . ."

Hill noted that the State had offered the evidence under the exception providing that prior similar acts were admissible if they show an absence of mistake on the part of the defendant. The elimination of the possibility of mistake seemed clearly essential to the Lawrence trial. If the Rabbi case was considered alone, a jury might have been tempted simply to accept Lawrence's word that he thought he was selling to the Rabbi, even though there was a sizeable body of evidence to contradict that argument. Lawrence had never been convicted of a crime before, and the jury might have been willing to give him the benefit of the doubt—forgiving him, in effect, for a single transgression in an otherwise blameless career.

The situation was thus a textbook example of the use of prior similar acts to show intent, and thus the absence of mistake. And the jury clearly believed that the absence of mistake had been demonstrated in the course of the trial.

Yet, Hill's decision contended that "the course of conduct actually introduced by the state indicates little more than that the appellant may have pursued like behavior in the past."

The prosecutors, Frank Murray and Mickey Goldsmith, who had

written the brief for the state in the Supreme Court appeal, were both baffled and outraged by the decision. The statement that the prior similar acts showed only that Lawrence had tried to frame people before simply did not get to the point. The issue is whether the demonstration of such acts serves a narrow purpose that falls within the rules of evidence—in this case, to show that the defendant had not been mistaken.

Goldsmith was willing to concede that the State might have presented the four similar cases after Lawrence claimed he was mistaken. But since the jury was going to hear them anyway, it seemed like a harmless error to put them into the "case in chief," rather than the rebuttal.

If the four cases Murray presented failed to meet the test established then Hill did not say why they failed.

Murray immediately filed with the court a petition to reargue the case, making the argument that the court had misapprehended the admissibility of prior similar acts. Murray also noted that Hill had misread the case on procedural grounds. In the pretrial conferences, Murray had informed Judge Costello that he intended to use the four similar acts in order to head off Lawrence's expected claim that he made a mistake. Costello had then told him that he could.

This ruling was set forth in the transcript, and Hill had apparently assumed that the ruling had come in response to an objection by Jack Welch, Lawrence's attorney. The significance of this mistake lies in the fact that unless Welch had objected to the use of the similar acts, he was not entitled to appeal the conviction using those grounds.

Actually, Welch had not objected to the similar acts until three of them had already been introduced into evidence in the trial itself. At that time, he remarked that he "renewed his objection" to the material.

While Murray was filing the request for a rehearing, Goldsmith sent the decision off to Irving Younger, a law professor at Cornell University, who is one of the nation's leading experts on evidence. Younger, interviewed later, said that, as far as he was concerned, the high court opinion was "pretty much unintelligible." When the circumstances of the case became known to him, he said it seemed clear that the use of the similar acts was justified to show the absence of mistake in accordance with the rules of evidence that have been in effect for over a hundred years.

Moreover, he said that the argument raised by Welch about the

search of Lawrence's car had no validity whatever. This was clearly
at variance with the feeling of the people connected with the case in
Vermont, including Goldsmith and Murray. They thought that
Welch's claim that the police could not possibly be justified in claiming they had good cause to search two places at the same time was a
threat to their case. This fear was reinforced by Goldsmith's inability
to discover any case law on the issue; in fact, Goldsmith considered
himself fortunate to discover language in a case that appeared to deal
with the issue—the analogy by a judge of the child's game, in which
one holds out two closed fists and asks someone to pick the hand that
holds the coin.

The reason there is no case law, Younger said, is that the argument is ridiculous on its face. Police have numerous cases in which
the loot from a crime or evidence they need has either been split up, or
could be located in one of two places. Saying they could only search
one of the two places is absurd, Younger said.

Any competent judge, when faced with such an objection from a
defense attorney, should simply say to the prosecutor: "I don't need to
hear from you," meaning that the argument should be rejected outright without the need for objection and argument.

Despite all the apparent drawbacks to the high court decision,
neither Murray nor Goldsmith expected the court to reconsider its
position. In mid-June, Murray resigned his office to go into private
practice, and William H. Sorrell, the new state's attorney, said that
he would try Lawrence again as soon as the Supreme Court ruled on
the reargument petition.

Murray, Goldsmith, and Sorrell were all confident that Lawrence could be convicted again. The State could not use the four
similar acts to show Lawrence had not been mistaken in framing the
Rabbi. In a new trial, however, the prosecution could bring out the
fact that he was now a convicted perjurer. The St. Albans convictions
ought to make a jury dubious about any Lawrence claim that he had
been mistaken in the Rabbi buy.

In mid-August, however, the Supreme Court stunned the prosecutors again: they agreed to hear rearguments on the case—a very
rare procedure. The decision did not say why they agreed to rehear—
it could have been that they meant to acknowledge their error on
Welch's failure to object to the prior similar acts. Or the justices could
be prepared to abandon the stand taken by Hill on the prior acts.

If either was to prove true, then the remaining uncertainty

would be whether or not they would rule on the Welch argument that the search of the Lawrence car should not have been allowed into evidence. The justices took no position on that argument, noting that the trial judge had issued no findings of fact to support his ruling that the car contents could be admitted into evidence.

The court could make a finding on that issue; it could send the issue back to the trial court for a finding of fact—without ordering a new trial—or it could remand the case to the trial court again. That would mean that Lawrence would be tried again sometime in late 1977.

In late August and early September of 1977, the first cracks appeared in the Lawrence veneer. He authorized his new attorney, John Maley, to begin plea bargaining with the new state's attorney, William Sorrell. Maley knew that it would be very difficult, if not impossible, to make a persuasive defense of his client. The only defense that Welch had mounted had been mistaken identity, and the first Lawrence jury had rejected that.

Of course, assuming that the Supreme Court renewed its decision to overturn that conviction, the State would no longer be able to use the four prior cases that tended to show Lawrence had a record of framing people and therefore had not been mistaken in his identification of the Rabbi; nevertheless, Lawrence would not be able to take the stand in a new trial without admitting that he was a convicted perjurer. Lawrence had had no record in the first Burlington trial, but he had subsequently been convicted in St. Albans, and this could now be used against him.

What Maley hoped for was that Sorrell would be willing to reduce the main charge against Lawrence—perjury. Any reduction in that charge would be a victory for Lawrence. But Sorrell would have no part of that. Frank Murray had been determined to see Lawrence convicted of the crime that had been the centerpiece of his career— lying about someone selling him drugs. Gensberg had not nailed Lawrence on this issue, settling instead for perjury convictions on Lawrence's testimony about his military record. There was no way that Murray was going to back away from the ultimate confrontation with Lawrence; that was what everyone had seemed to do when dealing with the man. Sorrell agreed with Murray. The perjury charge would stick.

What Sorrell was willing to do was to drop a second charge

against Lawrence that stemmed from the Rabbi case. That charge, false information, was a misdemeanor, and Lawrence had received a sentence of eight to twelve months on it, a sentence that was to run concurrently with the four- to eight-year sentence on perjury. The distinction between the false swearing—perjury—and false information was a technicality. The false information was the making out of the affidavit of probable cause on the Rabbi buy; the false swearing was simply swearing that the information was true.

The bargain that Maley struck with Sorrell contained the following elements: Lawrence would plead guilty to perjury. Sorrell would drop the misdemeanor charge: false information. Sorrell would agree to ask that the judge impose a sentence no greater than the original penalty of four to eight years. Lawrence would get credit for the time he had already served, about one year.

Sorrell told Maley what he would say to the judge on sentencing. He would tell Costello, Sorrell said, that he felt that perjury was a very serious crime and that perjury by a police officer was more serious still: the sentence ought to reflect that. But Sorrell agreed not to specifically object to any reduction of the four- to eight-year term, if the judge, drawing on the presentence investigation, decided that Lawrence had learned his lesson and might benefit from an earlier release from prison.

Finally, Sorrell agreed not to charge Lawrence with perjury in connection with his testimony at his own trial. This was simply a gambit on his part. If the State was going to charge Lawrence with perjury a second time, the charge should have been filed within two or three months of the trial itself, which was in January of 1975. An immediate defense, if a new charge was to be filed in mid-1977, would have been that Lawrence had not been given his constitutionally guaranteed speedy trial. But Sorrell felt that if Lawrence accepted this part of the bargain, it would be a tacit admission that he *had* committed perjury at the trial, and such a tacit admission would make it more difficult for Lawrence to claim that his plea bargain had been a tactical maneuver and that he had not, in fact, conceded that he had lied.

Although this bargain was the best that Lawrence was likely to get, he hesitated to go along. The problem was his mother. She had staunchly defended him and insisted on his innocence. But Lawrence was wearing down. Those who saw him in prison said he was growing desperate to get out. He was also described as depressed at his plight.

So in mid-September, he caved in. He would go for the deal, he told John Maley.

The decision was a break for the Supreme Court, most observers thought. They would not have to rehear the case; and the Hill decision would not have to go into the permanent record. When they were informed of the plea bargain, they reversed the conviction pro forma, and returned it to the lower court. The case was set for September sixteenth.

Lawrence was brought to Burlington by two sheriffs on a raw, cloudy Friday afternoon. Newspaper and television photographers had hoped to take his picture as he came into the building, but he was brought in through the basement of the court building on Pearl Street and taken to a room on the second floor.

Sorrell waited in his third-floor office for the proceedings to begin. Until the last minute, he was not sure that Lawrence would go through with the bargain. He had signed the stipulation that the plea bargain had been reached, but he would have to sign a waiver of his rights before the deal was firm. Lawrence had never hinted, in any way, that any of his buys were fraudulent, and Sorrell was prepared to see him refuse at the last minute to plead guilty.

But shortly after one, Sorrell got the word: Lawrence was ready. Lawrence's mother and father and girlfriend, Sue Ann Stearns, waited on a bench in the second-floor hallway, while a group of reporters and photographers stood nearby. Sorrell came downstairs and disappeared into the room; then he and Maley emerged to see Judge Costello in his chambers.

Shortly after 1:30, Lawrence emerged from the private room and walked quickly into the courtroom. Those who knew him were struck by his appearance. He was, as usual, dressed elegantly in a blue plaid suit, a pale shirt, and a red necktie. He was also tanned and every hair was in place. But he was thin, almost gaunt; the pudgy Paul Lawrence of his salad days was gone. His face was a mask.

When Costello entered the courtroom, Lawrence entered his plea: guilty to the charge of false swearing in the Rabbi case. Costello went over it carefully with him. He was actually saying he was guilty of this crime. Yes, he was. Costello told him he would not accept the plea if Lawrence was giving it only for tactical reasons. He would not accept it if Lawrence was not telling him he was guilty of this crime.

Lawrence assured him he was claiming that he was guilty. That was it. As he walked from the courtroom, Lawrence was met by Wadi Sawabini, a local television newsman who had interviewed Lawrence during his first trial. Lawrence had been talkative then, claiming that he was innocent, that he would be vindicated. He saw himself as a sort of Serpico then—the misunderstood good cop.

"Hey, what's happening, Man," said Sawabini.

"No comment," Lawrence replied.

He walked quickly to an elevator, descended to the basement, and got into the back seat of the sheriff's car. He was smoking his pipe, as they pulled away.

On Friday, October 7, Lawrence came in for sentencing. He was accompanied by his family. Costello held the sentencing in a small courtroom next to the main chamber, where Lawrence had pleaded guilty earlier.

Maley opened the proceedings with a lengthy statement to the effect that Lawrence had been rehabilitated and that he would no longer benefit by incarceration. Lawrence had suffered deeply because he had gone to jail, Maley said. Not only was he a pauper, but he had been deeply humiliated by having to rub elbows in prison with those people who had been his enemies.

Costello bridled at that line: the people of the state of Vermont are not to be construed as enemies of the policeman, he said sharply. He added, however, that he was impressed by the good record that Lawrence had compiled while in prison, and he elicited the information that Lawrence had undergone training as a printer. Lawrence also took up wood carving in prison.

When Costello asked Bill Sorrell for his views, the prosecutor delivered the statement he had agreed on with Maley as part of a plea bargain. The state did not agree that the remainder of Lawrence's sentence should be suspended, Sorrell said. The crime of perjury was a very serious one, particularly when committed by a policeman.

Still, Sorrell said, if the court saw reasons for reducing the sentence, the State would be "content" with that judgment. The alternative for Sorrell would have been to object to any lighter sentence for the defendant.

Finally, Costello asked if Lawrence had anything to say.

"I'm sorry and I regret this situation did occur," he said quietly. "All I can say is, I have suffered, and I would like a chance to rebuild my life."

Costello then gave him the chance, although not in so many words. He left the maximum sentence at eight years and reduced the minimum from four years to three. That would make Lawrence eligible for parole in the fall of 1978, six months earlier than under his original term. He would not suspend that sentence, Costello said. The sentence had to be maintained in order to provide a deterrent to other policemen who might be tempted to perjure themselves on the grounds that "everybody does it."

At the same time, however, Costello said he would recommend that Lawrence be made eligible for the extended furlough program, which amounts to an early release from prison. Under this program, he would get a two-week furlough from prison, go back for a day to report to his counsellor and then, provided he did not misbehave, he would get another two weeks off. That would continue until either he was paroled or he completed his sentence.

Costello said this system would enable the Corrections Department to keep a much tighter string on Lawrence than they could under a parole system, but the net effect, nonetheless, would be to see Lawrence freed.

Whether Lawrence would be, in effect, freed under that program was not certain in the fall of 1977. The recommendation for admission to the furlough program would have to come from Michael Coxon, the Superintendent of the Prison Farm where Lawrence had been incarcerated since mid-1976. Coxon said Lawrence had been a well-behaved prisoner and that he might recommend him for the program, but that a final decision had not been made.

The authority to grant admission to the program rested with Peter Profera, the Director of Adult Correctional Facilities for Vermont, and Profera sounded considerably more dubious about the Lawrence case than Coxon did. The program is used only in unusual cases, Profera said, adding that there would have to be a compelling reason why Lawrence should get out of prison early. "Actually," he said, "if the judge felt that strongly about it, he could have given him a different sentence."

Lawrence's eventual release date from prison thus remained uncertain, as did the method—furlough, parole, completed sentence. What was clear was that the criminal justice system, despite its failures, had ended Lawrence's career at last and that the man had been punished. Even if he were to get out of jail early, he had been obviously marked by imprisonment. It showed in his face, in his

subdued manner in the courtroom, in his plea of guilty, in his statement to the court that he was sorry about what he had done.

The flip-flopping on the Lawrence matter illustrated several
larger realities about law enforcement functioning in Vermont, and
probably elsewhere. One of those was that Lawrence got far more
protection from the courts and the legal process than any of his
victims did. Some observers felt that the trial judge, Costello, gave
Lawrence no particular breaks, but that the Supreme Court had
certainly looked after his interests.

At the same time, the quality of the high court decision was
strikingly deficient, understandable perhaps in a local court, but not
from the highest court in the state.

Finally, the case illustrated that even the performance of
Gensberg, one of the most enlightened officials to deal with Lawrence, could be faulted. Gensberg had brought six charges against
Lawrence in St. Albans, two of which involved Lawrence's false
testimony about his military record. The remaining charges went to
the heart of the case against Lawrence—the contention that he had
framed his victims.

Gensberg gained convictions on the first two counts without
difficulty, but he subsequently dropped the other four charges. He
said he did so on the grounds that he had not been able to secure a trial
date for the other four charges, and that rather than let more months
go by, he would withdraw the charges. Since Lawrence had already
been convicted in Burlington, and on two counts in St. Albans,
further prosecution would be "beating a dead horse."

It would be better, Gensberg said at the time, to begin the process
of rehabilitating the victims—studying all the cases developed by
Lawrence and granting pardons where deserved—at once, rather
than to wait for the Lawrence charges to be processed.

Once the Burlington conviction was overturned, however, it became clear that there might not ultimately be any convictions of
Lawrence for the central crime of his career—framing people on false
drug charges. He would always be a convicted perjurer, of course, but
lying about his military record is nowhere near as serious as framing
people. And if there was no conviction for that, then that fact could
encourage people to claim that the charges Lawrence brought against
the hippies of St. Albans might have been valid after all.

Gensberg has been criticized for this failure by other attorneys in the state, and he is now, three years later, somewhat defensive about it. But the die had been cast: a charge on the major issue would have had to come from the Rabbi case in Burlington. If Lawrence had been finally cleared on the Rabbi charge, then he would have been able to maintain his claim that all his drug buys were good.

The inability of anyone else to contradict that, despite the huge volume of evidence as to his deceptions and lies, will be one more monument to flaws in judgment that have marked the Lawrence case from the beginning.

Until the fall of 1977, Lawrence steadfastly maintained his innocence. He claimed he was "getting close to something big" when he was arrested, and he told *The New York Times* in the summer of 1976 that his arrest was politically motivated—that someone in Patrick Leahy's office was dealing drugs and that Leahy, then running for the Senate, wanted Lawrence out of the way.

After his conviction in Burlington, Lawrence gave to the press a long, rambling statement about the case, most of which was critical of Murray and Leahy. Most of the comments were meaningless—they involved such elements as the fact that Miles and Demag had made no buys in St. Albans and that Miles once gave other drug-unit members some souvenir pipes from a drug raid.

The most interesting element in the statement was the information that Lawrence had what he called an intelligence file that spoke of "influential people" in the Burlington area being involved in the drug traffic. One of these persons, Lawrence's statement said, was in the state's attorney's office.

Lawrence's statement said that although the intelligence file had been seized in the search of his apartment and had never been returned to him, he had a duplicate file and that it would be turned over to a federal agency in Washington, which he said would be investigating his case.

One is tempted to linger over this statement only if he is unfamiliar with the Lawrence career. Needless to say, no such federal investigation has taken place, nor has anyone seen any intelligence file. It was simply Paul Lawrence doing his thing, living by his wits. Whatever his faults, Patrick Leahy was no drug dealer, nor was he likely to be. Lawrence, it seemed, had stretched his method too far.

Sources

IT WAS A WARM SPRING THURSDAY NIGHT AND HANK Coleman had his mother's station wagon for the evening. He picked up Butch Baker at about seven, and they headed for Barrington Center, the shopping mall in the middle of town. They drove into the center, and as usual, found Paul Lawrence at the drugstore. He got in the front seat, and Hank pulled the wagon back onto County Road, headed north.

Butch and Hank had told their parents they were going to the library to study, but they almost never did that. They were more interested in drinking and raising hell than they were in studying. Tonight, they would cruise . . .

Hank headed first for Hill's Package Store on Route 6 in Seekonk, just over the border in Massachusetts. Paul was nineteen and taking a postgraduate course at Barrington High; he was old enough to get served at Hill's and at some of the other mom and pop liquor stores around Rehoboth, Massachusetts, a tiny rural town near the Rhode Island border.

It was getting dark when they got to Hill's, and Paul went in for an armload of GIQs (grand imperial quarts of beer) and a bottle of "Tango," a mixture of vodka and orange drink. It didn't take long to get an edge on, drinking beer and screwdrivers, while cruising the desolate back roads of Seekonk and Rehoboth.

By nine or so, they were back in Barrington, and Butch and Hank were pretty drunk. Both waited for Paul's cue on what to do. He was a year older and had a certain charisma, built of commonplace exuberance and rebellion. Hank and Butch were followers, dominated by Paul. Butch never quite understood why, but shortly after full darkness fell, the boys were driving to the Hampden Meadows section of town, toward the home of Norman Moors, the deputy chief of the Barrington Police Department. Hank and Butch did not know Moors, but Paul did: he had had a running feud with Moors and other members of the department for a couple of years.

They drove by the Moors house slowly. A typical one-family frame home, it was located just a block or so from Paul's home at 3 Greenwood Avenue. The Moors home was dark—empty for the evening. Hank parked a short distance down the street, near the corner, and Butch got quickly out of the car, carrying a GIQ. Paul had not told him to do it, but in a vague way he felt it was Paul's idea and he knew Paul would approve. Butch felt no animosity toward Moors.

He walked quickly toward the deputy chief's house and then walked onto the front lawn. In the front of the darkened house was a big picture window, and, taking aim, Butch fired the heavy bottle as hard as he could. He was turning to leave when he heard the heavy crash, and he trotted back to the car.

"They'll never catch us," Paul said as Butch got back into the car.

Having succeeded so well at the Moors home, the boys headed for Chief John Medici's home on Maple Avenue on the other side of town. On the way they stopped to steal a supply of white rocks that adorned the driveway of a house. Medici had a front window that would make a good target also . . .

What the boys didn't know was that Norman Moors had been sitting in his darkened living room when Butch threw the bottle. He leaped up when the bottle crashed against the shutter next to the window, breaking the shutter and falling to the porch. As he looked out, he saw a station wagon pull away, and he called the station with a description.

Lieutenant Mike Venditoulli was on Upland Way when he got the call about the bottle incident. Shortly thereafter, he saw the Coleman station wagon, and he could see that the occupants were drinking. That was more than enough to pull them over, and when he looked in the car, he saw both the heavy beer bottles and the white rocks.

"Drive to the police station and I'll follow you," he said.

"There's no way they can prove anything," Paul insisted as they swung the car around. "Deny everything, deny everything."

When they got to the police station, the three boys were taken first into a conference room, then taken into separate rooms for questioning. Butch denied everything. He continued to deny everything when they called his mother, since he was a juvenile. But someone broke down, and they found out that Butch had thrown the bottle. They put him on probation for that, after an appearance in juvenile court. Nothing happened to Paul.

Butch was not surprised. Paul always seemed to get off, although he was the wildest one in the crowd. But Paul's wildness was by no means unique. There was a deep sense of alienation among the teen-agers in Barrington in the early 1960s. A newspaper writer of the time said the town's major problem was suburban morality . . . "teenage drinking and the general mores of youngsters in a high-pressure town where executive fathers stretch themselves thin; where there's a surfeit of money, luxury, and, for wives at least, leisure."

To the visitor, the town would seem to be a suburban idyll; its sixteen thousand people live in a series of quiet neighborhoods on the northeast shoulder of Narragansett Bay. The town is cut by the Barrington and Warren rivers; it is notable for having the highest family income in the state; people live in big comfortable homes and their boats ride in tiny yacht basins. It is comfortable for the executives that move in and out of the town, but it can be dull for young people.

To the casual observer, the young people seemed to fall into three categories then: the athletes, the steady daters, and the partygoers. Some of them were deeply rebellious youngsters who got into juvenile scrapes and taunted the police, spent as little time in school as possible, and seemed to be constantly pursuing their favorite pastimes: drinking and going to parties. Paul Lawrence was one of those.

He lived in a red and white frame and brick colonial in a neighborhood of middle-class homes, not as pretentious as the bigger homes on Rumstick Road and Nyatt Point over on the bay, but comfortable nevertheless. Paul's family was deeply religious, and he served as an altar boy at St. Luke's Church; he continued to attend mass on Sunday even when he was drinking and fencing with the police. He attended LaSalle Academy for one year, but the rest of his high school years were spent at Barrington High School. A massive, low-slung red brick building on Lincoln Avenue, it is the centerpiece of what is considered one of the best school systems in Rhode Island.

Paul was an indifferent student, although all of his friends thought he was very bright. He was also something of an athlete, playing first string on the soccer team and running cross-country. To his soccer coach, George Gallipeau, Paul was a good kid who treated his coach with respect. The coach liked him, although he felt he didn't know him very well; he also thought no one else knew Paul very well.

Paul was a better than average player, but he wasn't an eager player, the coach thought. He also didn't have the stamina to be a great soccer player; he would not train hard enough, and Gallipeau suspected him of drinking too much beer. And although he and Paul got along well, Gallipeau was occasionally troubled vaguely by what he thought was Paul's willingness to flout authority and to annoy the police . . .

The people who knew the heavyset man with the moustache who appeared in police stations and courtrooms in Vermont ten years later probably would not recognize the Paul Lawrence of his Barrington years. The boy who stares out of yearbook pictures is lean, but well-built, with a baby face and a shock of short hair that scooped down over his forehead. The pictures of Paul on the soccer and cross-country teams and as a member of the junior class social committee are never smiling; he seems moody, quiet, almost petulant.

Perhaps the school atmosphere accounts for it, for Paul Lawrence was considered by his friends to be a notorious wild man and party crasher. In his senior year, he was one of what the kids called "The Magnificent Seven," the wildest of the partygoers. The more berserk one went at parties, the higher he stood in the estimation of his peers. The major activity of these kids was drinking. Geoff Reynolds, one of Paul's friends, would often load a cooler of beer into his old gray Falcon and drive it to school; the guys would drink the beer in the parking lot during the day.

By the time they were fifteen or sixteen, the kids in Barrington discovered the bars of Warren, a tiny town to the south. Barrington was a dry town; there were no bars, and the only places one could drink publicly were in the posh private clubs, such as the Rhode Island Country Club. But Warren was anything but dry.

Warren is a small, run-down village dotted with bars that are redolent of the town's nautical past. The Barrington kids discovered these havens early: the Rainbow Cafe, the Saint Joseph Polish Club. The Moonlight Cafe on Metacom Avenue was typical—an old ramshackle bar with a television set, a few tables, and a gas-burning stove. The clientele consisted of town workers and quahaugers, men with lined faces and big shoulders who spend their days hand-tonging hard-shelled clams off the floor of the bay: working-class people, different from Barrington adults—the executives and the housewives wrapped up in the garden and bridge clubs and the Junior League. There was a sort of cachet to rubbing shoulders with these older men, watching TV and drinking shots and beer . . . "a little spot of tea [Seagram Seven], please."

On nights before a dance, or before a football game, fifty or sixty kids would crowd into these bars, drinking and roistering, an occasional imbiber jumping onto the bar and racing its length, kicking over all the drinks, the wilder the better.

When they weren't at the bars, or driving around in someone's car, they were looking for a party at someone's house, preferably a house where the parents were not home. To people like Paul Lawrence and Butch Baker and the others, there was no such thing as a party you couldn't crash. And if the kids for some reason didn't like the family where the party was being held, they wrecked the house. Butch and the others would never forget a party at one house where someone pulled the phone out of the wall, somebody put the clothes of the woman of the house in the bathtub and turned on the water, and Paul Lawrence handed out the family Christmas presents to the kids at the party. "They were absolutely wild," Billy Reynolds said of those Barrington parties. "I've never seen anything like them."

Billy's brother Geoff was a rambunctious kid like Paul, and Paul used to come often to the Reynolds house to visit. Their sister, Polly, who was several years younger than her brothers, remembers Lawrence as the most charming of the youths who hung around. He would often come up to her room to talk, and he made a point of being pleasant to her parents. He would go out to the kitchen to make small talk with her mother, something for which most of the kids did not have the poise.

The kids, however, considered Paul an "Eddie Haskell," the youngster on the "Leave It to Beaver" television show who charms parents and then inspires their offspring to all sorts of mischief. Kids like Butch Baker and Hank Coleman (now solid, responsible citizens) didn't much trust Paul. Although they spent a lot of time with him, they were not truly close, and Butch, for one, thought he was the sneakiest kid he ever met.

One of Paul's favorite stunts, which he sometimes let Butch watch, was to call up someone's parents to tell them their son was drunk. "I hate to tell you this, Mrs. Blank, but your son is drunk and passed out behind the Moonlight," was the way the conversations would go. Another stunt, one with more menace, involved a call to the draft board about George Storey, one of the youngsters in town. Paul called the draft board, identified himself as Storey, and said he wasn't doing anything and would not mind getting drafted. Storey soon afterward found himself in Vietnam.

Butch himself got a draft notice the week he graduated from high school; he was the only kid he knew who got one at that time. Butch loved the army, but he wondered later whether Paul Lawrence had anything to do with the fact that he had been called.

A decade later, Butch Baker, Bill Reynolds, and his sister, Polly, spent a day driving around Barrington and Warren, reminiscing about Paul Lawrence and the way they had all grown up. None of them had been surprised when they opened *Time* magazine one day in 1974 to see Paul Lawrence, cop gone bad, framer of hundreds of people, staring at them from the pages. None of the three was surprised at all.

"He was infamous," said Bill Reynolds. And all three had what seemed like an inexhaustible fund of stories about wild Lawrence escapades, mostly in the company of three or four other local youths. There was the night that a gang of kids from nearby Riverside crashed a party at Paul's house, and he drove them off with a volley of gunshots from his bedroom window. And the impulse trip to Florida, when the son of a local car dealer took one of his father's cars and they took off in the middle of the winter, only to break down in Delaware.

Before the engine was cool, Paul Lawrence was back on the highway, hitchhiking north. The car was somebody else's problem.

Lawrence, they said, was prone to violence, charming, amoral, with a commitment only to a good time and a loyalty to no one, including his friends.

He was arrested on several occasions for minor scrapes, but the only thing that went on his record was a conviction for the "possession of malt beverages." Most of the time he was picked up for juvenile offenses, and Chief Medici, now retired, remembers Paul and his father coming to the sessions the local cops had on weekends to lecture errant youngsters on the need to obey the law.

Chief Medici was in the hospital in 1974 when the story about Paul Lawrence broke. He saw it in *Time,* and he scrawled across the top of the page, for the benefit of the next reader: "One bad cop."

The Victims

GARY BURBANK WAS HARD TO FIND. "LOOK FOR HIM AT Backstreet about four," one friend said. "He lives at Jack Welch's place on French Hill," said another. "There's no way to tell whether you'll find him." "He wrecked his truck so sometimes he crashes with friends. If you find him late in the day, he may be drinking . . . he's always into a bottle."

Late December 1976 . . . twenty degrees below zero. The road to John Welch's mounts French Hill outside St. Albans in a long curve, pitches over the top of a plateau, and winds down the other side, past the tiny shack where Jane Eaton, one of the other Lawrence victims, lives, past the swamp, now snow-covered and spiked with reeds, and finally past an old farmhouse flanked by a driveway. A short distance up the driveway, actually an old logging road, is the Welch place, a dilapidated cottage. An old car, its hood up and snow drifted into the engine compartment, stands out front.

Gary's friends said he had an electric blanket so he could survive the cold, and that he lived in one room, heated by a wood stove. It was impossible to see much through the front door, peering through the dirt and gloom; blankets had been hung over several of the windows.

The woodshed door beside the house was padlocked. Burbank was not home.

It took three days to find him, leaving messages with his friends. He was straight—sober—and we talked for an hour. He leaned forward, his elbows on his knees, speaking quietly and haltingly about his experiences with Paul Lawrence. Gary had a moustache, but no longer a beard, and he was dressed in the manner of the youth of the region—corduroy jeans and several layers of flannel shirts.

The first time I had seen Burbank was a couple of months earlier; it was in the evening at Backstreet, and Burbank had not seemed fully sober. At the time he seemed obsessed by his arrest by Lawrence and his subsequent conviction. He muttered about monstrous injustice, about a system that could permit such a thing. How could this happen, he asked over and over. No one had any answer.

Now he discussed the issue in more personal terms. Throughout his life, people had trusted him, he said.

"Suddenly, they didn't trust me or believe me when I said it was all bullshit," he said. "I didn't say I was a Goody Two-shoes. I made illegal left-hand turns, I smoked marijuana. I admitted these things to be sincere, straightforward—a real person, not one who never does anything wrong. But when you sell drugs, that's a real taboo. I heard people say, "If Gary was accused by the police, then he did it." Nothing I said made any difference.

"That has an effect on you," he said, seeming to search for the right words. "When you lose credibility, you lose a certain amount of contact with the foundations of being."

Gary was not only deeply wounded by the attitude of the community; he was devastated by the effect his experience had had on his family. Gary's father had left his mother when he was seven years old, and he had been very close to his mother and to his grandmother. From an early age, Gary had been the man of the house, a role he liked. Recently, his mother had married again.

After he was arrested, Gary's family stood by him, but their attitude was a burden in a way. "You know you are innocent, so what have you got to worry about?" they said to him. But Gary was less certain: he knew about the experience of other Lawrence victims, and he did not have the blithe confidence in local law enforcement that his parents did.

The defense cost Gary's mother, now Mrs. Dorothy Larry, six

thousand dollars, which the family could ill afford, and when Gary was convicted, he was fiercely angry.

"It destroyed my family," he said. "I had told the truth in court. I took a lie detector test. I spent money to get witnesses here, and they couldn't get on the stand. Anything he [Lawrence] could say against me was wide open. I could see when I went in there I was going to get railroaded."

As for an appeal, it seemed to him just one more way the system would squeeze money out of his family. In any case, he was totally alienated by then, sinking back into a simmering bitterness. The authorities in St. Albans were obviously corrupt. The heroin busts were the tip-off. If there was so much heroin around, where were the addicts, where were the people with tracks on their arms; why hadn't anyone suffered an overdose?

After the trial, Gary also struck out against his stepfather. He and his golfing buddies paid the taxes that supported the establishment; they were paying for all this bullshit, he thought. And they never had to worry about it happening to them.

Worst of all was the fact that the trial had, in a way, come between Gary and his grandmother. They had always been close, and the old woman loved him deeply. Until he was six, he and his parents had lived in the same house as his grandmother. When he was in high school, he worked as a stock boy at the W. T. Grant store on North Main Street, and he would eat lunch at his grandmother's house. She had been opposed to his working at Tuner's, and her attitude after the trial seemed to be: if you associate with that kind of people, that's what you've got to expect.

After the trial, Gary began to drink more heavily, and to drift, physically and emotionally.

"Not that I didn't drink before, but it was fun, not problem drinking. Afterwards, I would spend weeks doing absolutely nothing. I feared for my life because I was afraid that since some people thought I was guilty, some irate father would come gunning for me."

The arrest of Paul Lawrence in Burlington was not the end of the nightmare for Gary Burbank. Lawrence was still free at the time, and the authorities in St. Albans refused to admit they had been wrong in sponsoring and supporting Lawrence. Mayor Ken Kaye's remark that he and other city officials were still convinced they arrested the right people was particularly galling.

In late 1974, the psychological pressure growing out of his problem with Lawrence drove Gary to the Franklin County Mental Health Clinic to seek help. It was not just the Lawrence thing; he was what he called "severely emotional" over his experience in Vietnam, where he spent four years as a photographer on a ship. But the worst thing was that rage and bitterness over his false arrest were sapping his ability to cope with life.

In the winter of 1976–77, Gary was still drinking heavily, he said, but there were indications he was straightening out.

He had shaved off his beard at Christmas time for the sake of his grandmother. "I don't know how long she has to live," he said. He was also working some: he carried a briefcase, full of odds and ends, and he said he had lots of things going. He said he bought and sold cars, he wheeled and dealed. He was trying to market dried beans, and trying to put together some sort of truck-driving scheme.

He closed up his briefcase, and we left the office together. Outside it was getting dark, and cold.

"You can never know him as he was," said Gary Burbank's mother. "He's not the same person," she continued. "He was always such a calm, cool, placid individual who to me . . ." She stopped for a moment. "I can see a decided change in him. It's a defense mechanism — what's the use, everything I touch goes wrong. I don't think he can overcome it, he could never be the individual he was."

Mrs. Larry now lives in a small house on a quiet residential street in St. Albans. She has been a nurse at Krebs Hospital for many years; she knows many people in town, including George Hebert, the former police chief. She spoke at length, almost compulsively, about what Gary's arrest did to her and her family. Gary is her only son; she also has a daughter, Victoria, who is seven years younger. Gary's arrest not only badly damaged her son, it damaged her and her daughter.

"I'm on the defensive," she said. "I was so naive until this hit me. About the system and how an innocent person can be so badly hurt, economically and emotionally. I raised him to believe in gung ho America, the red, white, and blue. Justice will prevail. If you tell the truth, nothing will happen to you. I feel like a lamb led to slaughter."

"When this so crushingly came down on us and having never been involved before, we were totally shocked by it.

"I don't believe for a minute Carl Gregg didn't know what Paul Lawrence was," she said scornfully. "Look, these men aren't stupid. If *we* could learn everything about Paul Lawrence, how could *they* not know about Paul Lawrence? He certainly had to be an instrument . . ."

Most of Mrs. Burbank's friends and acquaintances, although sympathetic in some cases, thought Gary was guilty. If he wasn't guilty, why would the police have arrested him? Everyone knew there was a lot of drug traffic at Tuner's, and if he worked there, it was not surprising he got involved.

Mrs. Larry ran into this attitude shortly after Gary's arrest. She walked into a patient's room at the hospital, and the woman asked whether she was Gary Burbank's mother. She said she was.

"I'm sorry for you, but glad they caught him," the woman said. "If you play with fire you get burned."

She protested that he was innocent, but the patient, like most people she talked to, discounted that. They expected his mother to defend him.

Still, the heaviest burden for Mrs. Larry to bear now is the loss of close contact with her son. She said he feels guilty about the money he owes her for the defense. She is also unhappy about Gary's current life-style. "I don't think of him as the same person," she said. "I see him crying, I see him drink too much. I see him pace the floor . . . he's so frustrated."

Mrs. Larry's bitterness keeps spilling over as she talks. She said she had been a churchgoer, but that she would never go to her church again. "I feel like everybody there is a hypocrite." She paces the floor herself at night, hearing the jury foreman saying the word "Guilty."

"It's a terrible, sick feeling," she said. "I don't think I can ever put it aside."

For her mother, Mrs. Ida Lawton, Gary's grandmother, the nightmare will never go away. She was eighty-three at the time I talked to Gary's mother.

"She is not going to live long enough," Mrs. Burbank said. "She keeps saying, 'Is he free?' I say, 'Mother, he is not in jail, he is not on probation,' but I can't really make her understand . . ."

Jane Eaton was easy to find. She and Ruth Jette lived in a one-car garage that had been converted into a hovel. I visited them

one frigid morning, shortly after they had gotten up. Jane was trying
to light a fire in the potbellied stove in the middle of the room, pouring
kerosene on a few wet sticks while drying a bigger log in the oven of
the electric stove. "Roast elm," she called it. A pale light filtered
through the plastic covering a single front window, but it was enough
to see that winter living on French Hill could be incredibly
primitive—no running water, no toilet, just a cot covered with dirty
blankets. There was an electric stove that Gary Burbank had wired
up, the wood stove, an old chair. The walls were lined with insulation.

Jane's friends had warned that she would be hard to find sober.
She had been banned from Backstreet for tipping a table over on
someone, which she insisted was completely justified; but she was
clear-eyed as she tugged on a pair of heavy boots.

Otto Kremer had been right: Jane was beautiful. She was of
medium height and slim, with big hazel eyes, long auburn hair that
caught the sunlight, and a bright smile.

As she offered me the cabin's only chair, I wondered to myself
whether she, like Gary Burbank, had been deeply scarred by her
experience. Before I could ask, she brushed her hair out of her eyes,
smiled a wicked smile, and said: "It's because of Paul Lawrence that I
have to live like this."

Although she had been arrested and thrown in jail, and had
suffered like the others, the Paul Lawrence experience had passed
over her life like a shadow. The only aftermath she could point to was
a star-shaped scar in the middle of her forehead. The doctor told her it
was from a boil, and that the boil might have been caused by emotional strain.

Otherwise, Jane had been drifting, trying college briefly and
dropping out, doing occasional factory work or picking fruit, collect-
ing welfare and unemployment payments. She had used soft drugs for
some time, marijuana and speed mostly, some acid, and when I met
her, she drank heavily. Now she and Ruth Jette were planning to
leave the hovel on French Hill and travel; they could not say where
. . . perhaps to see friends in Connecticut, then maybe to the
Washington area.

"I've got itchy feet," she says simply. "I really like Vermont, but I
don't care for St. Albans. It's too big and I like small towns." She
doesn't care about Backstreet any more; the people there are into
clothes—she doesn't feel comfortable. She preferred the atmosphere

at Tuner's. And now she likes Bensons, the local bar so graceless and devoid of warmth or atmosphere as to make even drinking almost painful.

Traveling would soothe her spirit, she said. She and Ruth would have a "really good stash, perhaps four hundred dollars," and that would last them a long time. How long? A long time. "We ain't eatin' in no restaurants or sleepin' in motels," she said. It would be life in a van. But at least if they went south, it would be warmer.

Pain is one of Paul Lawrence's legacies. Gary Burbank feels it daily, years later, in the nagging realization that the powerful people of his community wanted to destroy him, were willing to go to great lengths to do so. Jane Eaton feels it another way: she is more alienated, thus less affected. She drifted after her arrest, as she had before.

Lawrence left a mark on all the lives he touched, regardless of the victim's background. Christine Currey has returned to the Buffalo area, and she seems to have a bright future. She is well-educated and comes from an affluent family: time ought to heal her wounds, there should be no lasting scars on her life. But there nevertheless seem to be. She is bitter about what happened to her; she cannot talk about it without becoming upset. Having been framed seems to engender a rage—it is harder to accept than other, apparently more serious, travails of life such as injury or the loss of a loved one.

The thread that runs through conversations with the victims is a combination of bitterness about being framed and a deep-seated need to understand. What was the *reason* for this, the victims want to know. They do not blame Lawrence alone: the rest of the community—the judge, the police, the prosecutor, the politicians, the general public—also are held responsible. It is hard for an observer to fathom how deeply the psychological damage runs. Virtually everyone has had the experience of being wronged in life—by family, by friends, by teachers, on the job. Yet somehow there is always an appeal to a larger world: you *can* be exonerated. But if you are attacked by the state, by the very institutions of society, where do you find justice, where is the refuge?

If you can be wronged by the police and the courts and the political structure, then how are you to be sure that everything is not poisoned? Should you expect to be cheated by clerks, by bank tellers, by gas station attendants? Perhaps there are no limits . . . perhaps the business of government is conspiracy. This kind of speculation, to which many of the victims seem driven, can lead to full-blown paranoia.

"How could they let this happen?"

Only the Lawrence victims know the full meaning of that question. Coping emotionally with that question is something that each of the victims has had to do, and they have had problems doing so. Statistics are a form of currency in our society, and in fact, the defense attorneys can recite a litany of instances where Lawrence's charges ruined lives: one man was divorced as a result of the charges against him; another suspect collapsed mentally and had to be institutionalized; others were alienated from their families. Ultimately, however, the Lawrence legacy defies cataloguing. No one knows for sure, nor can anyone measure the impact on each person.

Sonny Cross, the young hippie who was convicted of selling heroin and cocaine and who served several months in jail, has enrolled at Johnson State College and has become a serious student. He is working his way through school, with a part-time job in the administration office. But the Lawrence arrest hangs over him still. "I've got total paronoia," he said in the spring of 1977. "If I even get pulled over by a traffic cop, it's a really rotten scene . . ."

When Norman Young was released from prison in the spring of 1974, he went to New Mexico, where he worked in a mine. In his letters to his attorney, Jim Levy, Young has said he is doing well there. But he can scarcely talk or think about his experience with Lawrence in Vermont without breaking down.

"I never in my life felt so much bitterness as I did when I was convicted and I sat behind those bars knowing that all those arrested would be convicted of crimes they didn't commit," he wrote.

"My bitterness has really been a problem to me," he continued. "Last summer before I was busted I had a future planned for myself, but that went down the drain the day they put my name in their toilet bowl . . . Now I'll never be able to make a living in Vermont the way I wanted to. My name is marked in people's minds and not all of them will want to forget."

Otto Kremer lives with the pain daily, too. He can talk at length about Lawrence and about the politicians, philosophize about it, about the way the town was, and about what the bar was like: he's intelligent and articulate, and as a radical political activist he knows that the reality of Lawrence was probably not as bad as what might have happened if there was a right-wing coup in the United States (the expectation of many radicals). But the talk of a massive crackdown by the establishment was rhetoric, and Lawrence was reality. That is why Otto's hands shake slightly when you talk to him, and why he will tell you that you just don't forget about or get over something like the Lawrence frame-up.

That is why he tried the doctor and the antidepressant pills, and that is also why he gave them up: he is going to have to live with the effects of the Lawrence affair. And he knows it. What is more difficult to deal with is the realization that in many ways nothing has changed, at least not in a fundamental way. He still hears people say that as the most visible owner of Tuner's Place, he was the one who turned the young kids in St. Albans onto drugs.

In the spring of 1977, Otto sat at a restaurant in Berkshire, a small town north of St. Albans, eating a hamburger. A man sidled up to him and asked: "Can I buy some grass?"

"I don't sell grass," he said.

"Oh, I heard you were the one to see," the man said.

"I hardly even smoke it any more, let alone sell it," Otto said.

That's why his hands shake.

In the wake of the Lawrence arrest and conviction, Governor Salmon set up a commission to study all of the Lawrence cases and to recommend ways for the state to redress the wrongs suffered by his victims. In his investigation, Gensberg located 240 persons who had been convicted of drug-abuse charges either entirely or partially on the basis of evidence provided by Paul Lawrence. That was well below the six hundred arrests that had become attached to the Lawrence legend that had grown up in the press, but it was an enormous number nevertheless.

The figure of 240 included the dozens arrested in St. Albans, a few that Lawrence had arrested while police chief in Vergennes, and the arrests made in his five years as a member of the Vermont State Police. A large number of cases—Tony Badamo and Christine Currey were among them—were pending when Lawrence was arrested. Those cases were dropped immediately.

In the fall of 1976, the gubernatorial commission submitted its recommendations. Seventy-one persons convicted on the basis of evidence given by Lawrence should be pardoned, the commission said. Another twelve should not get pardons, the commission said, although its report noted that several of these involved cases where the conviction did not rest on Lawrence's word alone. He had worked with other police officers while in the state police. There were other cases where the suspect had admitted making a sale to Lawrence; those included some of the Brattleboro cases.

The report by the commission did not include names—part of the effort to rehabilitate the victims will be to clear the record of their arrest and convictions.

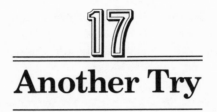

Another Try

WHEN PAUL LAWRENCE DRIFTED INTO VERMONT IN 1965, no one could predict the long shadow he would soon cast across the state. He had little to recommend him but a quick intelligence and an ability to live by his wits, honed by years of dueling with authority, from the police of his home town to the army officers he encountered at Fort Dix. His prospects for a career should have been poor: he had no college degree, a mediocre high school record, no work experience to speak of, and a less than honorable discharge from the army.

Yet Lawrence quickly found a niche for himself as a tough cop. He was transformed: he could arrest people. When he said they had done something wrong, prosecutors and juries believed him and the "wrongdoers" were swept away.

Lawrence was respected and believed, and that respect and credibility were a form of power over people, the sort of power that, despite his innate gifts, he had never had. Lawrence was determined to turn that power to his own purposes, and in so doing he increasingly played on the weaknesses and failure of the public and the officials with whom he dealt. He learned that he could manipulate his police superiors, juries, prosecutors, and judges. And when he could not manipulate them, he found that most of them lacked the resolution to move decisively against him.

In retrospect it seems fair to ask, was this a man so formidable and so persuasive that other men were inevitably blinded by his gifts or intimidated by his power? A look at Lawrence's career does not support such a conclusion. He was bright and quick, an excellent liar, but he was, as his career progressed, increasingly easy to see through. He made no long-range plans, so his charges and stories and scenarios were rife with inconsistency. He often overplayed his hand and got careless, thereby providing some of his targets with alibis when he had to do no more than be sure that the suspect was at a certain place at a certain time. As his career progressed and his arrest and conviction record grew, such mistakes increased in frequency.

To examine Lawrence's career, therefore, is to watch a seemingly relentless accretion of failures, stupidity, and omissions on the part of the public officials charged with guarding the public good and safety, and a corresponding failure of the system itself: a steady stream of people were convicted of crimes they did not commit. Lawrence was a test for these public officials and for the system, and it was a test largely failed. It was a rather rare test, for while cops who cut corners are common, those with Lawrence's nerve and ambition are not; but it was not a particularly difficult test. At virtually any stage in his career, a rigorous performance on the part of responsible public officials would have halted Lawrence's career. It was only after eight years of *failure,* culminating in a crescendo of injustice in St. Albans, that the man was finally stopped.

The end for Lawrence came when he went to Burlington and encountered a different set of individuals: Kevin Bradley was an unusual cop, Frank Murray a highly principled prosecutor. One could say that it was only a matter of time until Lawrence ran afoul of this type of public servant, but such an observation would be problematical. Eight years is a very long time to wait for that sort of confrontation. If Lawrence had stayed in St. Albans, he might have been able to prosecute his campaign indefinitely, establishing injustice as a way of life, as the norm rather than an aberration.

Why this opportunity existed there and then, and why it exists as a possibility in so many other places today, is clear from conversations with or examinations of the behavior of the officials who failed in the Lawrence case. They were not all bad men, far from it. Some were highly motivated. But they all had reasons, reasons that seemed — and in some cases, unfortunately, still seem — good enough to ignore Lawrence or to overlook the evidence. And in the case of St. Albans itself, some people there still believe that Lawrence helped their town, that he was their benefactor, and that they are the worse for his unmasking.

Others regret their failure deeply; some are deeply scarred by it, a benign fact of the Lawrence legacy. In this later response lies the hope that another Lawrence would find less fertile ground in which to plant injustice. Yet, full acceptance of responsibility is the exception in the Lawrence case, not the norm.

One of those scarred by the case is former Attorney General Kim Cheney. He was one who may have paid a price for his failure. In the November election following the Lawrence arrest in mid-1974, Cheney was defeated in his bid for reelection by Jerry Diamond, the former Windham County prosecutor. There is no way to tell whether or not he lost because of the Lawrence affair, but it probably was a contributing factor. Cheney was criticized by the left for failing to apprehend Lawrence himself and by conservatives for his quick decision to drop all prosecution of Lawrence cases before Lawrence himself had been tried. The career that Cheney lost had been a promising one in Vermont. A graduate of Yale Law School, Cheney was a young, liberal Republican who had moved up fast.

Cheney practices law in a small, second-story office in Montpelier, and he was willing to talk about the Lawrence case. He made no effort to excuse himself, although he had to struggle to suppress the bitterness he feels about Bill Keefe, his former deputy.

Keefe had assured him that Lawrence was reliable, that the defense attorneys in St. Albans were satisfied that the lie detector tests had shown their clients to be guilty. He had also been assured about the validity of the Lawrence cases by Ron Kilburn, whom he considered to have "impeccable integrity." Nevertheless, he had begun to change his mind on the issue after he talked to Jim Levy in the spring; that was why he went to Glenn Davis of the state police and urged him to bring in a narc to set up Lawrence. Davis went ahead with the plan, Cheney said, but it was too late by then — Burlington officials were already closing in on Lawrence. There was no way to gainsay his failure to read all the signs that were present as early as the February 1973 meeting with the St. Albans bar.

"Somewhere," he said quietly, "the clues were missing for me—I just didn't pick them up."

A man with a deserved reputation as a civil libertarian, Cheney is still bothered by his own and other officials' failures to stop Lawrence, but he also sees some positive reactions to the case. One of these is a statewide reluctance on the part of both the state police and local departments and county prosecutors to accept one-on-one drug cases. Although there may be an occasional exception, most law-enforcement officials are insisting that at least two cops take part in a drug sale, with the second man able to see the transaction. Most small departments have not enough men for an operation like that, so for at least the first three years after the Lawrence arrest, small departments have for the most part given up undercover drug work.

Cheney was one side of the Lawrence coin, a good man who was too trusting and who lacked the sensitivity to police malfeasance that inspired men like Murray and Bradley and Leahy. They were infuriated by the idea of Lawrence's depredations, and they acted swiftly and surely on far less information than Cheney had. Cheney likewise failed to understand Bill Keefe, who was the other side of the Lawrence coin. Keefe was an apparently honest man, but he was not bright enough to see through Lawrence, and he had no real understanding about the role he ought to play.

A deputy attorney general and the prosecutor of the first wave of St. Albans defendants, Keefe would not talk about the Lawrence case, but he appeared to have learned little from his experience, despite the fact that he was one of the few who suffered because of his mistakes. When Jerry Diamond took office in 1975, he removed Keefe as head of the criminal justice section of the attorney general's office. For a while, Keefe did odds and ends of legal work, including handling traffic cases. Diamond later permitted him to prosecute murder cases, which are relatively easy for a prosecutor.

Most murders are crimes of passion, not seriously planned crimes; prosecuting them is often a matter of bringing an obviously guilty party to court and keeping the defendant from successfully using the defense of insanity. Even in that role, however, Keefe has had his problems. In 1977, the Vermont Supreme Court overturned a murder conviction Keefe had obtained, partly because of errors by the trial judge, but also due to improper prosecutorial behavior on the part of Keefe.

Keefe seems to consider himself simply an arm of the police, rather than an officer of the court with an ultimate responsibility to see justice done. In a trial—the Gary Burbank trial was a good example—Keefe just hammers away with whatever evidence he has, even if that includes describing Burbank as the perpetrator of more than one hundred crimes against the state of Vermont because he smoked marijuana occasionally.

The manner in which Keefe brushed off the Champlain Security Systems Report about Lawrence, the way he utilized a faulty set of lie detector data, his refusal to confront information he received from people like Diamond, who had known Lawrence previously, his willingness to mislead his boss about the situation in St. Albans—all this leads to the conclusion that Keefe was not fit for the post he held.

Thus, Cheney and Keefe, two of the most important law enforcement officials in the state, faced with a sizeable body of evidence about Lawrence's background, refused, for different reasons, to act decisively. These were glaring failures. But there were many smaller failures as well.

When Lawrence came to Burlington to be a patrolman in 1966, no one checked the military records that would have shown that he had been given a less than honorable discharge for character and behavior disorders. If they had, someone might have had second thoughts about giving the man the badge, the power of arrest, and the other powers of a policeman. When he went to the Vermont State Police the following year, no one there checked those records either.

On his resumé, Lawrence always listed his discharge as honorable; and he testified in connection with a trial early in his career that he had served two years, reaching the rank of private. He was prepared from the beginning, in other words, to lie about his military record. A check by the state police would have disclosed that. In his report to the governor after Lawrence's arrest, Robert Gensberg noted:

"No one can fail to be impressed by the failure of the Vermont State Police to conduct an adequate background investigation as part of the employment process. In hiring a man who is going to be armed with a weapon, have the power of arrest, be entrusted with con-

traband material and expensive equipment, and represent and have
the full power of the law, the lack of any information relating to the
applicant's integrity, honesty, dedication to public service, and understanding of the professional standards that will be required of him
are damning in the extreme."

These omissions, apparently of such marginal importance in and
of themselves, continued to mount in the Lawrence case, raising the
question of how well justice is administered here, or in fact, in most
places. Jerry Diamond and his assistants spotted Lawrence as being a
suspicious operator early—in only a couple of months—and they
moved against him, but not in a finally decisive way. What they did
was understandable: they wrote to his superiors and said the man
was trouble. Diamond told Lawrence that unless he would take a lie
detector test, Diamond would not prosecute any more of his cases.
Lawrence refused, and he had to leave the county.

The state police never answered the letter from Garvan Murtha,
Diamond's deputy, but Diamond said later that the next couple of
narcs sent into his county by the state police came to him and, without
being asked, volunteered to take a lie detector test whenever Diamond wanted them to.

Diamond concluded from this, and undoubtedly accurately, that
the state police understood his complaint, and that they intended to
deal with it, at least to the point of precluding a similar problem with
Lawrence's successors. But that is a sizeable step from dealing with
Lawrence himself. And neither Diamond nor the state police did that.
Diamond was very young then, and perhaps it was unrealistic to hope
that he might do what Leahy and Murray ultimately did in Burlington. Moreover, Lawrence was apparently simply embellishing
his stories in Brattleboro, not faking buys altogether.

Still, there was no intrinsic reason why Diamond could not have
exposed Lawrence as a liar. And the failure to stop him in Windham
County undoubtedly encouraged him to think that juries in other
places could be manipulated so as to bring in guilty verdicts against
the dirty, longhaired drug users of the streets.

Even after Lawrence left the Windham County area, there was a
steadily growing body of evidence as to his unreliability; yet it was
four years before he would be forced to leave. And the manner of his
leaving was such as to solve the state police's problem, while turning
a dangerous rogue loose on the local communities of the state. If

Lawrence's official records had reflected the problems he had—if they had shown the unreliable testimony and Diamond's move to force him out of the Brattleboro area, the shooting spree at Farrell Distributing, the beating of an unarmed man with a flashlight— then even so unsophisticated a police officer as George Hebert might not have hired him in St. Albans, and even such weak public reeds as Michael McGinn, Ron Kilburn, and Bill Keefe might not have defended him so vigorously.

Why the Vermont State Police failed as they did must, like many of the judgments about the Lawrence case, be speculative. One likelihood is that the Vermont State Police is something less than a crack law-enforcement organization. Much of Vermont is rural; the job of the state police is therefore heavily involved with traffic control and the patrolling of lonely roads. There is only one metropolitan area in the state, and comparatively little crime.

The response of the Vermont State Police to the growing drug problems of the 1960s was therefore rather tentative: their drug unit normally had only four men, and the supervision was not particularly skilled. No one at the time knew much about drugs, and as Major Davis conceded, they had to learn as they went along.

Beyond that, the reason for the failure of the Vermont State Police to deal responsibly with Paul Lawrence seems to lie in the fortress mentality of the police, an "us against the world" feeling that showed up clearly in a conversation with Major Davis. He is the number-two man in the department, a career state police officer. He is responsible to the commissioner of public safety, who is a political appointee. Edward Corcoran, a former army officer, was commissioner at the time Lawrence left the department. He would not talk about the Lawrence case; he said he was one of those officials being sued by the Lawrence victims, and that his lawyer had advised him not to talk.

Davis would discuss the case, but he was cautious and defensive about it. He acknowledged that his department had had difficulty with drugs when the issue had first come up; it was hard to find good supervisors, and undercover men were difficult to handle. Finally, he said, they worked out a procedure that called for assigning a minimum of two men to a drug buy, and a practice of bringing undercover men back into uniform after a year or so. These procedures were adopted before the Paul Lawrence arrest, he said.

Asked specifically about the possibility of an officer faking buys, Davis said he had thought of that. "You're concerned with it," he said. "You always have to think of a person getting—I wouldn't say confused. You get people who accuse officers of doing this.

"You have to take the position that officers are human beings and are susceptible to, let's say, taking shortcuts. I'd hate to think of our trained and screened police officers doing anything illegal or being dishonest. But they are human beings and you need rigid controls, especially where they have liberty to perform . . ."

But Davis was evasive about the Lawrence case in particular. He was vague about how well he knew the man. He would not say he knew him well, yet he said that he had heard much more about Lawrence's work than he had about the work of many of the two hundred or so men under his command. He acknowledged that he had known about Jerry Diamond's complaints about Lawrence, but he dodged the question of what he had done about it.

"I don't recall what my response was, if any," he said. But he added: "We don't ignore that kind of thing."

Well, what about Lawrence?

"If the facts are so, it's a black mark to law enforcement generally."

If the facts are so?

"We have not one real solid actual case where Paul Lawrence did anything wrong," Davis said.

Were you suspicious of Lawrence?

"I'm suspicious of anyone who works under cover," he said.

Davis made these comments in late 1976, long after the bulk of the facts about Lawrence's career had come to light and had been detailed in the report from Robert Gensberg to Governor Salmon. Yet, Davis was conceding nothing—the failure to check Lawrence's military background, his performance at Farrell Distributing, the beating with the flashlight, his perjury in a drug case in the southern part of the state.

Yet, there can be no doubt that Davis was familiar with all this. In the winter of 1974, his superior, Corcoran, had told Dick Allard of St. Albans how bad an actor Lawrence was. Knowledgeable observers such as Jerry Diamond said it was obvious that the state police had forced Lawrence to resign.

Nothing would come out, however. Davis seemed to give voice to this fortress mentality when he said, "If once a guy is a state cop—it doesn't matter if he is a roofer now, and something bad appears in the paper, it always says, 'former state cop, or former FBI agent.' "

It may be true that when a member or former member of a supposedly elite organization gets into trouble, the organization is unfairly placed in a bad light. But covering up such incidents can have devastating consequences. In this case, the Vermont State Police may have improved the screening procedures that failed to filter out Paul Lawrence, but the fortress mentality—the flat refusal to deal with the Lawrence issue in a straightforward manner—is far more crucial. If another Paul Lawrence joins the state police and acts in a similar way, will the department get rid of him in its own private, insular manner, thereby protecting itself while inflicting another menace on society?

In St. Albans, a community which set some sort of record for injustice, there have been superficial changes, but the climate in which a man like Lawrence could flourish remains.

That is not because the actors are the same. All of the members of the city council of Lawrence's time are gone now. Keith Campbell is out of politics, working at his real estate business: bluff and hearty, he waves to the people he sees on the street, the pipe still clenched between his teeth. He refuses to talk about the Lawrence matter, but the comments he has made to reporters in the past have been that he suspects that Lawrence himself was framed.

There is no evidence for this view, but in St. Albans no evidence is required. Bob Hill, now an assistant judge in Franklin County Superior Court, also believes Lawrence was framed, although he won't say much else about the case. "Lawrence never should have gone to Burlington," he said one day in early 1977. "I think he was set up." But he would not say why he thought so.

Another official who would not talk was Judge Gregg. Gregg authorized the arrest of dozens, and presided over the trial of six, virtually all of whom would turn out to be innocent of the charges against them. That is an extraordinary record for one judge, yet no one apparently has thought he deserved a reprimand. Some defense attorneys criticized him, but none openly: they still had to appear in his court. (Gregg died of a heart attack in the spring of 1977.)

Police Chief George Hebert is gone now; he retired shortly after

Lawrence was busted. Raeldon Barker, the city manager, left for a job in the Midwest. No one can say whether these moves took place because of the Lawrence matter. Ken Kaye is still mayor, and still feels as he did when Lawrence was in town. In the summer of 1976, Kaye told *The New York Times* he wished that Lawrence could have acted legally, but that he, Kaye, was nevertheless sure that Lawrence had busted the right people.

And it is not only Lawrence supporters who feel that way. Dick Allard, who did as much as anyone on the city council to try to slow Lawrence down, thinks Lawrence had most of the suspects figured correctly. "I'm not saying he did all bad," Allard will say, meaning he is sure many of the victims were dealers, while describing at the same time how he thought the problems with Lawrence should have been obvious.

John Kissane believes that, too. Kissane is the lawyer who represented Christine Currey; he has lived for many years in St. Albans. "It could happen again, four or five years from now," he said.

Another indicator. Before Lawrence's trial, Augie Fernandez, who by that time had left the state police, went to St. Albans as a private investigator to help Lawrence prepare his defense. Fernandez believed Lawrence was getting a bad rap. When he was in the city, someone, he would not say who, indicated that he understood how things were, the implication being that it was all right to fake buys if the person was a known drug dealer. Augie was outraged. "What do you think I am, a criminal?" he said.

The man who was willing to acknowledge the scope and seriousness of the Lawrence campaign and the magnitude of the failure on the part of local officials was Ron Kilburn. In the fall of 1976, he was still the state's attorney for Franklin County and still prosecuting criminals in Judge Gregg's court.

Kilburn made no effort to escape the harsh judgment that his failure to spot Lawrence was a factor in the injustice that was wreaked. Kilburn said he had relied on his own instincts—on his confidence in his ability to talk to a man and determine if he was telling the truth.

"I always had the feeling that if a person said this is the truth, and I swear under oath . . . I gave too much credit to that," Kilburn said. "I see that in hindsight. I had that naïveté, that there is no one in law enforcement who would dare to be untruthful in that setting."

Kilburn also said he had too much faith in the adversary system. If a suspect was innocent, and given the tools that the defense always has—the right to depose all the state witnesses, for example—then the jury ought to determine the truth.

The material in the Champlain Security report was disturbing to him, Kilburn said, but when he questioned Lawrence about it, the man had a quick answer for every item. And Kilburn accepted them. "Paul Lawrence was a very rare person," he said. His office had no investigative capacity, Kilburn said; they had to rely on the Vermont State Police, and the state police were very complimentary to Mr. Lawrence.

As time went on, Kilburn said, he began to be disturbed about the Lawrence procedures—the big raids, more and more often attended by newspaper and television publicity. Lawrence, late in the spring of 1974, was making sure that the local press got called for all the busts, and Kilburn didn't like that. Furthermore, Lawrence was beginning to include in the busts cases on which the New York laboratory had not returned the drugs after testing.

Yet, Kilburn never succeeded in altering the situation, a fact he concedes, although he adds that he wanted to. He always seemed to be dealing with an accomplished fact: the buys had been made, the reports were all filled out and on his desk; why should he be holding this up? In the one instance he tried to, Kilburn said, a "prominent citizen" called to remonstrate with him. Why was he not cooperating? The "citizen" apparently was Keith Campbell, although Kilburn declined to confirm that.

"In a sense, I was busted too," he said, when asked how he had felt when Lawrence was arrested. Pat Leahy obviously had a solid case.

"I could have blown the whistle," Kilburn said quietly. "I could have said, no more drug prosecutions. I would have gotten heat for it. Lots of money had been spent . . .

"I was conned," he went on. "Judge Gregg was conned, other people in the city were conned. We've got to share the blame, it wasn't just Paul Lawrence."

Like Cheney, Kilburn was an essentially good man who sounds as if he has learned the lessons provided at such high expense by Paul Lawrence. It is very difficult to understand how he could have failed to see through the man, but one would be justified in taking his word that he did not. One might also be forgiven for suspecting that

Kilburn lacked the courage to deal harshly with Lawrence in the face of the community support for the man. It is thus hard to say how Kilburn might act the next time he faces a situation such as that presented by Lawrence's activities. Kilburn will certainly be a wiser man, but will he be a stronger one?

If the failure of the public officials at various levels of government in Vermont is a cause for disquiet, so is the failure of the juries of St. Albans. In some of the cases they sat on, there was no reason to disbelieve the evidence presented by Paul Lawrence and the other state witnesses. But in others, the contradictions were glaring. If the juries were a reflection of the public, as our system assumes they will be, then the ordinary folk of St. Albans were incapable of sound judgment in the consideration of the drug cases brought by Lawrence. In the Sonny Cross trial, they acquitted Cross where the evidence against him was unrebutted, and convicted him where the evidence against him was weak. They did so despite the fact that Lawrence proved himself to be a substantively poor witness. He failed to accurately describe Tuner's bar, even though he purportedly hung around there, and the jury overlooked this entirely—not just one juror or two, but every juror. Moreover, not a single juror changed his view of Lawrence's trustworthiness, even though he altered his story sharply in the Cross trial, when Peter Cleveland asked him about being cheated by Cross on a supposed drug deal.

If the jurors had exercised the most elementary discrimination, then they would have had to reject the scenario set forth by Paul Lawrence.

How could a supposed drug dealer, which Lawrence said he was posing as, be cheated so easily on a deal? And never protest? And then, apparently in full trust, make the same sort of deal again? The only answer is that the jurors never listened: the details were simply background noise to them.

The policeman carried with him onto the witness stand an aura of truth so bright that it blinded the jurors to the more modest light of fact. No one should think that this is rare: the policeman, moving easily in an authoritarian system, is often a very convincing witness in the courtroom. He is paid to do the bidding of society; it is his job, there is a heavy presumption that he is telling the truth. The suspect is from the beginning of the proceeding a lesser figure and—if he is young and alienated and poor—a much less impressive figure.

The litany of failures on the part of public authorities, the people of Vermont, and the City of St. Albans in the early 1970s, and the consequent damage, seems therefore not to be some monstrous coincidence, an accidental miscarriage of justice inspired by one unusual man, but rather something that threatens constantly at a time of social stress.

The American system assumes that if the policeman and the prosecutor and the judge and the jury, working in an adversary system, do their jobs with a normal amount of intelligence and honesty and courage, then justice will be done—injustice will be rare. That almost certainly is not the case. The system is exquisitely fragile, as demonstrated here. The system failed for the most part—it succeeded only where the individuals who manned its offices were themselves unusual. When tested by a man like Lawrence, in a period when the public was upset about the social menace posed by the use of drugs, the criminal justice system failed, and could fail again. The commitment to individual rights, to the right of individuals to wear their hair long or to hold different values from straight society is honored more in rhetoric than in action.

The presumption in our system is that a suspect is innocent until proven guilty. What the Lawrence case demonstrated is that that often is not so. The suspect, in effect, is presumed to be guilty. And, in the vast majority of criminal cases, the suspect *is* guilty. Acquitting those who are innocent is no easy process. There is a concept that both defense lawyers and prosecutors are officers of the court, and have a responsibility not only to the defendant or to the police, but to the finding of the truth. In the Lawrence affair, the prosecutors in St. Albans failed to discharge that aspect of their duty. That prosecutors do discharge it—that they do not simply serve as a rubber stamp for the actions of the police—is crucial.

There were positive aspects to the Lawrence experience. Some thoughtful officials could see the implications in the ease with which Lawrence framed his victims. They could see that undercover work ought to involve at least two officers, so that one would be a check against shortcuts and dishonesty by the other. But it is problematical how long that skepticism on the part of law-enforcement officials will last. The community attitudes in St. Albans encouraged an all-out effort on the part of the prosecution against drug users and hippies. That sort of attitude could prevail again. And only the most rigorous commitment on the part of police, prosecutors, and judges would prevent another Lawrence campaign.

The underlying issue, in short, is the attitude of law-enforcement officers: their willingness to grant a presumption of innocence and their skepticism about evidence in criminal cases. That is what is important, not the techniques that they use.

In the spring of 1977, Paul Lawrence was languishing in prison in Windsor, Vermont. Despite the ruin of his career and the prospect of more years in jail, he continues to live by his wits and enjoys some success.

Lawrence gets an occasional furlough from the prison, which he spends at his parents' home in Shelburne, Vermont, near Burlington. His current girlfriend, Sue Stearns, lives in an apartment nearby. I talked to Lawrence on the phone one day. He was innocent, he said, but would not offer any evidence he might have. The judge in the Burlington trial, Edward Costello, should have disqualified himself, Lawrence said. He, Lawrence, was investigating Costello's son at the time he was busted. Then there was the Leahy office involvement in the case . . . the case was political, he said. That was before his last guilty plea.

There is lingering speculation about what made Lawrence tick. Ron Kilburn thought the man figured that what he was doing was right because that was what the community wanted. There were some grounds for that, of course: significant elements of the community *did* want Lawrence to do what he did. Some would like him to be doing it still.

Others who watched Lawrence's career believe that Lawrence functioned under some sort of delusion. Nobody could tell so many lies and not get tripped up if he did not believe that what he was saying was the truth, they theorize. The flaw in that argument is that the Lawrence stories were full of holes—what was required was the willingness to look for them. Pat Leahy had the simplest and probably the most accurate view. "The man was just a vicious liar who wanted money and fame," he said.

While Lawrence worked for St. Albans, he made $160 per week. The city spent over $10,000 in drug-buy money, and authorities in Swanton kicked in at least $4,000 more. That is quite a salary supplement, in less than a year, to a man earning an annual salary of $8,300.

Lawrence also clearly relished publicity. He did his best to cultivate newspaper reporters, and some of them wrote stories quite
favorable to Lawrence. He did not become "Supercop" by word of
mouth alone.

No one can know for sure what drove him. His career was a
downward spiral, constantly moving away from the truth. At first he
embellished stories, then he fabricated them, until at the end he
seems to have scarcely told the truth at all. The roots of that behavior
may lie in Barrington, in the rebelliousness of his youth and in the
lack of loyalty to the kids he grew up with. Perhaps the wellsprings of
his behavior lie somewhere else. It would help, of course, if Lawrence
himself would talk candidly about his career, but that is not likely.
"Deny everything, deny everything," was his advice to Butch Baker
after Butch threw the bottle at the window in Barrington. And Lawrence followed that policy until his final guilty plea.

One does not *have* to look for deep psychological reasons for why
Lawrence did what he did. He found—probably in St. Albans—not
only that the embellishing of stories could be effective, but that no
buy need be made at all. You could find out from the local cops who the
hippies were, place them at a given location at a given time, and
simply claim that you made the buy. That way you got the kid into
jail, and you got to keep the buy money. Moreover, the local politicians would love you, and the local newspapers would celebrate your
exploits. One does not have to be unusually perceptive to discern the
advantages of such a course.

While this view is buttressed by a wealth of fact, there are some
things that have never been learned about Lawrence's operation.
That particularly involves the source of the drugs he used to frame
people. Bob Gensberg concluded that much of the heroin he planted
on victims came from the New York State laboratory. But there may
have been another source.

Gensberg's investigations turned up a series of phone calls from
Lawrence's home to a motel in Granby, Quebec. When investigators
went there, the motel clerk remembered having seen Lawrence there.
But Lawrence denied it. No one is sure of the significance of this—it
may have been one of Lawrence's dalliances, of which he was fond.
But at least one of the defense attorneys, who did not wish to be
identified, was privately investigating the possibility that Lawrence
had a drug connection somewhere, possibly in Canada.

This speculation is now fading, as is much of the data surrounding the Lawrence case. The public record may be expunged as part of the pardons. No one now needs to know where Lawrence got his drugs. The one certainty is that Lawrence himself will never tell. He has been denying everything since he was a boy, and is likely to go right on doing so.

It was inevitable that the series of drug frame-ups in Vermont would be known as the Paul Lawrence case. That is unfortunate, in a sense, for the affair was much larger than the activities of one man. It was a monstrous miscarriage of justice. It stained the image of law enforcement in the state, marred the reputations and damaged the careers of many law-enforcement officials, and left a trail of psychological wreckage in the lives of its victims.

It was an unusual case, but it was not farfetched, in the sense that it would not be likely to happen again. It *could* happen again, in Vermont or elsewhere.